A Register

of the Regiments

and Corps *of the*

British Army

The ancestry of the regiments and corps of the Regular Establishment

Edited by Arthur Swinson

with a Foreword by
Lieut.-General Sir Brian Horrocks
KCB, KBE, DSO, MC, LL.D (HON)

The Archive Press · London

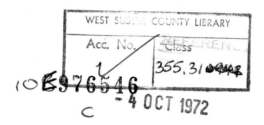
SBN 85591 000 3

© Archive Press Ltd   1972
22 Belsize Park Gardens
London N.W.3

Distributed by
Arms and Armour Press
2–6 Hampstead High Street
London N.W.3

Printed in Great Britain

ARCHIVE
MILITARY
REFERENCES

A Register
of the Regiments *and* Corps *of the* British Army

Contents

Foreword

Foreword

BY LIEUT.-GENERAL SIR BRIAN HORROCKS

KCB, KBE, DSO, MC, LL.D (HON)

I would like to congratulate all concerned on this really tremendous publication. Being a somewhat idle man myself, the colossal amount of work, research, checking and re-checking to produce this register fills me with awe. I have not the knowledge to check personally every single entry. I do not suppose anyone has, but the details of those regiments with which I am familiar seem absolutely accurate.

This register could not have been produced at a better moment because outside the Ministry of Defence it would be a brave man indeed who could boast that he knew accurately the organization of the British Army today, or what it was likely to be in the future.

Arthur Swinson gives a masterly summary explaining, as far as it is possible to do so, the highly complicated development of the British Army since Charles II came back to London in 1660 escorted through the streets by the Army of the Commonwealth. It was only when these Cromwellian stalwarts had been disbanded that our present regular army came into being.

A record of this sort will be of immense value in the future to military historians and I would also expect to find a copy in all regimental museums. It marks the end of an epoch, for, although we succeeded in winning the last two wars, we practically ruined ourselves in the process, and the Pax Britannica passed across to the other side of the Atlantic. So large reductions in our military formations were inevitable, both from a financial point of view and also because of our reduced commitments.

The reason why there has never been an accurate list of British regiments and corps, is that basically the Army is not popular in this country, and never has been since the tyrannical rule of Cromwell's Major Generals. We are also an island, and I have grown up in an age when the British Navy ruled the seas. Trouble in some distant corner of the wide flung British Empire was dealt with by the despatch of a cruiser, and the role played by soldiers, except in the really large scale wars when the whole country was involved is seldom, if ever, mentioned. Yet historians in the future will find that there are three major directions in which the Army has played a significant part in the development of the British Empire.

First, the maintenance of law and order in the home base—the United Kingdom—which usually meant, as it does at the present moment, dealing with trouble in Ireland.

Secondly, maintaining the balance of power in Europe. This involved taking part in some historic campaign such as the war of the Spanish Succession under Marlborough, or the Peninsular under Wellington, and most of the battle honours which you will see listed under the names of the different regiments were won in these wars.

But to my mind the *third* and most important role of all which is rarely mentioned, has surely been the protection which different regiments have afforded to those indomitable British merchants who in search of fresh markets spread our influence all over the world. This often involved spending many years in stinking garrisons overseas, where casualties from disease were often far greater than those suffered in some great campaign. There were no battle honours for this sort of operation and there was little glory to be won. To take just one instance at random, the first battalion The Queen's Regiment, suffered such heavy casualties from disease in the West Indies that they had to be reinforced by their new Second Battalion. Men were dying at the rate of thirty a month and by the end of 1795 the effective strength had fallen to 162 out of the original total of 661.

It was, however, during these terrible overseas garrison duties, when regiments were entirely dependent on their own resources, that the regimental family *esprit de corps* began to take root. In the beginning this regimental plant did not flourish to any marked degree, which was hardly surprising as regimental service in those early days makes terrible reading. Most regiments bore the name of their Commanding Officer to whom they belonged body and soul (these titles were, of course, subsequently replaced by numbers). The Royal Berkshire Regiment to take one example at random was raised by and called Trelawney's Regiment for some eight years. The commanding officers were given a certain sum of money with which to clothe and feed their regiments: everything depended, therefore, on their character. Discipline was of the most brutal: men were flogged in public for quite minor offences and pay was so little that the soldiers only pleasure lay in drinking the cheapest form of 'grog' that could be bought. Owing to the iniquitous system by which officers purchased their commissions battalions were often commanded by rich young men whom the troops hardly ever saw and who treated the men under them almost like cattle. Even the great Duke of Wellington himself served in five different regiments in six years, gaining a promotion each time. Under these circumstances the type of man who enlisted into the Army was the lowest of the low—all too often it was a case of the gibbet or military service. Yet the extraordinary fact always emerges that these men did in fact develop a pride in their own particular regiment.

The first high ranking officer to take any interest in administration and welfare of the men under his command was John Churchill, First Duke of Marlborough, known affectionately to the troops as Corporal John. His administrative arrangements were so good that by the time his army had marched right across Europe the troops were fitter and their morale higher than when they had started. This had much to do with his remarkable victory over the French at Blenheim, which altered the whole balance of power in Europe. Wellington, though not such an attractive character, was much the same; camp kettles, forage and food, appear more often in his despatches than do descriptions of military operations. With the exception of the appalling inefficiency and consequent suffering of the troops during the Crimean War, the standard of man management in the British Army has improved steadily over the years and is now second to none; each regiment has developed into a military family in the best sense of the word.

In August 1914, when I was just eighteen years of age, I conducted the first reinforcement to join my regiment, the Middlesex, who were part of the British Expeditionary force in France. Soon after the Battle of the Aisne I found myself in command of No. 16 Platoon. I was lucky, because my two chief mentors, Captain Gibbons, the Company Commander and Sergeant Whinney, my platoon sergeant, were both first-class at their jobs. Gibbons held me completely responsible for the welfare of the men in my platoon. Woe betide me if I attempted to have my own meal without first reporting to him 'All ranks in No. 16 Platoon fed Sir'. Once we arrived in pouring rain to find that a muddy field which had previously been over-populated by cows had been allocated as our bivouac area for the night. It was a depressing thought, but my spirits rose when the adjutant appeared and said that the officers could sleep in a house nearby where battalion H.Q. was billeted. Gibbons was furious 'If the men sleep out we sleep out'. My heart sank but I knew instinctively that he was right. But Gibbons's influence did not last long as on 21 October, 1914, at the Battle of Ypres, my platoon was surrounded by the enemy and I was wounded and taken prisoner. The war for me was over and my active military career had stopped for four years. I had, however, lasted for six weeks, which was three weeks longer than the average life of an Infantry Platoon Commander in the 1914–18 War. It was during this time that I learnt the vital importance of regimental *esprit de corps*, which is such a feature of all British infantry regiments; we were intensely proud of our nickname 'The Die Hards', which had been won on the battlefield of Albuhera on 16 May 1811, during the Peninsular War. Wellington had left behind a force under Marshal Beresford to hold up the French who were advancing under Marshal Soult to relieve the Fortress of Badajoz. Soult was too clever for Beresford and moved his main force under cover round our right flank while carrying out a dummy attack on the village itself. Suddenly the French columns were seen emerging from the woods. Beresford ordered the 57th Foot (Middlesex Regiment) to double to the threatened flank and hold up the French attack. The regiment got there in time and formed up in two ranks with Lieut.-Colonel Inglis, their Colonel, in front. Though completely outnumbered, time after time they beat back the French assaults. The corps of drums, many of whom were mere boys, began to waver. 'Steady the Drums and Fifes' called the C.O. This formed the subject of a picture by Lady Butler which hung in our mess for years and is now loaned to the School of Infantry. The ranks kept closing inwards owing to the severe casualties inflicted by the enemy fire. Inglis was badly wounded but refused to be evacuated, and lying in front of the regiment he cried 'Die hard, 57th, die hard'. The French never succeeded in breaking through and next day the 57th lay dead, in two ranks as they had fought. The casualties were so heavy that rations for one entire company were drawn next morning by a drummer boy in the small round cap with which they were issued in those days.

Since then the Duke of Cambridge's Own Middlesex Regiment, originally the 57th Foot, has been known as 'The Die Hards'. In the 1914–18 War the regiment raised forty-five battalions, of whom forty were operational and each man was proud to call himself a 'Die Hard'—such is the value of regimental tradition.

I regard this aspect of regimental life as so important that at the risk of making this foreword too long I would like to quote two other traditions of which their owners are justly proud.

The first is the Gloucestershire Regiment, which is the only regiment in the British Army to wear a badge on the front and back of their caps, in honour of the Battle of Alexandria in Egypt, when they were attacked by Napoleon's invincible Legions. Though heavily engaged to their front they were suddenly charged by another column from the rear. The order was given 'Rear rank right about face' and both attacks were beaten off.

The Royal Scots have a nickname of a somewhat different type. They are indeed of one the oldest fighting formations in the world and can claim descent from the Scottish Archer Guard which fought in the Crusades. They formed the élite bodyguard of the French Kings in about 1420. It was during this time when they were serving in France that they earned the nickname of Pontius Pilate's Bodyguard. They got it because of an argument which developed between them and their greatest rivals, the French regiment from Picardy, as to which was the oldest. The Picardy officers boasted that they were the direct descendants of the Legions which had been on duty in Jerusalem on the night of the Crucifixion. The officers of the Scots regiment confounded them by replying that had they themselves been on duty at the Sepulchre, the Body of Christ would never have left it, implying that they would not have slept at their posts as the original ancestors of the French regiment must obviously have done.

I have deliberately included these stories to show that many of our regiments had a colourful past which should justify the attention of military historians in the future, otherwise, alas, they may soon be forgotten.

The best description of regimental *esprit de corps* which I have ever read is the final paragraph in the short history of The Royal Fusiliers by Michael Foss, in the Famous Regiments Series. He writes

'The regiment of the Royal Fusiliers is an old institution. It has proved its worth a hundred times in the past, but the days of its greatest value are gone. It has always been a little conservative, sometimes a little inefficient. But it sought out the hearts of its soldiers, and when it found them it raised those men to deeds they did not know they were capable of. Though sometimes stiff and silly and narrow-minded, the Royal Fusiliers have steadily insisted that the soldier is an individual with the strengths and failings of ordinary men. In the thinking of the regiment war is not glorified. Only courage and fortitude receive the respect and admiration that these qualities deserve. The regimental traditions have been the greatest humanizing influence on the conduct of the British Army. And unless it is humane an army is barbaric.'

It is always sad when old friends depart. In the last few years many famous old regiments which I have known so well have disappeared from the army list, merged into larger formations. In many ways something of this sort was inevitable. The young will not mind it so much as the old. I remember well the words of a very wise old general who once said to me 'One good Commanding Officer is worth a ton of tradition with mould on it'. My only worry, and it is a very serious one, is that this reorganization is bound to sever the close ties which now exist between our County regiments and the Territorial Army. The main strength of our military system of recent years has lain in the fact that regimental roots were planted deep into the British countryside in the shape of the T.A. This ensured the closest possible link between civilian and military worlds and built up a unique county and family *esprit de corps*, which exists in no other army in the world. This, I am afraid, will no longer exist.

Let me end with that classic quotation from the last chapter of Fortescue's *History of the British Army*: 'The bulk of the Empire despised and derided the stone which became the headstone of the corners. They were not worthy of such an army. Two centuries of persecution could not wear out its patience. Two centuries of thankless toil could not abate its ardours. Two centuries of conquest could not awake it to insolence. Dutiful to its masters, merciful to its enemies; it clung steadfastly to its old simple ideals—obedience, service, sacrifice.'

BRIAN G. HORROCKS

Introduction

Introduction

BY THE EDITOR AND PUBLISHER

John S. Farmer's work, *The Regimental Records of the British Army*, was published in 1901. Now increasingly rare and missing from many reference libraries, it remains an indispensable work to any student of the regimental system of the army. *The Records and Badges of Every Regiment and Corps in the British Army* by H. M. Chichester and G. Burges-Short (1900), another standard work on the subject, has recently been reprinted. But since these works first appeared the British Army has undergone the most thorough reorganization in its history, and, should their authors return today, they would find the Army almost unrecognizable. Many famous regiments have disappeared; some through amalgamation and others through disbandment. New regiments and corps have come into being. There have been changes in title and in function, and new formations have appeared such as the 'Large Regiments'. Since 1945 the changes have been particularly important.

It seemed to us that an urgent need had arisen for a reference work in which one could trace the ancestry of the regiments and corps which are on the Regular Establishment today.* *A Register of the Regiments and Corps of the British Army* has been produced to fill that need.

The following information concerning each regiment is given:

Date of Formation	Nicknames
Changes of Title	Mottoes—if any
Principal Campaigns	Dates of Amalgamation
and Battles	Date of Disbandment

Where amalgamations have taken place, page references are given both to the units concerned and to the unit subsequently brought into being.

* The Volunteers, Militia and Territorial Units will be the subject of another volume of this series.

It must be confessed that when embarking on this work we imagined that in general the authorities named above were accepted as accurate by the regiments and corps concerned. Here we were mistaken, and indeed so many errors have been pointed out that we can only conclude that Farmer and Chichester and Burges-Short worked from published sources without consulting regimental historians and archivists. Should this be so, then the value of the present work needs no emphasizing, for we have received magnificent co-operation and help from almost every regiment and corps now serving in the British Army, and from officers concerned with the interests of units now lost through disbandment or amalgamation. This help has been of especial benefit when deciding whether past units (many of them in existence for only a few years) may be said to be the forerunners of regiments later permanently established. In these instances we have followed the advice of the regiments concerned noting the existence of unconnected previous units, however, to complete the record.

In order to keep the work down to a handy size, compact enough for general use it has been necessary to make a selection of the campaigns and battles—the number varies enormously from one regiment to another—but wherever possible each regiment has been allowed to comment upon the selection to be listed and in most cases its recommendations have been followed. This has resulted in some anomalies; for example the battle of Neer Landen may seem to be important to some regiments and unimportant to others who fought in it. Its inclusion or exclusion therefore has been determined by the space available and the judgment of editor and the regiment concerned. All major battles such as Blenheim or Waterloo have, of course, been included wherever applicable. For a full list of all campaigns and battles it is necessary to consult the particular regimental history for which this work does not pretend to be a substitute.

In general the campaigns and battles listed may or may not appear now, or have appeared in the past, on the Colours but in the case of the 1st and 2nd World Wars, only those honours selected to be borne on the Colours, Guidons or Standards have been listed, for in these great conflicts most regiments gained far more battle honours than could possibly be listed in a single volume.

Despite the above it must be emphasized that the present

work is not largely concerned with battle honours—a complex subject which may be pursued elsewhere. Many battle honours, of course, were awarded many years after the units concerned had ceased to enjoy a separate identity. As indicated above, battles and campaigns have been included to give a general idea of the service of a unit. Thought necessary, this policy has led to a number of difficulties (and no doubt inconsistencies) in terminology. It seems to us, for example, that while anyone interested in military history will know that 'Peninsula 1809–14' indicates service under the Duke of Wellington in Spain and Portugal during the Napoleonic Wars, 'Burma 1824–6' may not be immediately recognizable as referring to the First Burma War. All minor campaigns have therefore been listed by name. In general place names have been modernized, i.e. Kabul, instead of Cabool, though on occasions where regiments have preferred the earlier spelling (which may agree with the honour on their Colour) such requests have been respected.

About mottoes, the only point to mention is that where one was taken by a regiment of foot before 1881 and later adopted by a post-1881 linked regiment that fact has been noted.

A word concerning the general shape of the work may be helpful. The order in which regiments and corps are listed is as follows:

1. The Cavalry Regiments as they existed up to 1922—in order of seniority.
2. Cavalry Regiments formed by the amalgamations of 1922.
3. Cavalry Regiments formed by the amalgamations of 1958 onwards.
4. The Regiments of Foot Guards.
5. The Regiments of Foot from 1 to 25 under the titles they held in 1958.
6. The Regiments of Foot from 26 onwards.
7. The Regiments formed in 1881 by the linking of the above Regiments of Foot under the titles they held in 1958 or on disbandment.
8. Regiments formed by the amalgamations since 1958.
9. The Regiments of the Gurkha Brigade of which came on to the British Establishment in 1948.
10. Royal Regiment of Artillery, Royal Horse Artillery, Royal Tank Regiment.
11. The Corps.

Wherever possible within categories, seniority in the Army List has been observed, but the overriding factor has been the historical development of the army.

A close examination of the above table may appear to disclose an anomaly between the Regiments of Foot numbered 1 to 25 and those numbered from 26 onwards. As the entire history of The Suffolk Regiment, for example, from its formation in 1685 to its amalgamation with The Royal Norfolk Regiment in 1959 appears on one sheet, it may seem odd that to trace The Worcestershire Regiment one has first to look under the 29th and the 36th Foot. There is, however, a good reason for such an arrangement.

The Regiments of Foot existed as individual corps for periods of up to two centuries and more—two-thirds the length of time the British Army has existed. When the first 25 Regiments of Foot were given a second battalion in 1857* they continued as they were, merely changing their names, but when the 29th and 36th Foot became the 1st and 2nd Battalions The Worcestershire Regiment, a radical change took place and a new corps was born. Our differentiation would therefore seem to be justified.

A student, for instance, may read of the exploits of the 58th Regiment of Foot at Quebec (1759). By consulting the index he will find details of its service until 1881, then, following the references at the foot of each page, he will learn that it became linked with the 48th (Rutlandshire) Regiment to form The Northamptonshire Regiment and that on 1 June 1960, this corps amalgamated with The Royal Lincolnshire Regiment to form The 2nd East Anglian Regiment (Duchess of Gloucester's Own Royal Lincolnshire and Northamptonshire) and that on 1 September 1964, the unit was incorporated into a 'large regiment' and re-named The 2nd (Duchess of Gloucester's Own Lincolnshire and Northamptonshire) Battalion the Royal Anglian Regiment. He will also learn, unfortunately, that sub-titles were dropped in 1968 and that by 1971 The Royal Anglian Regiment had reorganized its four battalions into three, the fourth battalion reducing to an independent company, 'Tiger Company', The Royal Anglian Regiment.

As anyone who has entered the field of regimental history

* Many regiments had raised second battalions at earlier times, notably during the Seven Years' War and the Napoleonic Wars. Some regiments, including the Royal Scots, the 60th and the Rifle Brigade, had always had more than one battalion.

will know, the dangers of falling into error are enormous. We owe a great debt to the many officers, historians and other specialists who checked the entries with which they were concerned. In many cases they pointed out errors which had originated in earlier works and supplied us with information unobtainable elsewhere. In particular we should like to thank the following:

Colonel R. M. Adams (Historical Officer, Royal Signals)

Major J. F. Ainsworth (The Royal Sussex Regiment)

Lt.-Colonel M. Armstrong (Royal Corps of Transport)

Major H. Barker MBE (Queen's Own Highlanders)

Lt.-Colonel J. S. Barkworth (3rd Carabiniers (Prince of Wales's Dragoon Guards))

Major D. Baxter (The Royal Anglian Regiment)

Major J. K. W. Bingham (Royal Tank Regiment)

Lt.-Colonel E. A. T. Boggis (Duke of Edinburgh's Royal Regiment)

Major G. A. N. Boyne JP (The Royal Irish Rangers)

Major S. E. M. Bradish-Ellames (The Blues and Royals)

Colonel C. R. Buchanan

Lt.-Colonel John Busby (Bedfordshire and Hertfordshire Regiment)

Captain J. O. Campbell (Royal Army Medical Corps)

Major A. V. M. Chapman MBE, TD (The Black Watch)

Major A. L. Clark (The Royal Leicestershire Regiment)

Colonel J. M. Clift (The Royal Hampshire Regiment)

Kenneth J. Collins Esq., MA (The Queen's Own Royal West Kent Regimental Museum)

Major R. M. Collins (9th/12th Royal Lancers)

Colonel H. C. B. Cook OBE (The Staffordshire Regiment)

Major W. G. Cripps (The Royal Norfolk Regiment)

Major C. M. Cusack (Royal Pioneer Corps)

Major I. M. Elliot (Brigade of Gurkhas)

Colonel D. A. D. Eykyn DSO, DL (The Royal Scots)

Colonel J. M. Forbes (The Green Howards)

Lt.-Colonel J. E. E. Fry MC (The Duke of Cornwall's Light Infantry)

Lt.-Colonel G. P. Gofton-Salmond (The Sherwood Foresters)

Major G. A. S. Graham MBE (17th/21st Lancers)

Lt.-Colonel G. C. E. Grew (Royal Army Chaplains Department Centre)

Colonel E. A. Harding (The Gloucestershire Regiment)

Lieutenant B. Harris (13th/18th Royal Hussars)

Major A. J. R. Harrison (Scots Guards)

Lt.-Colonel P. St. C. Harrison (The King's Own Scottish Borderers)

Colonel W. A. Heal OBE (The Suffolk Regiment)

Captain A. A. Hedley (16th/5th The Queen's Royal Lancers)

J. G. Hook Esq. (Coldstream Guards)

Captain T. W. Jackson (4/7th Royal Dragoon Guards)

Lt.-Colonel I. Jarman MBE (The South Wales Borderers)

Lt.-Colonel J. Jeffrey OBE (The Loyal Regiment)

Major E. Jessup (The Royal Anglian Regiment)

Lt.-Colonel D. A. Johnson (Ministry of Defence)

Miss Ailsa S. Kelly (Durham Light Infantry Museum and Arts Centre)

Major C. R. D'I. Kenworthy (The Gordon Highlanders)

D. W. King Esq., OBE, FLA (Chief Librarian, War Office Library, Ministry of Defence)

Brigadier J. H. S. Lacey CBE, BA (The Corps of Royal Engineers)

Major E. L. Kirby MC, TD, DL (The Royal Welch Fusiliers)

Major T. V. Leckie (Queen's Royal Irish Hussars)

Major G. F. Lane-Fox (The Blues and Royals)

Lt.-Colonel W. W. Leary BEM (Intelligence Corps)

Major C. M. Leggett (The Royal Irish Rangers)

Major D. H. C. Gordon Lennox (Grenadier Guards)

Major E. D. Lloyd-Thomas (The Royal Regiment of Wales)

Major A. B. Mainwaring-Burton (Irish Guards)

Major A. E. Matthews (The Royal Ulster Rifles)

Brigadier P. W. Mead CBE (Royal Artillery Institution)

Miss L. Milliard BA (Royal Museum and Public Library, Canterbury)

Major D. C. MacDonald Milner (Welsh Guards)

Major J. H. Mott OBE (The York and Lancaster Regiment)

Major J. S. F. Murray (15th/19th The King's Royal Hussars)

Major G. G. Norton (The Parachute Regiment)

Lt.-Colonel A. G. D. Palmer MC (The Royal Green Jackets)

G. Archer Parfitt Esq. (The King's Shropshire Light Infantry)

Lt.-Colonel R. M. Pratt DSO (The Royal Regiment of Fusiliers)

E. J. Priestley Esq. (Assistant Keeper (Military History) City of Liverpool Museums)

Colonel N. S. Pope DSO, MBE (Light Infantry)

Major F. J. Reed (The Queen's Regiment)

Lt.-Colonel J. D. Ricketts DSO (The Worcestershire Regiment)

Brigadier B. L. Rigby CBE (The Cheshire Regiment)

Major F. H. Robson (5th Royal Inniskilling Dragoon Guards)

Lt.-Colonel A. Rowland OBE, MC (1st The Queen's Dragoon Guards)

Lt.-Colonel M. Ryan OBE (The Royal Regiment of Fusiliers)

Lt.-Colonel G. C. B. Sass (The Lancashire Regiment)

Lieutenant M. I. Scott-Dalgleish (10th Royal Hussars)

Major T. P. Shaw MBE (The Royal Regiment of Fusiliers)

Lt.-Colonel T. B. G. Slessor (Argyll and Sutherland Highlanders)

Major Dick Smith (The Middlesex Regiment)

Lt.-Colonel N. Smyth (The Border Regiment)

Brigadier J. F. Snow CBE (The Light Infantry)

Air Commodore R. H. S. Spaight CBE

Lt.-Colonel C. L. Speers (The Duke of Edinburgh's Royal Regiment)

Lt.-Colonel G. N. B. Spencer (The Devonshire and Dorset Regiment)

Major T. R. Stead (The Essex Regiment)

Major J. S. Sutherland MBE (The Queen's Own Hussars)

Lieutenant C. P. Thompson (11th Hussars)

B. Thirkill Esq., BEM (King's Dragoon Guards)

W. A. Thorbush Esq. (Scottish United Services Museum)

Mrs Edith Tyson FMA (City of Lancaster Museum and Art Gallery)

Major M. Urban-Smith MC (14th/20th King's Hussars)

Lt.-Colonel A. C. M. Urwick (Light Infantry)

Lt.-Colonel D. V. W. Wakely MC (The Dorset Regiment)

T. A. Walden Esq., Director, City of Leicester Museums and Art Gallery

The Warden, Royal Army Chaplains Department Centre

Brigadier Webb-Carter (The Duke of Wellington's Regiment)

Lt.-Colonel J. E. B. Whitehead (The Cameronians (Scottish Rifles))

Captain A. J. Wilson (The Royal Highland Fusiliers)

Lt.-Colonel F. R. Yorke (The Prince of Wales's Own Regiment of Yorkshire)

No doubt some errors and omissions still remain and we should be glad to have them pointed out to us so that corrections may be made in a future edition.

ARTHUR SWINSON, *Editor*

July, 1970   PETER ELSTOB, *Publisher*

Arthur Swinson died suddenly a few weeks after finishing the first draft of his book. This caused publication to be delayed but with the help of John Keegan and other authorities *A Register of Regiments* has been brought up to date.

December, 1971   PETER ELSTOB, *Publisher*

Some Notes on the Formation and Development of the British Army

Some Notes on the Formation and Development of the British Army

BY THE EDITOR

It came into being and grew in the most haphazard manner possible, though, when one considers the traditional unpopularity of standing armies in England, this fact is not surprising. On the whole it is true to say that the army has remained in being through the last three centuries because the nation has never quite been able to do without it. Even so, it has often been reduced to a token force, and on one occasion at least almost disappeared altogether. In wars, of course, its numbers have immediately swelled, by tens of thousands in the 17th, 18th and 19th centuries, and by millions in the 20th. Till the mid-18th century at least, many of the regiments raised were ephemeral, and disappeared before the ink was dry on the next peace treaty. Of twelve regiments raised in 1688 only two, the 16th and 17th Foot survived on the Regular Establishment; and one only has to read the history of Marlborough's wars to learn of such forgotten units as Rooke's, Paston's, Deloraine's, Inchiquin's and Ikerryn's Foot. Hurriedly raised and trained, and lacking tradition, it is amazing that they fought so well. Many regiments which did eventually find a place on the Establishment were raised and disbanded several times, often under different titles or with a different number, before their identity became secure. The changing pattern is quite understandable; till the mid-18th century, there was little or nothing for an army to do, when England happened to be at peace. Only a few battalions were employed in India, to bolster the East India Company's forces, and overseas garrisons were reduced to a minimum. With the steady growth of the Empire, however, and the transfer of India to the Crown, colonial wars proliferated and from 1847 onwards there was the added responsibility of the guardianship of the North-West Frontier. From 1789 to 1966 there was not a single year in which British troops were not in action somewhere in the world.

But to begin at the beginning: when Charles II came back to London in 1660, he was escorted through the streets by cavalry of the Army of the Commonwealth*, which had ruled England since 1647. At this time it numbered 65,000, and the monarchy could not be considered secure, until it were disbanded. So General George Monck, the former Parliamentary commander-in-chief, now knighted by the King and appointed master of the horse, took the job in hand, and prepared a scheme which was soon adopted by Parliament. Matters would go ahead at a leisurely pace, all arrears of pay being settled, and the regiments broken up one at a time, the order being decided by lot. Monck's own regiments of foot, together with units taken over by the Duke of York and Duke of Gloucester, would be disbanded last. To reduce the risk of discontent, an Act was passed enabling ex-soldiers to enter trades without the formality of apprenticeship. If everything went well, the Army of the Commonwealth—with the exception of the regiments above mentioned—would disappear by the early months of 1661.

But then there occurred one of those minor events which are destined to change the course of history. An obscure sect known as the 'Fifth Monarchy Men' decided to stage an insurrection, which was not put down until Monck's regiment of foot went into action. This incident graphically illustrated the need for a permanent force, and the disbandment of Monck's regiment and the troop of horse-guards was hurriedly countermanded. In addition, the King ordered that a new regiment of guards should be raised together with a regiment of horse in eight troops, and a troop of horse-guards. The Duke of York's troop of horse-guards, then serving in Dunkirk, was summoned home.

So the foundations of the new army were laid, but it was still necessary to abolish the existing army in compliance with the Act passed through Parliament. So on 14 February 1661 there took place on Tower Hill the famous scene in which Monck's regiment of foot, formed up by companies, solemnly laid down its arms, paused, then took them up again as the Lord General's

* He also brought three troops of his own Life Guards. (See page 3.)

Regiment of Foot-Guards, to be known to history as the Coldstream Guards. Coldstream was the Scottish village from which they had begun the long march to London, so prefacing the return of constitutional monarchy. The Coldstream is therefore the oldest regiment and sole survivor of Cromwell's army, a fact which is emphasized by its proud motto, 'Nulli Secundus', or Second to None.

In order of precedence, however, it is second to the regiment of guards raised by the King for his own protection, known in 1660 as the King's Royal Regiment of Guards, and from 1815 as the Grenadier Guards. In its ranks were included many Cavaliers who had refused to surrender in the battle of Dunkirk Dunes on 24 May 1658, where a mixed force of Royalists and Spaniards were routed by the English. The three troops of Life Guards, after a further 128 years as independent troops, were to be absorbed into the 1st and 2nd Life Guards, the senior regiments of the army. By 1662 another regiment had arrived on the scene; Le Régiment d'Hebron, a body of mercenaries, which from 1625 to 1633 had been in the service of Gustavus Adolphus of Sweden, and from 1633, of the French throne. At the request of King Charles, Louis XIV agreed that the regiment should come to England on temporary loan, and so it took its place at the head of the British line regiments under its old title, the Royal or Scots Regiment. In 1662 it went back to France for some years but later came to find a place on the British Establishment and to claim its precedence.

Once having been raised or brought into service, regiments had to be paid for, and Charles adopted the customary expedient among royalty of marrying a wealthy princess, Catherine of Braganza. Apart from half a million pounds in silver, she brought him the overseas possessions of Bombay and Tangier. The latter, under constant threat from the Moors, had to be supplied with a garrison, and so the Earl of Peterborough was prevailed upon to raise a regiment of foot and a troop of horses. These units survived as the Queen's Own Regiment of Foot, later known as The Queen's Royal Regiment (West Surrey), and The 1st The Royal Dragoons.

The next regiment to join the Establishment came from Holland. At this time there were no less than three English regiments and four Scots regiments in the service of the Dutch Republic. With the struggle between Britain and Holland, the second Dutch War, (the British captured New Amsterdam and renamed it New York) the foreign troops were told peremptorily that they must either swear an oath of allegiance to the States-General or be cashiered. The English officers refused point-blank, and made their way to England where they formed the Holland Regiment, known from 1708 down to the present day as The Buffs.

It is interesting to note that the Scots officers, with few exceptions, decided to remain with their Dutch masters and it was a century before their successors sought to enter the British Army. When they did so eventually it was as the 94th Regiment, later to become the 2nd Battalion The Connaught Rangers. The Regiment was disbanded in 1922.

In 1672, to the disgust of his people, Charles II allied himself with France in the war against Holland. A force of 6,000 British troops served in this conflict, under command of the Duke of Monmouth, and, from those disbanded on the declaration of peace two years later, were formed three English regiments which took service under the Prince of Orange. Later two of these were to become regiments of the line in the British service.

With great difficulty Charles managed to keep his regiments in being, and in 1680 even managed to form another unit for service in Tangier—the 2nd Tangier Regiment, eventually, after many vicissitudes, to be called The King's Own Royal Regiment (Lancaster).

On 6 February 1685 Charles died, to be succeeded by his brother James, a soldier who had fought in no less than four campaigns under Turenne, apart from his service with the Spaniards. Thoroughly trained in the military arts, and even in military administration, James lusted for glory, and was even more determined than his predecessor that the army should remain in being. The Monmouth Rebellion of 1685 helped to further his plans, and, although the Tangier regiments were already back home, he demanded the return of three foot and three horse regiments from Holland. Though these remained for a short period, before coming over for good in 1688, two established their precedence as the 5th and 6th Regiments of the Line, eventually being known as The Royal Northumberland Fusiliers and The Royal Warwickshire Regiment. Choosing his moment, James enlarged his army still further by raising eight new cavalry regiments and twelve of infantry. The first of the foot regiments was the Ordnance Regiment raised to act as escort to the artillery. In 1689 it took the title of the Royal Fusiliers, and with minor variations was to hold this until a few years ago. The other regiments raised at this time were to take their place in the Line as the 8th, 9th, 10th, 11th, 12th, 13th, 14th and 15th, known in due course as the King's Regiment (Liverpool), the Royal Norfolk Regiment, the Royal Lincolnshire Regiment, the Devonshire Regiment, the Suffolk Regiment, the Somerset Light Infantry, the West Yorkshire Regiment, (The Prince of Wales's Own) and the East Yorkshire Regiment (The Duke of York's Own). The cavalry regiments were later to become the 1st to 6th Regiments of Dragoon Guards, and the other two after periods as dragoons and light dragoons, the 3rd The King's Own Hussars and the 4th The Queen's Own Hussars. For garrison duties, James had formed thirty independent companies, and his army had therefore grown to formidable proportions.

But the cost to the nation was immense for those times, and when James asked Parliament for the sum of £1,400,000 to maintain it, he was grudgingly given half that sum. In a fury he prorogued parliament and did not summon it again during the rest of his reign.

Even by 1685, however, the English people had grown tired of James, and detested the Catholic cause he espoused. By 1688 a message had gone to William of Orange, beseeching him to come over with his army. Hearing of this development, James raised twelve new regiments of foot, from which there emerged the 16th and 17th Foot. The army now totalled 40,000 men; but whether it would repel William or welcome him with open arms became a matter of increasing doubt. Before long the doubt was resolved, and deserted by lord and commoner alike, James signed an order for the disbandment of the army on 11 December and five days later fled the country.

Before going further, it may be mentioned that, for the first twelve years of the army's existence, the words 'regiment of foot' and 'battalion' were synonymous: they signified a unit of twelve companies, the companies varying in strength from 120 men in war to as few as 50 in peace. In 1672, however, the First Guards were increased to a strength of twenty companies, organized into two battalions, and this precedent was followed in several other regiments. It may also be interesting to note that it was James who decreed that an additional company of grenadiers should be added to each regiment or battalion, composed of the tallest men who, so it was imagined, could throw the grenade furthest.

As might have been expected, the expulsion of the Catholic King James II provoked violent reactions in France, where Louis XIV promptly declared war on Holland. England, therefore, found herself reminded of treaty obligations, and shipped a force of ten battalions under Lieutenant-General Lord Marlborough. The Royal Scots finding themselves commanded by the Duke of Schomberg (William's unwise appointment) marched as far as Ipswich en route for embarkation, mutinied, seized four cannon, and turned north for Scotland. Overtaken by a large force under General Ginkell, the Scots surrendered, and after a few ringleaders had been punished, sailed in good order for the Maas. Here the men deserted by the hundred, but their place was taken by willing recruits, and the regiment remained in being.

But the mutiny had a salutary effect on the House of Commons, which was frightened into passing the first Mutiny Act. It is often stated that the continuance of the British Army was dependent on the annual renewal of this Act, but, as Sir John Fortescue has pointed out, this is not so: 'The statute simply empowered the King to deal with certain military crimes for which the civil law made no provision. It made a great parade of the statement that the raising or keeping of a standing army in time of peace is against the law, but the standing army was in existence for nearly thirty years before the Mutiny Act was passed, and continued to exist, as will be seen, for two short but distinct periods between 1689 and 1701 without the help of any Mutiny Act.' Nevertheless the Act was a measure of immense importance in the history of the army. It will be found in full in the Appendix.

A few days before the Royal Scots mutinied there had come serious news from Ireland, where James's viceroy, the Duke of Tyrconnel, had called on the Irish to rise in his cause. Some of the regiments in the Irish establishment went over to him, while others split into Catholic and Protestants and prepared to join sides accordingly. The English Government realized that Ireland must be reconquered by force of arms, and estimates were prepared for raising six regiments of horse, two of dragoons (i.e. mounted infantry), and twenty-five of foot. So the army continued to grow. Lord Forbes' Regiment, brought over by King James in 1688 and having eluded disbandment by

William on his accession, took its place in the Line as the 18th Royal Irish. The next units to be established were three regiments raised to support the Protestant cause in 1688: the first was a cavalry regiment raised by the Earl of Devonshire among his tenantry in Derbyshire, known for many years as the Black Horse, and then as the 7th Dragoon Guards; the second, a regiment of foot raised at Exeter, later known as the 20th, and then the Lancashire Fusiliers; and the third, Colonel Francis Luttrell's Regiment, later to take precedence as the 19th Foot. Of the nine other regiments raised in 1689, only three survived, as the 22nd, 23rd and 24th of the Line (The Cheshire Regiment, The Royal Welch Fusiliers and The South Wales Borderers). Six others, Drogheda's, Lisburn's, Kingston's, Ingoldsby's, Roscommon's and Bolton's only survived a few years before disbandment.

These ephemeral corps, and indeed the regiments destined to survive on the Establishment, were in a deplorable condition, their uniforms threadbare or in tatters, their boots disintegrating, and even their weapons largely defective. The men themselves were sullen and undisciplined, and the quality of their officers varied from indifferent to corrupt and stupid. Fortunately, the campaign in Flanders came to an end after only one serious engagement at Walcourt, but then James Claverhouse, the Earl of Dundee, called the Highland clans to insurrection, and in Edinburgh Lord Leven raised a new regiment in two hours. First known as the Edinburgh Regiment of Foot, it took its place as the 25th, and from 1887 became known as the King's Own Scottish Borderers. Before 1689 was out, yet another regiment came into being; the 26th Regiment of Foot, better known as the Cameronians, the descendants of the old Cameronian Guard of the 'Lords of Convention'. The name was taken from Richard Cameron, a famous preacher.

Meanwhile, throughout 1689, the troubles went on in Ireland, where the Protestants made their base at Enniskillen, the town in northern Ireland which was crowded with refugees from Munster and Connaught. Here, to harass the rebellious Irish, were organized no less than three regiments which were to survive on the Establishment: the 5th The Royal Irish Lancers, the 6th Inniskilling Dragoons and the 27th Inniskilling Regiment of Foot, later to become the 1st Battalion The Royal Inniskilling Fusiliers.

Throughout the 1690s the war in Flanders continued, costly to both sides. Two regiments formed at this time were to survive, Colonel Sir John Gibson's as the 28th Foot (later the 1st Battalion The Gloucestershire Regiment) and Colonel Thomas Farington's, as the 29th Foot (later the 1st Battalion The Worcestershire Regiment). In 1697, with the conclusion of the Peace of Ryswick, France was exhausted and William of Orange could show one costly success—the capture of the town and citadel of Namur. The British Army in Flanders was in a miserable state, with its money and credit exhausted; pay was in arrears, and, not for the first time, there was a complete administrative breakdown.

In 1697 ten regiments were disbanded, and Robert Harley (Earl of Oxford), moved in the House of Commons that all regiments raised since 1680 should be submitted to the same fate. The motion was carried with acclamation. The attitude of the members is understandable, even if the state of Europe did not justify disarmament on such a scale; arrears of pay due to the army since 1692 amounted to almost a million and a quarter sterling, apart from subsistence which almost doubled the figure. These debts could not be met. But the clamour from officers and men who had done their duty in the face of the enemy grew so insistent that the House, being forced to make part payment, petitioned the King to appoint an independent commission to examine the grievances. In December Harley was able to push through a motion reducing the army to 7,000 men, with 12,000 on the Irish establishment. On 26 March 1699 the House went even further, declaring that all regiments, save those excepted by proclamation, should be disbanded. The Mutiny Act, which had expired in April 1698, was not renewed, so the officers commanding such units of the army that were left had no powers to enforce discipline. England lay virtually at the mercy of France; and William threatened to abdicate. As for the British Army, its career showed every appearance of coming to an end after a mere twenty-eight years of existence.

However, it survived, if in a skeleton form. 3,000 men were designated as marines; the 7th Fusiliers were transferred temporarily to the Dutch service; and a minute establishment of artillery was maintained—four companies each of thirty men under twelve officers. It was from this unpromising fragment that the Royal Regiment of Artillery was to grow. Only ten engineer officers were retained in the whole of England.

In 1701, however, the situation changed dramatically, for Britain found herself embroiled in the great conflict to be known as the War of the Spanish Succession. Yet again the enemy was Louis XIV, and a force was needed to serve in Flanders. Having been reduced to a skeleton the army had now to find thousands of recruits. Regiments raised them again; and when news arrived of troubles in the West Indies, four new regiments had to be raised. Two of these, Brudenell's and Mountjoy's, were disbanded when the emergency was over, but the others, Lord Charlemont's and Lord Donegal's served on, taking precedence as the 35th and 36th Foot respectively. Later they became the 1st Battalion The Royal Sussex Regiment and the 2nd Battalion The Worcestershire Regiment. The years 1701 and 1702 saw the appearance of many other distinguished regiments:

Colonel Thomas Sanderson's Regiment of Marines	(30th Foot)
Colonel George Villier's Regiment of Marines	(31st Foot)
Colonel Edward Fox's Regiment of Marines	(32nd Foot)
Colonel the Earl of Huntingdon's Regiment of Foot	(33rd Foot)
Colonel Lord Lucas's Regiment of Foot	(34th Foot)
Colonel the Earl of Donegal's Regiment of Foot	(35th Foot)
Colonel Thomas Meredith's Regiment of Foot	(37th Foot)
Colonel Lillingston's Regiment of Foot	(38th Foot)
Colonel Coote's Regiment of Foot	(39th Foot)

Six of these were to serve in Spain under the Earl of Peterborough while one of them, the 37th, was to serve under Marlborough and earn its first great battle honour at Blenheim in 1704. Many years later it was to become the 1st Battalion The Hampshire Regiment.

It was the Marlborough Wars, with the four great victories of Blenheim, Ramilies, Oudenarde and Malplaquet, which established the British Army as a major force in Europe; and though with the Peace of Utrecht in 1713 its numbers were reduced, there was no danger of anything approaching total disbandment. Successive revisions of the Mutiny Act established rates of pay for the various ranks, and abolished some of the more notorious deductions by the Paymaster-General, Secretary-at-War, commissaries, and muster-masters, though not unhappily the shilling in the pound due to the Queen. The Colonels, of course, continued to regard their regiments as private property, and would do so for many years yet. As captain-general the Duke of Marlborough upheld the purchase of commissions, as Wellington would do over a century later.

One concomitant of the above system was that Regiments of the Line were named after their Colonels, which meant that they changed fairly frequently, and sometimes in the middle of a battle. Such a system must have made staff work and administration extremely difficult, especially when, as often happened, there were two or more colonels with the same name. (This, of course, happened with the regiments known as the Green Howards and the Buff Howards.) Curiously enough, the system continued right through Marlborough's wars and right on until the year 1751, when it was ended by the Duke of Cumberland. The means of his doing so were curious and are not generally known. In 1747 he issued a clothing regulation which contained the following paragraph:

> 'In the centre of each colour is to be painted or embroidered in gold Roman characters the number of the rank of the Regiment within a wreath of roses and thistles.'

By the term 'rank' was meant precedence, and to comply with the instructions, the regiments were forced to confirm their precedence with the Secretary-at-War. So there developed a conscious recognition of precedence, and regiments came to refer to themselves by numbers rather than by their Colonel's name. In 1751 this custom was reinforced by a Royal Warrant, and from then onwards regiments took the identity which was to last for exactly 130 years. The royal warrant also applied to cavalry of the line, and so we see the Black Dragoons become the 6th (Inniskilling) Dragoons, and the Queen's Own Dragoons become the 7th Queen's Own Dragoons.

It may be mentioned here that between the Peace of Utrecht and 1751, several more regiments had joined the Establishment, some formed from units which had fought under Marlborough; amongst the cavalry, units which came to be known as the 9th Lancers, the 10th, 11th, 12th, 13th and 14th Hussars. There were also nineteen regiments of foot. One of the senior of these began its career as Independent Companies of Invalids, and later became the 41st (The Welsh) Regiment of Foot. The Black Watch, the oldest Highland Regiment in the army also dates from this period, being formed from Independent Companies of Highlanders. Also must be mentioned the 60th Regiment of Foot, which after many changes in title—from

1755 to 1824, it was known first as the 62nd (Royal American) Regiment, and then as the 60th (Royal American) Regiment—it became The King's Royal Rifle Corps. By 1900, having four regular battalions, it had gained more honours than any other regiment in the British Army.

It was the Seven Years' War which raged over many theatres from 1756 to 1763, that saw the next great expansion of the army. Britain was fully stretched, fighting France and then Spain in Europe, Canada and India. 1759 came to be known as the *annus mirabilis* of Britain arms, for this was the year not only of Minden but Quebec and the naval victory in Quiberon Bay. In the following year Coote decisively defeated the French in India at the battle of Wandewash. The formation of no less than five cavalry regiments and forty infantry regiments dates from this period: of the cavalry, the 15th Light Dragoons, later to become the 15th The King's Hussars, the 16th Light Dragoons which later became the 16th The Queen's Lancers, the 18th Light Dragoons which were later re-numbered the 17th and turned into lancers, fourthly a regiment popularly known as 'The Drogheda Light Horse', which in 1858 was named the 18th Hussars, and last the 19th Light Dragoons. The infantry regiments are far too numerous to mention here; they range from the 54th Foot (later to become the 2nd Battalion The Dorset Regiment), to the 109th Foot, which, as the Honourable East India Company's 3rd (Bombay European) Regiment, was to join the British Establishment in 1861, later to become the 2nd Battalion The Prince of Wales' Leinster Regiment (Royal Canadians). Mention must be made, however, of the distinguished Scottish Corps which, owing to William Pitt's wise instinct, made their appearance at this time. Among these was the unit originally raised as the 2nd Battalion 42nd Royal Highlanders which after a period as the 73rd (Perthshire) Regiment rejoined the parent corps. The two regiments of foot, 71st and 74th, which went to form the Highland Light Infantry both date from 1758, and both were to experience extraordinary vicissitudes. The 72nd and 78th (the parent regiments of the Seaforth Highlanders) date from 1756, and both were disbanded at the end of the Seven Years' War. The 75th (Stirlingshire) Regiment which after being disbanded or dispersed into Independent Companies became in 1881 the 1st Battalion The Gordon Highlanders, dates from 1758, but the 2nd Battalion was not raised until the Napoleonic Wars.

The Queen's Own Cameron Highlanders, the 79th, remained for many years the only single battalion regiment in the army.

In the American War of Independence (1775–1781) each of the 64 companies of the Brigade of Guards contributed 15 men to form a guards battalion and before the war was over most of the regiments of foot had become involved. It was in America, at the Battle of Stillwater, that the 62nd Regiment earned their nickname 'The Springers' because they acted as light infantry to whom the command 'Spring up!' was given and, despite the 125 lb load they carried, obeyed. When the 23rd (Royal Welch Fusiliers) had to surrender at Yorktown the colours were saved by two officers who wrapped them round their bodies. No less than 49 regiments carry one or more American battles on their colours.

Many of the regiments which went to form famous Irish corps date from shortly after this period: 83rd and 86th—The Royal Irish Rifles; 87th and 89th—The Royal Irish Fusiliers; 88th and 94th—The Connaught Rangers; 100th and 109th—The Prince of Wales's Leinster Regiment; 101st and 104th—The Royal Munster Fusiliers; 102nd and 103rd—The Royal Dublin Fusiliers.

It is interesting to note that, by 1763, the regiments which were to serve Britain so well during the next two centuries, were already formed, even though there were still to come a bewildering number of changes in title and number, apart from other forms or reorganization. The few exceptions may be noted, especially as they were all to gain great distinction. The 98th (Argyllshire Highlanders) Regiment of Foot, later renumbered the 91st, which became the 1st Battalion The Argyll and Sutherland Highlanders dates from 1794. From this year also dates the 92nd (Highland) Regiment of Foot, which became the junior battalion of the Gordon Highlanders. The last of the trio is the Rifle Brigade, raised as the Corps of Riflemen in 1800. The men forming it came from many units, and for a large part of the 19th century the regiment had four regular battalions. Its first battle honour, Copenhagen, dates from the year after it was formed.

From Waterloo to 1858, a period of no less than forty-three years, the British Army lived on the glories of Wellington's victories in the Peninsula and at Waterloo. Weapons, organization, command structure, the brutal penal code, and the system of purchasing commissions, all remained very much as they were. The prestige and authority of the Duke of Wellington, who had lived on until 1852, were so immense that few dare question his judgments—and within increasing age, he naturally grew more conservative. Long after the purchase of commissions had proved itself a stultifying and corrupting influence on the army, he was still defending it, oblivious to social and technical changes.

Then two great events occurred within a few years; the Crimean War which broke out in 1854, and the Indian Mutiny of 1857. The inept staff work, and the incompetence of Lord Raglan and other commanders, displayed in the Crimea, contrasted with the extreme gallantry of the troops, as brilliantly recorded in *The Times* and other papers, convinced the country that something drastic must be done: that the army must be reformed from top to bottom. After the Mutiny it became clear —as it should have done before—that the Government of the Indian sub-continent could no longer be left to the somnolent offices of the East India Company, and responsibility must be assumed by the Crown. So there was initiated the bitter debate as to whether the European troops necessary for duty in India should be provided by the British Army, or whether a separate force should be organized. Though the die-hards of the John Company were outraged, the latter course was adopted, and the nine European battalions serving the East India Company were incorporated into the British Army. The native army, which had been disrupted during the Mutiny, was totally reorganized, and became the Indian Army, a superb fighting force and a factor of stability in south-east Asia which was to hold the North-West Frontier, serve in many minor wars, and render great service to the British Empire and Commonwealth in two World Wars.*

Another major development of this period was that the senior twenty-five regiments of foot were again given a second battalion. For the most part one battalion would be serving at home, keeping the other battalion abroad up to strength with drafts. But it was in 1868 that the major reforms began, with the appointment of Edward Cardwell as Secretary of State for War. Only a few of his measures need be mentioned here: the placing of the Commander-in-Chief and his staff

* *A Register of the Regiments of the Indian Army*, in the Archive Military References, is in preparation.

in direct subordination to the Secretary of State; the abolition of the purchase of commissions; and the introduction of a twelve-year service period, divided between colour and reserve service. But it was his last reform, completed only after he had left office, which had its greatest impact on the regimental system. Perhaps it is best summed up in this passage from Major Eric Sheppard's *Short History of the British Army*:

'. . . the Regular Army and the separate reserve forces, such as the Militia and Volunteers, who were liable for home service only, were welded into one homogenous army by the establishment throughout the country of regimental districts, into which units of all these forces were brought into direct and intimate conjunction; each district normally comprised two line battalions (of which one would be on service abroad), a regular depot feeding both in peace time, two militia battalions, which it was hoped would supply recruits in war, and a proportionate number of volunteer units. Each pair of regular battalions, at first merely linked, were later formed into one regiment and renamed accordingly . . .'

This final measure, which did not materialize until 1881, and came into effect during the next twelve months, caused tremendous opposition both from the Horse Guards and from the regiments themselves. How on earth, it was asked, could a proud corps like the 68th (Durham Light Infantry) Regiment run in harness with the 106th Bombay Light Infantry? How could the 63rd (West Suffolk) Regiment be fused with the 96th Regiment—previously known as 'The Queen's Germans'—to form the Manchester Regiment? What would happen to *esprit de corps* and regimental loyalty? The anomalies were many and incredible; regiments raised in Wales found themselves based in England; regiments who had detested each other found themselves kith and kin; regiments proud of their precedence found themselves relegated to the status of a second battalion. It would be many years, and, in fact a whole new generation of officers and men would emerge, before the army ceased to curse its great benefactor, Edward Cardwell. By then the wisdom of his reforms, not the least the linking of most regiments to counties, was recognized. Loyalty to the battalion took its place within the greater loyalty to the regiment; and it was significant that when, by the chances of war, two battalions of a regiment came together, the bond was recognized at once and with great enthusiasm.

It should be mentioned here that Cardwell's linking system applied only to regiments from the 26th Foot and below, the senior regiments having already been given a second battalion, as noted. So the most senior of the linked regiments was the Cameronians (26th and 90th) while the most junior was the Royal Dublin Fusiliers (102nd Royal Madras Fusiliers and 103rd Royal Bombay Fusiliers). Perhaps it should be mentioned that another Irish regiment, The Royal Munster Fusiliers, also came from two European Regiments of the East India Company, the 101st Royal Bengal Fusiliers and the 104th Bengal Fusiliers. As these John Company regiments were largely composed of Irishmen the anomaly is not so great as it may seem. Of the cavalry, two regiments joined the British Establishment: the 1st Bengal European Cavalry which became the 19th (Prince of Wales's Own) Hussars in 1861, and the 2nd Bengal European Light Cavalry which was renamed the 20th Hussars in 1860.

In general one can say that the regimental system which had been evolved by 1881, at the end of the Cardwell reforms, was —despite some amalgamations and disbandments—the system which was to serve in two World Wars. There was, however, another series of reforms which must be mentioned here, although, so far as basic organization was concerned, they affected the regular units less than others. These were the reforms instituted by Richard Haldane, who became Minister of War in the Liberal Government of 1906. First the General Staff (formed two years previously) was made into a working reality instead of an abstraction; the Regular Army at home was organized into a strike force of six infantry divisions and one cavalry division; the Militia became the Special Reserve; and the Yeomanry and Volunteers were completely reorganized to form the Territorial Force, which provided fourteen infantry divisions and fourteen cavalry brigades. All Territorial units were linked to Regular units, the latter supplying adjutants, and much advice and assistance. The Territorial Force, of course, was granted only a few years to form and train before it was tested in the greatest conflict up to that time in world history. It may be sufficient to say here that it survived with great credit, and went on to serve in the Second World War.

Between the two World Wars there was remarkably little change in the regimental system, or in nomenclature. In 1921, however, regiments were given the opportunity of changing their titles and many did so, often adopting names by which they were popularly known for their official titles. So the Princess of Wales's Own (Yorkshire Regiment) became The Green Howards (Alexandra, Princess of Wales's Own Yorkshire Regiment), and the Prince of Wales's Own (West Yorkshire Regiment) varied its title to The West Yorkshire Regiment (The Prince of Wales's Own).

More far-reaching effects were felt among the cavalry, eighteen regiments being amalgamated to form nine. Among these were the 1st and 2nd Life Guards which formed The Life Guards; the 3rd Dragoon Guards and the Carabiniers (6th Dragoon Guards) which formed the 3rd Carabiniers (Prince of Wales's Dragoon Guards); and the 5th Dragoon Guards and the Inniskillings (6th Dragoon Guards) which formed the 5th Royal Inniskilling Dragoon Guards.

The next development, an unhappy one, was the disbandment of several Irish regiments, on the formation of the Irish Free State. These were the Royal Irish Regiment, the Connaught Rangers, The Prince of Wales's Leinster Regiment (Royal Canadians), the Royal Munster Fusiliers, and the Royal Dublin Fusiliers. All five went out of existence on 31 July 1922. The Royal Irish Rifles, which had in 1921 been renamed The Royal Ulster Rifles, soldiered on.

These fine regiments could not be replaced, though of course many officers and men served on in other regiments. It would be 1948 before any new infantry regiments appeared on the Army List, and these came from the Indian Army, now tragically split with the creation of independent India and Pakistan. They were four regiments of the Brigade of Gurkhas, who came on to the Establishment. How long they will remain, as Britain pulls back from her Far Eastern commitments, it is hard to say. But if there is fighting to be done in jungle or mountain territory their incredible skill and courage will be a welcome addition to our infantry.

The regiments of the British Army which served throughout the Second World War from 1939 to 1945, and indeed those who served in Korea in the early 1950s, would have been perfectly recognizable, with few exceptions, to anyone leaving the colours in 1881. But now rapid changes were to occur. With the exception of those belonging to the senior Guards regiments, all second battalions were to go, so that the line regiments were reduced to one battalion, the state from which Edward Cardwell had rescued them seventy years earlier. Then from 1958 onwards comes a complete process involving renaming, brigading, amalgamating, forming the amalgamated regiments into 'large regiments', disbanding, and the close association of regiments into divisions. The old notion of the regiment as a finite and almost sacred body has been deliberately eroded and officers are being cross-posted, as the requirements of the service demand. There have been strong hints that in Whitehall the regimental system is regarded as unwieldy, uneconomic and unnecessary, and that it will be replaced by a Royal Corps of Infantry. Whether this will happen, and indeed, whether all the drastic reforms will operate for the best, it is as yet impossible to say. Only time and the exigencies of action can give any definite answer. Meanwhile, though recognizing that the disappearance of any corps must bring grief to those who have loved and served it, one must realize that with the shrinking of the British Empire, the change in political situations, the shift of international alliances, and the rapid development of weaponry, the army's role has changed. It has been said and with some justice that the British Army has always prepared for the last war rather than for the next; let us hope that the many changes we have seen since 1958 are an indication that this will not happen again.

Such wider aspects apart, the inescapable fact is that many familiar names have disappeared from the Army List and many new names have appeared: The Blues and Royals, The Queen's Regiment, The Royal Regiment of Fusiliers, The Royal Anglian Regiment, The Royal Irish Rangers, The Royal Highland Fusiliers, and others. How long these will last it is impossible to say—some have been reduced in size during the few years since formation—but as long as they do, they will carry the traditions and honours of regiments which are now history.

So far these notes have been exclusively concerned with the infantry and cavalry regiments, to the exclusion of the other branches of the service. The reason is first that, taking part in all campaigns and battles, the Corps do not have battle honours, and it has therefore been possible to find space for historical notes on the relevant pages. Secondly, many of the Corps appeared late in the Army's history, no less than eighteen of them being formed since the Crimean War, though one may identify their forerunners among specialist units. In some ways the British Army has been slow to recognize the services to be rendered by highly trained specialists; it was not until 1716 for example that the Royal Engineers broke free from the artillery, and a further forty-one years were to pass before its officers gained military rank. The Royal Regiment of Artillery was not founded until 1716 either, and it is extraordinary to realize that in such great battles as Blenheim and Oudenarde, and indeed in all his campaigns, the Duke of Marlborough relied on the Train of Artillery, an irregular force raised by royal warrant and disbanded on the cessation of hostilities. Probably the innate conservatism of the military authorities is nowhere more evident than in the field of intercommunication or signalling. Though signalling has presented a problem to all armies and in all ages, it was not until 1920 that the Royal Corps of Signals was formed; and it is interesting to note that the Signals struggled to become independent of the Royal Engineers as two centuries previously the latter had struggled to become independent of the artillery. Of the remaining Corps, probably none has survived such vicissitudes and changes of title as the Royal Corps of Transport; on no less than three occasions has the Corps (or to be more accurate, its forerunners) been disbanded, the last occasion being as recent as 1857.

Whether, with further technological development, the various corps and departments of the army will suffer the upheavals experienced by the cavalry and infantry, it is impossible to say, but there are no indications at the moment.

The Royal Artillery has switched from shells to rockets, where necessary, and will no doubt cope with guided missiles without losing its identity or its name. The Royal Engineers will adapt itself to new techniques as these are developed—as it has always done in the past—and the same applies to the Royal Corps of Signals. And even if tanks are superseded by some form of robot there is no reason to suppose that the Royal Armoured Corps will be unable to accept the challenge.

No doubt further changes in the British Army will come— and indeed a few are already presaged—but it is hoped that this work will serve as a link between past and present. No army however advanced or even automated can afford to let its traditions be forgotten.

ARTHUR SWINSON

British Regimental
Organization, 1972

British Regimental Organization, 1972

Most of today's British regiments have been in continuous existence for a long time; if this seems self-evident it would be well to reflect that such a statement cannot accurately be made of any other country. It might be expected, since age and continuity are hallmarks of British institutions, that the Army would have had an evolutionary rather than a revolutionary history, but it would be wrong to suppose that a path of development different from that of continental armies was deliberately chosen. The oceans and Royal Navy along with Parliament and Crown spared the British Army many of the upheavals, political and military, which upset continuity in the growth of institutions in Europe and America. Nevertheless, during the last century at least, conscious efforts were made to keep venerable regiments alive almost for their own sakes, for respect for tradition has become a national characteristic, nowhere stronger than in the Army. It is a tribute both to the flexibility of the British regimental system and to the good sense of the soldiers who run it that ways have always been found to reconcile tradition with efficiency.

The purpose of *A Register of Regiments* is to chronicle those reconciliations and to provide a clear guide to the ancestry of any existing regiment or corps or to the descent of an ancestor regiment.

Let us start with the CAVALRY. The organization of cavalry regiments is best understood by looking at an Army List for a year shortly before the First World War. This would show thirty one mounted regiments in three groups: three regiments of The Household Cavalry, seven of Dragoon Guards and twenty-one of Dragoons, Hussars or Lancers. The Household Cavalry were the monarch's personal troops; Dragoon Guards were regiments of horse who, when the government was trying to increase the numbers of mounted infantry (dragoon) regiments in 1746, were persuaded by the bribe of a guards title to accept that despised role. In practice they fairly swiftly reverted to pure cavalry while keeping the honorific 'Guards'. The third group had largely evolved from mounted infantry regiments who, disliking their dismounted duties found ways to avoid it and succeeded, by the end of the 18th century, in becoming ordinary cavalry regiments. Some became light cavalry and during the Napoleonic Wars and after these were given the dress, equipment and titles of Hussars and Lancers, largely for faddish reasons. Eventually only the 1st, 2nd and 6th retained their ancient Dragoon title. The last three pre-First World War cavalry regiments were East India Company European regiments which were absorbed into the regular establishment in 1858.

The order of battle of the cavalry remained unaltered until 1922 when, room having to be found in a drastically reduced army for the Tank Corps, the cavalry regiments were naturally chosen for reduction. The amalgamation was done by seniority and took place strictly within the three groups with the exception of that between the 5th Dragoon Guards and the 6th Dragoons. Among the cavalry regiments numbered from one to twenty-one Lancer married Lancer and Hussar married Hussar. This programme produced the order of battle in which the cavalry fought the Second World War.*

The latest great round of reductions in the cavalry began in the late 1950s and would now seem to have run its course. Once again amalgamation was by seniority within groups with two exceptions: the Royal Horse Guards joined with the 1st Dragoons and the 3rd Dragoon Guards with the Royal Scots Greys (2nd Dragoons). It is not only sentimentalists who will regret the passing of the last two pure Dragoon regiments from the Army List, though the title has been saved from extinction in the new regiment, The Blues and Royals (Royal Horse Guards and 1st Dragoons).

The ancestry of regiments of the INFANTRY is a good deal more difficult to follow than that of cavalry. Once more the best starting point is probably an old Army List, say for 1870. This will reveal three sorts of infantry regiments: Foot Guards; the Rifle Brigade; and 109 regiments of Foot which, since the abandonment of titling by name of Colonels in 1751, or since

* For operational purposes The Life Guards and The Royal Horse Guards took the field (mixed) as the 1st and 2nd Household Cavalry Regiments.

their raising (whichever was later), had carried numbers. Most of the numbered regiments would also be seen to bear a territorial title, there having been a general grant of such titles in 1782, and some also to describe themselves as Fusiliers or Light Infantry—functional distinctions no longer of real significance. It would also be seen that the first 25 regiments had two battalions, whereas the remainder had only one.

This disparity led in 1871 to the most famous and still perhaps the most important reorganization which the British Infantry has ever undergone, that carried through by the Liberal War Minister, Edward Cardwell. Believing that the two-battalion system was the only one by which the Empire might be effectively garrisoned, he determined to link the single-battalion regiments into pairs and form new regiments from them. Thus emerged the 'County' regiments of the First and Second World Wars, so-called from the county or other local title that each adopted in 1881. In doing so, of course, most regiments had to shed a title that they had carried since 1782. But that grant had not attached the regiments to the counties whose names they bore. That of 1881 did, each regiment being given a depot in its eponymous locality.

The old numbers, however, did not die with Cardwell. They remained, of course, the basis of the order of precedence. They continued in private use within the regiments, 1st and 2nd battalions commonly referring to each other by their pre-Cardwell numbers ('I strop my razor 52 times', a 2nd Ox and Bucks officer was fond of remarking, 'and when I get to 43 I spit'—testimony that Cardwell's arranged matches were for many years not always happy ones). And, in the great reorganization of the 1950s and 1960s, some were officially readopted as the most convenient way of commemorating the origins of regiments newly amalgamated.

This latest reorganization did not bring about the first disbandments of modern times (those had been suffered by the five southern Irish regiments in 1922) nor the first amalgamations (those were the work of Cardwell), but its results were more destructive of the historic character of British infantry than any hitherto. In 1948 all second battalions (except those of the senior Foot Guards) had been disbanded, so that all 1st Battalions junior to the first 25 now represented two historic regiments of Foot (60th and 79th excluded for reasons explained in the text). Furthermore, all these now single-battalion regiments had been grouped, since 1946, in administrative brigades with territorial designations (e.g. East Anglian Brigade, containing all the East Anglian regiments). Then, from 1958 onwards, amalgamations were ordered by the War Office between regiments of these brigades, in order of juniority, so as to reduce the superfluity of infantry in the Army; disbandment was offered as the alternative, which at first no regiment chose. As the rate of reduction quickened, however, a number did so in the late 1960s, while other regiments, with official encouragement, opted for inclusion in a 'large regiment', a refuge which promised the chance to preserve, if in somewhat ghostly fashion, the identities of all those which joined. Thus the Royal Anglian Regiment, now (1971) of three battalions and one independent company, incorporates seven of the old pre-Cardwell numbered regiments of Foot.

In 1971 all infantry except the Parachute Regiment and the Ghurka Regiments were arranged for administrative reasons in six divisions: The Guards, Scottish, Queen's, King's, Prince of Wales's and Light (see page lix). Whether the 'divisional' system foreshadows the reduction of the Foot to six super-large regiments is not known. Given the proved resilience of the regimental system it seems unlikely.

JOHN KEEGAN

December, 1971   Royal Military Academy

NOTE

None of the following units are included in this volume of Archive Military References: The Militia, Volunteers, Yeomanry, Special Reserve or regiments of the Territorial Army, the Indian Army or of the Colonies. No ephemeral or disbanded regiments are listed except, for reasons of historical clarity, the Irish Regiments disbanded in 1922.

LATE CORRECTIONS

After some sheets had been printed it was discovered that *Ramillies* and *Suvla* had been mis-spelt. The correct spellings are given where possible.

pages 11, 14, 20, 49, and 56
The amalgamation of the 3rd Carabiniers (Prince of Wales's Dragoon Guards) and The Royal Scots Greys (2nd Dragoons) took place in July 1971 to form: The Royal Scots Dragoon Guards (Carabiniers and Greys). Of the 53 battle honours previously carried on the Standards of the two regiments all but 'Shivebo', 'Bremen' and 'France and Flanders, 1914–1918', appear on the new Standard.

page 27
Titles after 1783 should read:
1783–1807   The 7th, or Queen's Own Light Dragoons.
1807–1921   The 7th (Queen's Own) Hussars.
1921–1958   The 7th Queen's Own Hussars.

page 42
First title: *Burgoyne's* Light Horse.

page 61
The Grenadier Guards. The title granted in 1815 to the First Regiment of Foot Guards was for having defeated the Grenadiers of the French Imperial Guards at Waterloo.

page 63
Date of third campaign should read: 1673.

page 124
Dates for the first title should read: 1689–1751.
Motto should read: 'Nec aspera terrent' (Nor do difficulties deter).

page 148
Dates of second title should read: 1743–1748.

page 149
Dates of second previous unit should read: 1748–1757.

page 156
In 1921 the title varied to: The Middlesex *Regiment* (Duke of Cambridge's Own).

page 168
Date of Cherbourg should read: 1758.

page 176
Sixth campaign/battle should read: 1803 Laswarree.

Orders of Precedence

SYMBOLS

Infantry regiments are single battalion unless marked
** Two battalions
† Three battalions
‡ Four battalions

I ORDER OF PRECEDENCE OF CAVALRY AND INFANTRY REGIMENTS, 1870

CAVALRY REGIMENTS

1st Life Guards
2nd Life Guards
Royal Horse Guards
1st The King's Dragoon Guards
2nd Dragoon Guards (Queen's Bays)
3rd The Prince of Wales's Dragoon Guards
4th Royal Irish Dragoon Guards
5th Princess Charlotte of Wales's Dragoon Guards
6th Dragoon Guards (Carabiniers)
7th The Princess Royal's Regiment of Dragoon Guards
1st Royal Dragoons
2nd Royal North British Dragoons (Scots Greys)
3rd King's Own Hussars
4th Queen's Own Hussars
5th Royal Irish Lancers
6th Inniskilling Dragoons
7th Queen's Own Hussars
8th King's Royal Irish Hussars
9th Queen's Royal Lancers
10th Prince of Wales's Own Royal Hussars
11th Prince Albert's Own Hussars
12th Prince of Wales's Royal Lancers
13th Hussars
14th King's Hussars
15th King's Hussars
16th Queen's Lancers
17th Lancers
18th Hussars
19th Hussars
20th Hussars
21st Hussars

FOOT GUARDS

1st (or Grenadier) Guards†   Coldstream Guards**   Scots Fusilier Guards**

REGIMENTS OF FOOT, 1870

1st The Royal**
2nd The Queen's Royal**
3rd East Kent (The Buffs)**
4th King's Own Royal**
5th Northumberland Fusiliers**
6th Royal 1st Warwickshire**
7th Royal Fusiliers**
8th The King's**
9th East Norfolk**
10th North Lincolnshire**
11th North Devonshire**
12th East Suffolk**
13th 1st Somersetshire Prince Albert's Light Infantry**
14th Buckinghamshire**
15th Yorkshire East Riding**
16th Bedfordshire**
17th Leicestershire**
18th Royal Irish**
19th 1st Yorkshire North Riding**
20th East Devonshire**
21st Royal North British Fusiliers**
22nd Cheshire**
23rd Royal Welsh Fusiliers**
24th 2nd Warwickshire**
25th King's Own Borderers
26th Cameronian
27th Inniskilling
28th North Gloucestershire
29th Worcestershire
30th Cambridgeshire
31st Huntingdonshire
32nd Cornwall Light Infantry
33rd Duke of Wellington's
34th Cumberland
35th Royal Sussex
36th Herefordshire
37th North Hampshire
38th 1st Staffordshire
39th Dorsetshire
40th 2nd Somersetshire
41st Welsh
42nd Royal Highland (The Black Watch)
43rd Monmouthshire Light Infantry
44th East Essex
45th Nottinghamshire (Sherwood Foresters)
46th South Devonshire
47th Lancashire
48th Northamptonshire
49th Princess Charlotte of Wales's Hertfordshire
50th Queen's Own
51st 2nd Yorkshire West Riding King's Own Light Infantry

52nd Oxfordshire Light Infantry
53rd Shropshire
54th West Norfolk
55th Westmoreland
56th West Essex
57th West Middlesex
58th Rutlandshire
59th 2nd Nottinghamshire
60th King's Royal Rifle Corps‡
61st South Gloucestershire
62nd Wiltshire
63rd West Suffolk
64th 2nd Staffordshire
65th 2nd Yorkshire N. Riding
66th Berkshire
67th South Hampshire
68th Durham Light Infantry
69th South Lincolnshire
70th Surrey
71st Highland Light Infantry
72nd Duke of Albany's Own Highlanders
73rd Perthshire
74th Highland
75th Stirlingshire
76th
77th East Middlesex
78th Highland, Rossshire Buffs
79th Cameron Highlanders
80th Staffordshire Volunteers
81st Loyal Lincoln Volunteers
82nd Prince of Wales's Volunteers

83rd County Dublin
84th York and Lancashire
85th Buckinghamshire Volunteers The King's Light Infantry
86th Royal County Down
87th Royal Irish Fusiliers
88th Connaught Rangers
89th Princess Victoria's
90th Perthshire Volunteers Light Infantry
91st Argyllshire Highlanders
92nd Gordon Highlanders
93rd Sutherland Highlanders
94th
95th Derbyshire
96th
97th Earl of Ulster's
98th
99th Lanarkshire
100th Prince of Wales's Royal Canadians
101st Royal Bengal Fusiliers
102nd Royal Madras Fusiliers
103rd Royal Bombay Fusiliers
104th Bengal Fusiliers
105th Madras Light Infantry
106th Bombay Light Infantry
107th Bengal Infantry
108th Madras Infantry
109th Bombay Infantry
Rifle Brigade The Prince Consort's Own‡

II REGIMENTS OF INFANTRY, 1914

Pre-Cardwell Numbers
Infantry of the Line have two battalions unless otherwise marked

Grenadier Guards†
Coldstream Guards†
Scots Guards**
Irish Guards (one battalion)
1 Royal Scots (Lothian Regiment)
2 Queen's Royal West Surrey
3 The Buffs (East Kent)
4 King's Own (Royal Lancaster)
5 Northumberland Fusiliers
6 Royal Warwickshire
7 Royal Fusiliers‡
8 King's (Liverpool)
9 Norfolk
10 Lincolnshire
11 Devonshire
12 Suffolk

13 Prince Albert's Somerset Light Infantry
14 Prince of Wales's Own West Yorkshire
15 East Yorkshire
16 Bedfordshire
17 Leicestershire
18 Royal Irish
19 Alexandra, Princess of Wales's Own Yorkshire
20 Lancashire Fusiliers
21 Royal Scots Fusiliers
22 Cheshire
23 Royal Welsh Fusiliers
24 South Wales Borderers
25 King's Own Scottish Borderers

26/90 Cameronians (Scottish Rifles)
27/108 Royal Inniskilling Fusiliers
28/61 Gloucestershire
29/36 Worcestershire‡
30/59 East Lancashire
31/70 East Surrey
32/46 Duke of Cornwall's Light Infantry
33/76 Duke of Wellington's (West Riding)
34/55 Border
35/107 Royal Sussex
37/67 Hampshire
38/80 South Staffordshire
39/54 Dorset
40/82 Prince of Wales's Volunteers (South Lancashire)
41/69 Welsh
42/73 Black Watch (Royal Highlanders)
43/52 Oxfordshire and Buckinghamshire Light Infantry
44/56 Essex
45/95 Sherwood Foresters (Nottinghamshire and Derbyshire)
47/81 Loyal North Lancashire
48/58 Northamptonshire
49/66 Princess Charlotte of Wales's Royal Berkshire
50/97 Queen's Own Royal West Kent

51/105 King's Own Yorkshire Light Infantry
53/85 King's Shropshire Light Infantry
55/77 Duke of Cambridge's Own Middlesex‡
60 King's Royal Rifle Corps‡
62/99 Duke of Edinburgh's Wiltshire
63/96 Manchester
64/98 Prince of Wales's North Staffordshire
65/84 York and Lancaster
68/106 Durham Light Infantry
71/74 Highland Light Infantry
72/78 Seaforth Highlanders (Ross-shire Buffs, the Duke of Albany's)
75/92 Gordon Highlanders
79 Queen's Own Cameron Highlanders
83/86 Royal Irish Rifles
87/89 Princess Victoria's Royal Irish Fusiliers
88/94 Connaught Rangers
91/93 Princess Louise's Argyll & Sutherland Highlanders
100/109 Prince of Wales's Leinster (Royal Canadians)
101/104 Royal Munster Fusiliers
102/103 Royal Dublin Fusiliers
The Rifle Brigade (Prince Consort's Own)‡

III PRECEDENCE OF CORPS, 1971

1 The Life Guards and The Blues and Royals
2 Royal Horse Artillery*
3 Royal Armoured Corps
4 Royal Regiment of Artillery (Royal Horse Artillery excepted)
5 Corps of Royal Engineers
6 Royal Corps of Signals
7 Regiments of Foot Guards
8 Regiments of Infantry
9 Special Air Service Regiment
10 Army Air Corps
11 Royal Army Chaplains' Department
12 Royal Corps of Transport
13 Royal Army Medical Corps
14 Royal Army Ordnance Corps

15 Corps of Royal Electrical and Mechanical Engineers
16 Corps of Royal Military Police
17 Royal Army Pay Corps
18 Royal Army Veterinary Corps
19 Small Arms School Corps
20 Military Provost Staff Corps
21 Royal Army Educational Corps
22 Royal Army Dental Corps
23 Royal Pioneer Corps
24 Intelligence Corps
25 Army Physical Training Corps
26 Army Catering Corps
27 General Service Corps (defunct)
28 Queen Alexandra's Royal Army Nursing Corps
29 Women's Royal Army Corps

* But on parade, with their guns, to take the right and march at the head of the Household Cavalry.

IV PRECEDENCE OF REGIMENTS OF THE ROYAL ARMOURED CORPS, 1971

1 Queen's Dragoon Guards
2 Royal Scots Dragoon Guards (Carabiniers and Greys)
3 4/7th Dragoon Guards
4 5th Royal Inniskilling Dragoon Guards
5 Queen's Own Hussars
6 Queen's Royal Irish Hussars
7 9/12th Royal Lancers (Prince of Wales's)
8 Royal Hussars (Prince of Wales's Own)
9 13/18th Royal Hussars (Queen Mary's Own)
10 14/20th King's Hussars
11 15/19th The King's Royal Hussars
12 16/5th The Queen's Royal Lancers
13 17/21st Lancers
14 The Royal Tank Regiment

V PRECEDENCE OF INFANTRY REGIMENTS, 1971

Pre-Cardwell Numbers

The Royal Scots (The Royal Regiment)	1
The Queen's Regiment	2, 3, 31, 35, 50, 57, 70, 77, 78 and 107
The King's Own Royal Border Regiment	4, 34 and 55
The Royal Regiment of Fusiliers	5, 6, 7 and 20
The King's Regiment	8, 63 and 96
The Royal Anglian Regiment	9, 10, 12, 16, 17, 44, 48, 56 and 58
The Devonshire and Dorset Regiment	11, 39 and 54
The Light Infantry	13, 32, 46, 51, 53, 68, 85, 105 and 106
The Prince of Wales's Own Regiment of Yorkshire	14 and 15
The Green Howards (Alexandra, Princess of Wales's Own Yorkshire Regiment)	19
The Royal Highland Fusiliers (Princess Margaret's Own Glasgow and Ayrshire Regiment)	21, 71 and 74
The Cheshire Regiment	22
The Royal Welch Fusiliers	23
The Royal Regiment of Wales	24, 41 and 69
The King's Own Scottish Borderers	25
The Royal Irish Rangers (27th (Inniskilling) 83rd and 87th)	27, 83, 87, 89 and 108
The Gloucestershire Regiment	28 and 61
The Worcestershire and Sherwood Foresters Regiment (29th/45th Foot)	29, 36, 45 and 95
The Queen's Lancashire Regiment	30, 40, 47, 59, 81 and 82
The Duke of Wellington's Regiment (West Riding)	33 and 76
The Royal Hampshire Regiment	37 and 67
The Staffordshire Regiment (The Prince of Wales's)	38, 64, 80 and 98
The Black Watch (Royal Highland Regiment)	42 and 73
The Duke of Edinburgh's Royal Regiment (Berkshire and Wiltshire)	49, 62, 66 and 99
Queen's Own Highlanders (Seaforth and Camerons)	72, 78 and 79
The Gordon Highlanders	75 and 92

The Argyll and Sutherland Highlanders (Princess Louise's)   91 and 93
The Parachute Regiment   —
The Brigade of Gurkhas   —
The Royal Green Jackets   43, 52 and 60

VI DIVISIONAL ORGANIZATION OF INFANTRY, 1971

The Guards Division
Grenadier Guards
Coldstream Guards
Scots Guards
Irish Guards
Welsh Guards

The Scottish Division
The Royal Scots
Royal Highland Fusiliers (Princess Margaret's Own Glasgow and Ayrshire Regiment)
The King's Own Scottish Borderers
The Black Watch (Royal Highland Regiment)
The Queen's Own Highlanders (Seaforth & Camerons)
The Gordon Highlanders
The Argyll and Sutherland Highlanders

The Queen's Division
The Queen's Regiment
The Royal Regiment of Fusiliers
The Royal Anglian Regiment

The King's Division
The King's Own Royal Border Regiment

The King's Regiment
The Prince of Wales's Own Regiment of Yorkshire
The Green Howards (Alexandra, Princess of Wales's Own Yorkshire Regiment)
The Royal Irish Rangers
The Queen's Lancashire Regiment
The Duke of Wellington's Regiment (West Riding)

The Prince of Wales's Division
The Devonshire and Dorset Regiment
The Cheshire Regiment
The Royal Welch Fusiliers
The Royal Regiment of Wales
The Gloucestershire Regiment
The Worcestershire and Sherwood Foresters Regiment (29th/45th Foot)
The Royal Hampshire Regiment
The Staffordshire Regiment (The Prince of Wales's)
The Duke of Edinburgh's Royal Regiment (Berkshire and Wiltshire)

The Light Division
The Light Infantry
The Royal Green Jackets

The Cavalry
Regiments

The 1st Life Guards

With the 2nd Life Guards, originated as follows:

In 1639 a number of Royalists formed themselves into a bodyguard to protect Charles I. After his execution in 1649 they crossed the Channel to offer their services to his son, later Charles II.

In 1656 he formed them into a Corps of Life Guards under Lord Gerard.

In 1656 Parliament established a body of horse to be called General Monck's Troop of Life Guards, Monck then being commander-in-chief of the Army of the Commonwealth.

At the restoration of 1660 when Charles arrived at Dover, he was attended both by the King's Life Guard, organized into three troops, and Monck's Troop of Life Guards.

On the 30 June 1660 Parliament passed a resolution bringing on to the Establishment the Duke of York's Life Guards, raised in Flanders.

By an order of 26 January 1661 Charles II established his Household Cavalry as 'His Majesties own Troope of Guards, His Highness Royall the Duke of Yorke his Troope of Guards, and his Grace the Duke of Albermarle his Troope of Guards.'

TITLES

1661–1788	The Life Guards
	In 1788 the troops were re-constituted to form:
1788–1922	The 1st and 2nd Life Guards

PRINCIPAL CAMPAIGNS, BATTLES, etc.

1673	Maestricht	1815	Netherlands
1690	Boyne	1882	Egypt
1692–7	Flanders	1882	Tel-el-Kebir
1692	Steenkirk	1884–5	Khartoum
1693	Neer Landen	1889–1900	South Africa
1743	Dettingen	1900	Relief of Kimberley
1812–14	Peninsula		Paardeberg
1815	Waterloo	1914–18	*See* The Life Guards

continued overleaf

3

NICKNAMES

The Cheeses   The Piccadilly Butchers
The Tin Bellies   The Patent Safeties

April 1922   Amalgamated with the 2nd Life Guards to form:
THE LIFE GUARDS

see page 4   2nd Life Guards
see page 48   The Life Guards

The 2nd Life Guards

(For origins see 1st Life Guards)

TITLES

1660–1788   The Life Guards
            In 1788 the troops were re-constituted to form:
1788–1922   The 1st and 2nd Life Guards

PRINCIPAL CAMPAIGNS, BATTLES, etc.

1673	Maestricht	1815	Netherlands
1689–70	Flanders	1882	Egypt
1689	Walcourt	1882	Tel-el-Kebir
1694–97	Flanders	1884–5	Khartoum
1695	Namur	1899–1900	South Africa
1743	Dettingen	1900	Relief of Kimberley
1812–14	Peninsula		Paardeberg
1815	Waterloo	1914–18	*See* The Life Guards

NICKNAMES

The Cheeses   The Cheese Mongers
The Tin Bellies

April 1922   Amalgamated with 1st Life Guards to form:
THE LIFE GUARDS

see page 3   1st Life Guards
see page 48   The Life Guards

The Royal Horse Guards (The Blues)

Soon after the restoration Charles II adopted Colonel Unton Croke cavalry regiment which now styled itself 'the Royal Regiment'. In December 1660 this unit was disbanded. By royal warrant of 26 January 1661 was raised the Earl of Oxford's Regiment of Horse, many of the officers having previously served under Unton Croke. In 1819 the regiment finally established itself without question as part of the Household Cavalry.

TITLES

At various times the Regiment was designated:
His Majesty's Regiment of Horse
The King's Regiment of Horse
The First Horse
The Horse
The First Regiment of Horse
The Earl of Oxford's Regiment of Horse
The 'Blew' Guards
The King's Regiment of Horse Guards
The Royal Regiment of Horse Guards
His Majesty's Own Regiment of Horse Guards
The Oxford Blues

1750–1819	The Royal Horse Guards (Blue)
1819–1969	The Royal Horse Guards (The Blues)

PRINCIPAL CAMPAIGNS, BATTLES, etc.

1685	Sedgemoor	1812–14	Peninsula
1689–90	Flanders	1813	Vittoria
1689	Walcourt	1815	Waterloo
1690	Boyne	1882	Egypt
1742–5	Flanders	1882	Tel-el-Kebir
1743	Dettingen	1884–5	Nile
1745	Fontenoy	1901–2	South Africa
1758–62	Germany		
1760	Warburg	1914–18	IST WORLD WAR
1761	Kirk Denkern		Battle honours
1762	Wilhelmstahl		selected to appear on
1794	Flanders		the Standard:
1794	Beaumont		Le Cateau
1794	Willems		Marne, 1914

continued overleaf

1914–18	Messines, 1914	1939–45	selected to appear on
	Ypres, 1914, '15, '17		the Standard:
	Gheluvelt		Souleuvre
	Fresenberg		Brussels
	Loos		Nederrijn
	Arras, 1917		N.W. Europe, 1944–5
	Sambre		Iraq, 1941
	France & Flanders		Palmyra
	1914–18		Syria, 1941
			El Alamein
1939–45	2ND WORLD WAR		North Africa, 1942–3
	Battle honours		Italy, 1944

NICKNAMES

The Oxford Blues   The Blue Guards   The Blues

1 April 1969	Amalgamated with The Royal Dragoons (1st Dragoons) to form: THE BLUES AND ROYALS (Royal Horse Guards and 1st Dragoons)

see page 17 The Royal Dragoons (1st Dragoons)
see page 57 The Blues and Royals (Royal Horse Guards and 1st Dragoons)

6

The 1st King's Dragoon Guards

Raised chiefly near London during the Monmouth Rebellion.

TITLES

1685–1714	The Queen's (or 2nd) Regiment of Horse
1714–46	The King's Own Regiment of Horse
1746–1959	The 1st King's Dragoon Guards

PRINCIPAL CAMPAIGNS, BATTLES, etc.

1685	Sedgemoor	1855	Sevastopol
1690	Boyne	1860	China
1691	Aughrim	1860	Taku Forts
1692–7	Flanders	1860	Pekin
1693	Neer Landen	1879	South Africa
1695	Namur	1901–2	South Africa
1702–14	Flanders and Germany	1914–18	1ST WORLD WAR
1702	Liege		Battle honours
1703	Huy		selected to appear on
1704	Schellenberg		the Standard:
1704	Blenheim		Somme, 1916
1705	Neer Hespen		Morval
1706	Ramillies		France & Flanders,
1708	Oudenarde		1914–17
1708	Lisle	1919	Afghanistan (3rd
1709	Tournay		Afghan War)
1709	Malplaquet		
1711	Bouchain	1939–45	2ND WORLD WAR
1742–6	Flanders		Battle honours
1743	Dettingen		selected to appear on
1745	Fontenoy		the Standard:
1758–63	Germany		Beda Fomm
1760	Warburg		Defence of Tobruk
1761	Kirk Denkern		Defence of Alamein
1762	Wilhelmstahl		Line
1763	Groebenstein		Advance on Tripoli
1793–5	Flanders		Tebaga Gap
1794	Cateau		Tunis
1794	Beaumont		North Africa, 1941–43
1815	Waterloo		Monte Gamino
1815	Netherlands		Gothic Line
1854–5	Crimea		Italy, 1943–4

continued overleaf

NICKNAMES

Bland's Dragoons   The K.D.G.'s
The Trades Union

1 January
1959

Amalgamated with The Queen's Bays (2nd Dragoon Guards) to form:
THE 1st THE QUEEN'S DRAGOON GUARDS

see page 9   Queen's Bays (2nd Dragoon Guards)
see page 56   1st The Queen's Dragoon Guards

The Queen's Bays (2nd Dragoon Guards)

The Regiment was formed from four troops raised as follows: in Hounslow by Sir John Talbot, in Edgware by Mr. John Lloyd, in Yorkshire by Sir Michael Wentworth, in London by Lord Aylesbury. The Regiment was first commanded by Henry, 2nd Earl of Peterborough.

TITLES

1685–8	Colonel the Earl of Peterborough's Regiment of Horse
1688–1711	The 3rd Regiment of Horse
1711–27	The Princess of Wales's Own Royal Regiment of Horse
1727–46	The Queen's Own Royal Regiment of Horse
1746–1872	The 2nd Queen's Dragoon Guards
1872–1921	The 2nd Dragoon Guards (Queen's Bays)
1921–1959	The Queen's Bays (2nd Dragoon Guards)

PRINCIPAL CAMPAIGNS, BATTLES, etc.

1690	Boyne
1691	Aughrim
1695	Namur
1704–10	Spain
1707	Almanza
1710	Almanara
1710	Saragosa
1715	Jacobite Rebellion
1745	Jacobite Rebellion
1760–3	Germany
1760	Warburg
1761	Kirk Denkern
1762	Wilhelmstahl
1763	Groebenstein
1793–5	Flanders
1793	Dunkirk
1794	Tournay
1809	Flushing
1858	Indian Mutiny
1858	Lucknow
1901–2	South Africa

1914–18   1ST WORLD WAR
Battle honours selected to appear on the Standard:

1914–18	Mons
	Le Cateau
	Marne, 1914
	Messines, 1914
	Ypres, 1914, '15
	Somme, 1916, '18
	Scarpe, 1917
	Cambrai, 1917–18
	Amiens
	Pursuit to Mons

1939–45   2ND WORLD WAR
Battle honours selected to appear on the Standard:

Somme, 1940
Gazala
El Alamein
El Hamma
Tunis
North Africa, 1941–43
Coriano
Lamone Crossing
Rimini
Argenta Gap

continued overleaf

The Queen's Bays (2nd Dragoon Guards)

NICKNAMES
The Bays   The Rusty Buckles

MOTTO
'Pro Rege et Patria' (For King and country)

1 January 1959	Amalgamated with the 1st King's Dragoon Guards to form: THE 1st THE QUEEN'S DRAGOON GUARDS
see page 7	1st King's Dragoon Guards
see page 56	1st The Queen's Dragoon Guards

The 3rd Dragoon Guards (Prince of Wales's)

Formed from old regiments of Horse raised in Worcester-shire, Oxfordshire, Bedfordshire and at St. Albans and Dorking.

TITLES

1685–7	Colonel the Earl of Plymouth's Regiment of Horse
1687–1746	The 4th Regiment of Horse
1746–65	The 3rd Regiment of Dragoon Guards
1765–1921	The 3rd (Prince of Wales's) Dragoon Guards
1921–2	The 3rd Dragoon Guards (Prince of Wales's)

PRINCIPAL CAMPAIGNS, BATTLES, etc.

1689	Scotland	1760	Warburg
1691–7	Flanders	1762	Wilhelmstahl
1692	Steenkirk	1763	Groebenstein
1693	Neer Landen	1793–5	Flanders
1695	Namur	1793	Dunkirk
1702–14	Flanders and Germany	1794	Cateau
		1794	Tournay
1704	Blenheim	1809–14	Peninsula
1706	Ramillies	1809	Talavera
1708	Oudenarde	1811	Albuera
1709	Malplaquet	1813	Vittoria
1710	Bethune	1868	Abyssinia
1715 } 1745 }	Jacobite Rising	1901–2	South Africa
		1914–18	*See* 3rd Carabineers
1758–63	Germany		(Prince of Wales's
1759	Minden		Dragoon Guards)

NICKNAMES

The Old Canaries

April 1922   Amalgamated with The Carabiniers (6th Dragoon Guards) to form:
3rd CARABINIERS (PRINCE OF WALES'S DRAGOON GUARDS)

see page 14   The Carabiniers (6th Dragoon Guards)
see page 49   3rd Carabiniers (Prince of Wales's Dragoon Guards)
see page 56   The Royal Scots Dragoon Guards

The 4th Royal Irish Dragoon Guards

Raised in various English counties—at London, Lichfield, Grantham, Durham and Morpeth.

TITLES

1685–90	Colonel the Earl of Arran's Cuirassiers. Also, the 6th Horse
1690–1746	The 5th Horse
1746–88	The 1st Irish Horse or the Blue Horse
1788–1921	The 4th (Royal Irish) Dragoon Guards
1921–2	The 4th Royal Irish Dragoon Guards

PRINCIPAL CAMPAIGNS, BATTLES, etc.

1691–97	Flanders	1914–18	1ST WORLD WAR
1692	Steenkirk		Battle honours
1693	Neer Landen		selected to appear on
1695	Namur		the Standard:
1811–13	Peninsula		Mons
1812	Ciudad Rodrigo		Le Cateau
1812	Badajos		Retreat from Mons
1812	Leira		Marne, 1914
1854	Balaclava		Aisne, 1914
1855	Sevastopol		Messines, 1914
1882	Egypt		Ypres, 1914, '15
1882	Tel-el-Kebir		Somme, 1916, '18
1884–5	Nile		Cambrai, 1917, '18
			Pursuit to Mons

NICKNAMES

The Buttermilks   The Mounted Micks

MOTTO

'Quis separabit?' (Who will separate?)

April 1922	Amalgamated with the 7th Dragoon Guards (Princess Royal's) to form: THE 4th/7th ROYAL DRAGOON GUARDS

see page 15   7th Dragoon Guards (Princess Royal's)
see page 50   4th/7th Royal Dragoon Guards

The 5th Dragoon Guards (Princess Charlotte of Wales's)

Originally raised as a Troop of Cuirassiers at Lichfield, Kingston-upon-Thames, Chester, Bridgnorth, Bristol, etc. They wore cuirasses till 1688, and again between 1707–14.

TITLES

1685–7	Colonel The Duke of Shrewsbury's Regiment of Horse
1687–1717	The 6th (or 7th) Regiment of Horse. (During this period it was also known by the Colonel's name, e.g. in 1687 as Coy's Horse and in 1794 as Cadogan's Horse)
1717–1788	The 2nd (or 'Green') Irish Horse
1784–1804	The 5th Dragoon Guards
1804–1921	The 5th (Princess Charlotte of Wales's) Dragoon Guards
1921–22	The 5th Dragoon Guards (Princess Charlotte of Wales's)

PRINCIPAL CAMPAIGNS, BATTLES, etc.

1690	Boyne	1812	Salamanca
1695	Namur	1813	Vittoria
1703–12	Flanders and Germany	1814	Toulouse
		1854–5	Crimea
1704	Blenheim	1854	Balaclava
1706	Ramillies	1855	Sevastopol
1708	Oudenarde	1899–1902	South Africa
1709	Malplaquet	1900	Ladysmith
1759–62	Germany	1914–18	*See* 5th Royal
1794–5	Flanders		Inniskilling
1811–14	Peninsula		Dragoon Guards
1812	Badajos		

NICKNAMES

The Old Farmers   The Green Horse

MOTTO

'Vestigia nulla retrorsum' (No going backward)

April 1922	Amalgamated with The Inniskillings (6th Dragoons) to form: THE 5th ROYAL INNISKILLING DRAGOON GUARDS

see page 26   The Inniskillings (6th Dragoons)
see page 51   5th Royal Inniskilling Dragoon Guards

13

The Carabiniers
(6th Dragoon Guards)

The Regiment was originally formed from troops of Horse raised in various English counties and took the title of Carabiniers when armed with carbines in 1692.

TITLES

1685–90	The Queen Dowager's Regiment of Horse
1690–2	The 8th (or 9th) Regiment of Horse
1692–1745	The First Regiment of Carabiniers. The King's Carabiniers
1745–88	The 3rd Irish Horse
1788–1826	The 6th Regiment of Dragoon Guards
1826–1921	The 6th Regiment of Dragoon Guards (Carabiniers)
1921–2	The Carabiniers (6th Dragoon Guards)

PRINCIPAL CAMPAIGNS, BATTLES, etc.

1685	Monmouth Rebellion	1760	Warburg
1690	Boyne	1762	Wilhemstahl
1691	Aughrim	1793–5	Flanders
1692–7	Flanders	1794	Tournay
1692	Steenkirk	1806	Buenos Aires
1693	Neer Landen	1807	Monte Video
1695	Namur	1855	Sevastopol
1702–14	Flanders and Germany	1857–8	Indian Mutiny
		1879–80	2nd Afghan War
1704	Blenheim	1899–1902	South Africa
1706	Ramillies	1900	Relief of Kimberley
1708	Oudenarde	1914–18	See 3rd Carabiniers
1709	Malplaquet		(Prince of Wales's
1760–3	Germany		Dragoon Guards)

NICKNAMES

The Carbs   Tichborne's Own

April 1922	Amalgamated with the 3rd Dragoon Guards to form: 3rd CARABINIERS (PRINCE OF WALES'S DRAGOON GUARDS)

see page 11	3rd Dragoon Guards (Prince of Wales's)
see page 49	3rd Carabiniers (Prince of Wales's Dragoon Guards)
see page 56	The Royal Scots Dragoon Guards

The 7th Dragoon Guards (Princess Royal's)

In 1688 five regiments of horse raised by James II marched with the Earl of Devonshire to meet the Princess Anne on her flight from London. On accession she commissioned them for permanent service.

TITLES

1688–90	Colonel The Earl of Devonshire's Regiment of Horse; also the Tenth Horse.
1690	Schomberg's Horse
1690–1720	Colonel the Duke of Leinster's Horse; also the 8th Horse.
1720–46	Colonel (afterwards Earl) Ligonier's Horse
1746–88	The 4th (or 'Black') Irish Horse
1788–1921	The 7th (The Princess Royal's) Dragoon Guards
1921–2	The 7th Dragoon Guards (Princess Royal's)

PRINCIPAL CAMPAIGNS, BATTLES, etc.

1690	Boyne	1846–47	South Africa (First Kaffir War)
1692–7	Flanders		
1695	Namur	1857–8	Indian Mutiny
1702–14	Flanders and Germany	1882–4	Egypt
		1882	Kassassin
1704	Blenheim	1882	Tel-el-Kebir
1706	Ramillies	1900–02	South Africa
1708	Oudenarde		
1709	Malplaquet	1914–18	IST WORLD WAR
1742–5	Flanders		Battle honours
1743	Dettingen		selected to appear on
1745	Fontenoy		the Standard:
1760–3	Germany		La Bassée, 1914
1760	Warburg		Somme, 1916, '18
1761	Kirk Denkern		Amiens
1762	Wilhelmstahl		Hindenburg Line
1763	Groebenstein		Pursuit to Mons

NICKNAMES

The Black Horse   The Blacks   The Ligoniers
The Virgin Mary's Bodyguard   Straw-boots

MOTTO

'Quo fata vocant' (Where fate calls)

continued overleaf

The 7th Dragoon Guards (Princess Royal's)

April 1922   Amalgamated with the 4th Royal Irish Dragoon Guards
to form:
THE 4th/7th ROYAL DRAGOON
GUARDS

see page 12   4th Royal Irish Dragoon Guards
see page 50   4th/7th Royal Dragoon Guards

The Royal Dragoons (1st Dragoons)

Originated in the Troops of Horse engaged in the defence of Tangier from 1661–84.

TITLES

1661–83	The Tangier Horse
1683–90	The King's Own Royal Regiment of Dragoons
1690–1751	The Royal Regiment of Dragoons
1751–15 May 1961	The 1st (Royal) Dragoons
15 May 1961–9	The Royal Dragoons (1st Dragoons)

PRINCIPAL CAMPAIGNS, BATTLES, etc.

1661–84	Tangier	1914–18	1ST WORLD WAR
1690	Boyne		Battle honours
1694–7	Flanders		selected to appear on
1695	Namur		the Guidon:
1705–10	Spain		Ypres, 1914–15
1706	Barcelona		Frezenberg
1707	Almanza		Loos
1710	Almanara		Arras, 1917
1710	Saragossa		Amiens
1715	Jacobite Rising		Somme, 1918
1742–5	Flanders		Hindenburg Line
1743	Dettingen		Cambrai, 1918
1745	Fontenoy		Pursuit to Mons
1760–3	Germany		France and Flanders,
1760	Warburg		1914–18
1762	Wilhelmstahl	1939–45	2ND WORLD WAR
1793–5	Flanders		Battle honours
1794	Cateau		selected to appear on
1794	Tournay		the Guidon:
1809–14	Peninsula		Nederrijn
1811	Fuentes d'Onor		Rhine
1812	Salamanca		North West Europe,
1813	Vittoria		1944–5
1815	Waterloo		Syria, 1941
1854–5	Crimea		Knightsbridge
1854	Balaclava		El Alamein
1855	Sevastopol		Advance on Tripoli
1884	Egypt		North Africa, 1941–3
1899–1902	South Africa		Sicily, 1943
1900	Relief of Ladysmith		Italy, 1943

continued overleaf

The Royal Dragoons (1st Dragoons)

NICKNAMES
The Royals

MOTTO
'Spectemur agendo' (Let us be judged by our deeds)

1 April 1969	Amalgamated with The Royal Horse Guards (The Blues) to form: THE BLUES AND ROYALS (ROYAL HORSE GUARDS AND 1st DRAGOONS)

see page 5 — The Royal Horse Guards (The Blues)
see page 57 — The Blues and Royals (Royal Horse Guards and 1st Dragoons)

The Royal Scots Greys (2nd Dragoons)

continued overleaf

TITLES

1681–May 1692	A Regiment of Dragoons
May 1692–1707	The Royal Regiment of Scots Dragoons (circa 1702 the regiment was known unofficially as 'Scots Greys' or 'Grey Dragoons'.)
1707–51	The Royal Regiment of North British Dragoons
1751–86	2nd Royal North British Dragoons
1786–1877	2nd Royal North British Dragoons (Scots Greys)
1877–1921	2nd Dragoons (Royal Scots Greys)
from 1921	Royal Scots Greys (2nd Dragoons)

PRINCIPAL CAMPAIGNS, BATTLES, etc.

1694–7	Flanders
1702–13	Germany
1704	Blenheim
1706	Ramillies
1708	Oudenarde
1709	Malplaquet
1715	Jacobite Rising
1742–8	Flanders
1743	Dettingen
1745	Fontenoy
1758–63	Germany
1759	Minden
1760	Warburg
1761	Kirk Denkern
1762	Wilhclmstahl
1765	Groebenstein
1793–5	Flanders
1794	Tournay
1815	Waterloo
1854–5	Crimea
1854	Balaclava
1854	Inkerman
1855	Sevastopol
1899–1902	South Africa
1900	Relief of Kimberley
	Paardeburg
1914–18	1ST WORLD WAR Battle honours

1914–18	selected to appear on the Guidon:
	Retreat from Mons
	Marne, 1914
	Aisne, 1914
	Ypres, 1914, '15
	Arras, 1917
	Amiens
	Somme, 1918
	Hindenburg Line
	Pursuit to Mons
	France and Flanders, 1914–18
1939–45	2ND WORLD WAR Battle honours selected to appear on the Guidon:
	Hill 112
	Falaise
	Hochwald
	Aller
	Bremen
	Merjayun
	Alam El Halfa
	Alamein
	Nofilia
	Salerno

19

The Royal Scots Greys (2nd Dragoons)

NICKNAMES

The Bubbly Jocks   The Bird-catchers

MOTTO

'Second to none'

In 1971 [July]   To be amalgamated with the 3rd Carabiniers (Prince of Wales's Dragoon Guards) to form:
THE ROYAL SCOTS DRAGOON GUARDS (CARABINIERS AND GREYS)

see page 49   3rd Carabiniers (Prince of Wales's Dragoon Guards)
see page 56   The Royal Scots Dragoon Guards (Carabiniers and Greys)

The 3rd The King's Own Hussars

TITLES

1685–1714	The Queen Consort's Own Regiment of Dragoons
1714–51	The King's Own Regiment of Dragoons
1751–1818	The 3rd (King's Own) Dragoons
1818–61	The 3rd (King's Own) Light Dragoons
1861–1921	The 3rd (King's Own) Hussars
1921–58	The 3rd The King's Own Hussars

PRINCIPAL CAMPAIGNS, BATTLES, etc.

1690	Boyne	1914–18	Retreat from Mons
1691	Aughrim		Marne, 1914
1694–7	Flanders		Aisne, 1914
1695	Namur		Messines, 1914
1702–8	Spain		Ypres, 1914, '15
1707	Almanza		Arras, 1917
1715	Jacobite Rising		Cambrai, 1917, '18
1742–5	Flanders		Somme, 1918
1743	Dettingen		Amiens
1745	Fontenoy		France & Flanders,
1745	Jacobite Rising		1914–18
1746	Culloden	1939–45	2ND WORLD WAR
1801–14	Peninsula		Battle honours
1812	Salamanca		selected to appear on
1813	Vittoria		the Guidon:
1842	Kabul		Sidi Barrani
1845–6	1st Sikh War		Buq Buq
1845	Mudki		Beda Fomm
1846	Sobraon		Sidi Suleiman
1848–9	2nd Sikh War		El Alamein
1849	Chillianwallah		North Africa, 1940–42
1849	Gujerat		Citta della Pieve
1902	South Africa		Citta di Castello
1914–18	1ST WORLD WAR		Italy, 1944
	Battle honours		Crete
	selected to appear on		
	the Guidon:		

NICKNAMES

The Moodkee Wallahs   Bland's Dragoons

MOTTO

'Nec aspera terrent' (Nor do difficulties deter)

continued overleaf

3 November Amalgamated with the 7th Queen's Own Hussars to form:
1958   THE QUEEN'S OWN HUSSARS

see page 27   7th Queen's Own Hussars
see page 55   The Queen's Own Hussars

The 4th Queen's Own Hussars

Formed from Independent Troops, raised at Warminster, Shaftesbury, Shepton Mallet, Glastonbury, Frome, Wincanton, and elsewhere, and named in honour of William III and Mary and afterwards Queen Anne.

TITLES

1685–1702	The Princess Anne of Denmark's Dragoons
1702–51	Named after various Colonels as a Regiment of Hussars
1751–88	The 4th Dragoons
1788–1818	The 4th, or Queen's Own Dragoons
1818–61	The 4th, or Queen's Own Light Dragoons
1861–1921	The 4th, (The Queen's Own) Hussars
1921–2	The 4th Queen's Own Hussars

PRINCIPAL CAMPAIGNS, BATTLES, etc.

1689	Scotland	1914–18	Mons
1690	Boyne		La Cateau
1692–7	Flanders		Marne, 1914
1692	Steenkirk		Aisne, 1914
1693	Neer Landen		Ypres, 1914, '15
1706–8	Spain		S. Julien
1707	Almanza		Arras, 1917
1742–8	Flanders		Cambrai, 1917
1743	Dettingen		Somme, 1918
1809–14	Peninsula		Amiens
1809	Talavera		
1810	Busaco	1939–45	2ND WORLD WAR
1811	Albuera		Battle honours selected to appear on the Guidon:
1812	Salamanca		Ruweisat
1813	Vittoria		Alam el Halfa
1839	1st Afghan War		El Alamein
1839	Ghazni		Coriano
1854–5	Crimea		Senio Pocket
1854	Alma		Rimini Line
1854	Balaclava		Argenta Gap
1854	Inkerman		Proasteion
1855	Sevastopol		Corinth Canal
1914–18	1ST WORLD WAR Battle honours selected to appear on the Guidon:		Greece, 1941

continued overleaf

NICKNAME

Paget's Irregular Horse

MOTTO

'Mente et manu' (With heart and hand)

24 October 1958   Amalgamated with the 8th King's Royal Irish Hussars to form:

THE QUEEN'S ROYAL IRISH HUSSARS

see page 29   8th King's Royal Irish Hussars
see page 55   The Queen's Royal Irish Hussars

The 5th Royal Irish Lancers

TITLES

1689–1704	The Royal Irish Dragoons; also Wynne's Dragoons; also Brigadier Ross's Dragoons (under Marlborough)
1704–56	The Royal Dragoons of Ireland. Also by Colonel's name
1756–99	The 5th (Royal Irish) Dragoons; then disbanded, 1799, but brought back into service in 1858
1858–1921	The 5th (Royal Irish) Lancers
1921–2	The 5th Royal Irish Lancers

PRINCIPAL CAMPAIGNS, BATTLES, etc.

1690	Boyne	1914–18	1ST WORLD WAR
1692	Flanders		Battle honours
1702–14	Flanders and Germany		selected to appear on the Guidon:
1704	Blenheim		Mons
1706	Ramilies		Le Cateau
1708	Oudenarde		Retreat from Mons
1709	Malplaquet		Marne, 1914
1743–8	Flanders		Aisne, 1914
1745	Fontenoy		Messines, 1914
1885	Suakin		Ypres, 1914, '15
1899–1902	South Africa		Cambrai, 1917
1900	Defence of Ladysmith		St. Quentin
			Pursuit to Mons

NICKNAMES

The Daily Advertisers   The Redbreasts
The Irish Lancers

MOTTO

'Quis Separabit' (Who will separate?)

April 1922	Amalgamated with the 16th The Queen's Lancers to form: THE 16th/5th THE QUEEN'S ROYAL LANCERS

see page 54	16th/5th The Queen's Royal Lancers
see page 42	16th The Queen's Lancers

The Inniskillings
(6th Dragoons)

Originally part of the forces raised for the defence of Inniskilling in 1681.

TITLES

1689–1751	Colonel Sir Albert Cunningham's Regiment of Dragoons, the title later being varied with each Colonel. Also about 1715 took temporarily the title of 'The Black Dragoons'.
1751–1921	The 6th, or Inniskilling Dragoons (later varied to the 6th (Inniskilling) Dragoons
1921–2	The Inniskillings (6th Dragoons)

PRINCIPAL CAMPAIGNS, BATTLES, etc.

1690	Boyne	1794	Cateau
1691	Aughrim	1794	Tournay
1715	Dunblane	1815	Waterloo
1742–8	Flanders	1854–5	Crimea
1743	Dettingen	1854	Balaclava
1745	Fontenoy	1855	Sevastopol
1746	Roucoux	1881	Transvaal
1758–63	Germany	1884–90	Bechuanaland, Natal
1759	Minden		and Zululand
1760	Warburg	1899–1902	South Africa
1762	Kirk Denkern	1914–18	*See* 5th Royal
1762	Wilhelmstahl		Inniskilling
1763	Groebenstein		Dragoon Guards
1793–5	Flanders		

NICKNAMES

The Skillingers   The Old Inniskillings

April 1922	Amalgamated with the 5th Dragoon Guards to form: **THE 5th ROYAL INNISKILLING DRAGOON GUARDS**

see page 13   5th Dragoon Guards (Princess Charlotte of Wales's)
see page 51   5th Royal Inniskilling Dragoon Guards

The 7th Queen's Own Hussars

Formed in Scotland from Independent Troops of Horse that fought at Killiecrankie. Disbanded in 1713, but re-formed two years later.

TITLES

1690–1715	Cunningham's Dragoons
1715–27	The Princess of Wales's Own Royal Dragoons
1727–51	The Queen's Own Dragoons
1751–83	The 7th, or Queen's Own Dragoons
1783–1821	The 7th, or Queen's Own Light Dragoons
~~1805–1958~~	~~The 7th Queen's Own Hussars~~
1805–1921	The 7th (Queen's Own) Hussars
1921–58	The 7th Queen's Own Hussars

PRINCIPAL CAMPAIGNS, BATTLES, etc.

1694–7	Flanders	1914–18	**1ST WORLD WAR**
1695	Namur		Battle honours
1711–13	Flanders and		selected to appear on
	Germany		the Guidon:
1715	Jacobite Rising		Khan Baghdadi,
1742–9	Flanders		Sharqat
1743	Dettingen		Mesopotamia,
1745	Fontenoy		1917–18
1760–3	Germany		
1760	Warburg	1939–45	**2ND WORLD WAR**
1762	Wilhelmstahl		Battle honours
1793–5	Flanders		selected to appear on
1794	Cateau		the Guidon:
1808–9	Peninsula		Egyptian Frontier,
1809	Benevente		1940
1809	Corunna		Beda Fomm
1813–14	Peninsula		Sidi Rezegh, 1941
1814	Orthes		North Africa, 1940–1
1815	Waterloo		Ancona
1838–9	Canada		Rimini Line
1858	Indian Mutiny		Italy, 1944-45
1858	Lucknow		Pegu
1881	Transvaal		Paungde
1896	Rhodesia		Burma, 1942
1901–2	South Africa		

continued overleaf

The 7th Queen's Own Hussars

NICKNAMES

The Old Saucy Seventh   The Lily-white Seventh
Young Eyes   Old Straws—(or Strawboots)

3 November Amalgamated with the 3rd King's Own Hussars to form:
  1958   THE QUEEN'S OWN HUSSARS

see page 21   3rd The King's Own Hussars
see page 55   The Queen's Own Hussars

The 8th King's Royal Irish Hussars

Composed originally of loyal Protestants who had fought at the Boyne.

TITLES

1693–1751	Colonel Henry Cunningham's Regiment of Dragoons, the title later changing with the Colonel's name.
1751–75	The 8th Dragoons
1775–7	The 8th Light Dragoons
1777–1822	The 8th or the King's Royal Irish Light Dragoons
1822–1921	The 8th (The King's Royal Irish) Hussars
1921–58	The 8th King's Royal Irish Hussars

PRINCIPAL CAMPAIGNS, BATTLES, etc.

1704–13	Spain	1914–18	Bapaume, 1913
1706	Barcelona		Rosières
1707	Almanza		Amiens
1710	Almanara		Albert, 1918
1710	Saragossa		Beaurevoir
1794–5	Flanders		Pursuit to Mons
1795	Cape of Good Hope		France and Flanders,
1800	Kaffir War		1914–18
1801	Egypt		
1802–22	India	1939–45	2ND WORLD WAR
1854–5	Crimea		Battle honours
1854	Alma		selected to appear on
1854	Balaclava		the Guidon:
1854	Inkerman		Villers Bocage
1855	Sevastopol		Lower Maas
1858	Indian Mutiny		Roer
1879–80	2nd Afghan War		Rhine
1900–2	South Africa		North-West Europe
			1944–5
1914–18	1ST WORLD WAR		Buq Buq
	Battle honours		Sidi Rezegh, 1941
	selected to appear on		Gazala
	the Guidon:		El Alamein
	Givenchy, 1914		North Africa, 1940–2
	Somme, 1916, '18	1950–1	Korea
	Cambrai, 1917, '18	1951	Imjin

NICKNAMES

The Cross Belts	The Georges	The Dirty Eighth

continued overleaf

MOTTO

'Pristinae virtutis memores' (The memory of former valour)

24 October 1958	Amalgamated with the 4th Queen's Own Hussars to form: THE QUEEN'S ROYAL IRISH HUSSARS

see page 23   4th Queen's Own Hussars
see page 55   The Queen's Royal Irish Hussars

The 9th Queen's Royal Lancers

The senior of several Regiments of Dragoons reformed in 1715, which had disbanded after the Peace of Utrecht.

TITLES

1715–51	Major-General Owen Wynne's Regiment of Dragoons. The title later changed with the Colonel's name.
1751–83	The 9th Dragoons
1783–1816	The 9th Light Dragoons
1816–30	The 9th Lancers
1830–1921	The 9th (or Queen's Royal) Lancers
1921–60	The 9th Queen's Royal Lancers

PRINCIPAL CAMPAIGNS, BATTLES, etc.

1715	Jacobite Rising	1914–18	Marne, 1914
1798	Irish Rebellion		Aisne, 1914
1806	Buenos Aires		Messines, 1914
1807	Walcheren		Ypres, 1914, '15
1811–13	Peninsula		Somme, 1916, '18
1843	Punniar		Arras, 1917
1846	1st Sikh War		Cambrai, 1917, '18
1846	Sobraon		Rosières
1848–9	2nd Sikh War		Pursuit to Mons
1849	Gujerat		
1857–8	Indian Mutiny	1939–45	2ND WORLD WAR Battle honours selected to appear on the Guidon:
1857	Delhi		
1858	Lucknow		
1878–90	2nd Afghan War		Somme, 1940
1879	Charasiah		North-West Europe, 1940
1879	Kabul		Gazala
1880	Kandahar		Ruweisat
1889–1902	South Africa		El Alamein
1900	Relief of Kimberley		El Hamma
1914–18	1ST WORLD WAR Battle honours selected to appear on the Guidon: Retreat from Mons		North Africa, 1942–3 Lamone Bridgehead Argenta Gap Italy, 1944–5

NICKNAMES

The Delhi Spearmen   The Magpies

continued overleaf

11 Septem- Amalgamated with 12th Royal Lancers (Prince of Wales's)
ber 1960   to form:
            THE 9th/12th ROYAL LANCERS
            (PRINCE OF WALES'S)

see page 37   12th Royal Lancers (Prince of Wales's)
see page 56   9th/12th Royal Lancers (Prince of Wales's)

10th Royal Hussars (Prince of Wales's Own)

Raised in Hertfordshire and adjoining counties.

TITLES

1715–51	Colonel Humphrey Gore's Regiment of Dragoons. Later the title changed with the Colonel's name.
1751–83	The 10th Dragoons
1783–1806	The 10th, or Prince of Wales's Own Light Dragoons
1806–11	The 10th or Prince of Wales's Own Hussars
1811–1921	The 10th, The Prince of Wales's Own Royal Hussars
1921–69	10th Royal Hussars (Prince of Wales's Own)

PRINCIPAL CAMPAIGNS, BATTLES, etc.

1746	Falkirk	1914–18	1ST WORLD WAR
1746	Culloden		Battle honours
1758—63	Germany		selected to appear on
1759	Minden		the Guidon:
1760	Warburg		Ypres, 1914, '15
1760	Campen		Frezenberg
1761	Kirk Denkern		Loos
1762	Wilhelmsthal		Arras, 1917, '18
1763	Groebenstein		Somme, 1918
1808–14	Peninsula		Avre
1808	Sahagun		Amiens
1809	Benevente		Drocourt-Quéant
1809	Corunna		Pursuit to Mons
1813	Vittoria		France & Flanders,
1813	Pyrenees		1914–18
1814	Orthes		
1814	Toulouse	1939–45	2ND WORLD WAR
1815	Waterloo		Battle honours
1855	Eupatoria		selected to appear on
1855	Sevastopol		the Guidon:
1878–9	2nd Afghan War		Somme, 1940
1878	Ali Masjid		Saunnu
1884	Egypt		Gazala
1889–1902	South Africa		El Alamein
1900	Relief of Kimberley		El Hamma
			Tunis
			Coriano
			Santarcangelo
			Valli di Commacchio
			Argenta Gap

continued overleaf

10th Royal Hussars (Prince of Wales's Own)

                    NICKNAMES
                    Baker's Light Bobs   The Don't Dance Tenth
                    The Chainy Tenth   Later known as The Shiny Tenth
                                            or The Shiners

1969   Amalgamated with the 11th Hussars (Prince Albert's
                    Own) to form:
                    THE ROYAL HUSSARS (PRINCE OF
                    WALES'S OWN)

see page 35   11th Hussars (Prince Albert's Own)
see page 57   The Royal Hussars (Prince of Wales's Own)

34

The 11th Hussars
(Prince Albert's Own)

Raised in Essex and adjoining counties. According to tradition the Regiment was first mounted on grey horses and bore the motto 'Motus Componere'. Its present title was bestowed because it escorted the Prince Consort on the occasion of his marriage to Queen Victoria.

TITLES

1715–51	Brigadier-General Philip Honywood's Regiment of Dragoons. Later the title changed with the Colonel's name.
1751–83	The 11th Dragoons
1783–1840	The 11th Light Dragoons
1840–1921	The 11th Prince Albert's Own Hussars
1921–69	The 11th Hussars (Prince Albert's Own)

PRINCIPAL CAMPAIGNS, BATTLES, etc.

1715	Jacobite Rising	1854	Inkerman
1746	Culloden	1855	Sevastopol
1760–3	Germany	1897–8	North-West Frontier
1760	Warburg	1899–1902	South Africa
1761	Kirk Denkern		
1762	Wilhelmstahl	1914–18	1ST WORLD WAR
1763	Groebenstein		Battle honours
1793–5	Flanders		selected to appear on
1793	Valenciennes		the Guidon:
1794	Cateau		Le Cateau
1794	Tournay		Retreat from Mons
1799	Holland		Marne, 1914
1801	Egypt		Aisne, 1914
1801	Aboukir		Messines, 1914
1801	Alexandria		Ypres, 1914, '15
1805	Hanover		Somme, 1916, '18
1811–13	Peninsula		Cambrai, 1917, '18
1811	El-Bodon		Amiens
1812	Salamanca		France & Flanders,
1812	Burgos		1914–18
1815	Quatre Bras	1936	Palestine
1815	Waterloo	1938–9	Palestine
1826	Bhurtpore		
1854–5	Crimea	1939–45	2ND WORLD WAR
1854	Alma		Battle honours
1854	Balaclava		selected to appear on
			the Guidon:

continued overleaf

The 11th Hussars (Prince Albert's Own)

1939–45	Villers Bocage	1939–45	Sidi Rezegh, 1941
	Roer		El Alamein
	Rhine		Tunis
	Egyptian Frontier,		Italy, 1943
	1940	1953–6	Malaya
	Siddi Barrani	1961	Kuwait
	Beda Fomm		

NICKNAMES

The Cherry-pickers   The Cherubims

MOTTO

'Treu und Fest' (True and steadfast)

| 1969 | Amalgamated with the 10th Royal Hussars (Prince of Wales's Own) to form:
THE ROYAL HUSSARS (PRINCE OF WALES'S OWN) |

see page 33   10th Royal Hussars (Prince of Wales's Own)
see page 57   The Royal Hussars (Prince of Wales's Own)

The 12th Royal Lancers (Prince of Wales's)

Originally raised in Berkshire, Buckinghamshire and Hampshire.

TITLES

1715–51	Brigadier-General Phineas Bowles's Regiment of Dragoons. Later the title changed with the Colonel's name.
1751–68	The 12th Dragoons
1768–1816	The 12th (The Prince of Wales's) Light Dragoons
1816–17	The 12th (The Prince of Wales's) Lancers
1817–1921	The 12th (Prince of Wales's Royal) Lancers
1921–60	The 12th Royal Lancers (Prince of Wales's)

PRINCIPAL CAMPAIGNS, BATTLES, etc.

1794	Corsica	1914–18	Aisne, 1914
1801	Egypt		Messines, 1914
1801	Aboukir		Ypres, 1914, '15
1801	Alexandria		Arras, 1917
1809	Walcheren		Cambrai, 1917, '18
1811–14	Peninsula		Somme, 1918
1812	Salamanca		Sambre
1813	Vittoria		
1815	Waterloo	1939–45	2ND WORLD WAR Battle honours selected to appear on the Guidon:
1851–3	South Africa		
1854–5	Crimea		
1855	Sevastopol		
1858	Indian Mutiny		Dyle
1899–1902	South Africa		Dunkirk, 1940
1900	Relief of Kimberley		North-West Europe, 1940
1914–18	1ST WORLD WAR Battle honours selected to appear on the Guidon: Mons Retreat from Mons Marne, 1914		Chor es Sufan Gazala El Alamein Tunis North Africa, 1941–3 Bologna Italy, 1944–5

NICKNAME

The Supple Twelfth

continued overleaf

The 12th Royal Lancers (Prince of Wales's)

11 September 1960	Amalgamated with the 9th Queen's Royal Lancers to form: THE 9th/12th ROYAL LANCERS (PRINCE OF WALES'S)

see page 31   9th Queen's Royal Lancers
see page 56   9th/12th Royal Lancers (Prince of Wales's)

The 13th Hussars

Raised in the Midlands.

TITLES

1715–51	Colonel Richard Munden's Regiment of Dragoons. Later the title varied with the Colonel's name.
1751–83	The 13th Dragoons
1783–1861	The 13th Light Dragoons
1861–1922	The 13th Hussars

PRINCIPAL CAMPAIGNS, BATTLES, etc.

1715	Jacobite Rising	1899–1902	South Africa
1745	Jacobite Rising	1900	Relief of Ladysmith
1810–14	Peninsula		
1811	Campo Mayor	1914–18	1ST WORLD WAR
1811	Albuera		Battle honours
1811	Arroyo dos Molinos		selected to appear on
1812	Badajos		the Colours:
1813	Vittoria		France & Flanders,
1814	Toulouse		1914–16
1815	Waterloo		Kut al Amara, 1917
1854–5	Crimea		Baghdad
1854	Alma		Sharqat
1854	Balaclava		Mesopotamia,
1854	Inkerman		1916–18
1855	Sevastopol		

NICKNAMES

The Green Dragoons   The Ragged Brigade
The Evergreens   The Geraniums
The Great Prestonpans

MOTTO

'Viret in Aeternum' (It flourishes forever)

April 1922	Amalgamated with the 18th Royal Hussars (Queen Mary's Own) to form: THE 13th/18th ROYAL HUSSARS (QUEEN MARY'S OWN)

see page 44 18th Royal Hussars (Queen Mary's Own)
see page 52 13/18th Royal Hussars (Queen Mary's Own)

The 14th King's Hussars

Raised in the South of England by Colonel Dormer.

TITLES

1715–20	Brigadier-General James Dormer's Regiment of Dragoons
1720–76	The 14th Dragoons. Frequently known by the Colonel's name.
1776–98	The 14th Light Dragoons
1798–1830	The 14th, or Duchess of York's Own Light Dragoons
1830–61	The 14th King's Light Dragoons
1861–1921	The 14th (King's) Hussars
1921–2	The 14th King's Hussars

PRINCIPAL CAMPAIGNS, BATTLES, etc.

1715	Jacobite Rising	1848	Ramnuggur
1745	Jacobite Rising	1849	Chillianwallah
1794–5	Flanders	1858	Indian Mutiny
1808–14	Peninsula	1900–2	South Africa
1809	Douro	1900	Relief of Ladysmith
1809	Talavera	1914–18	1ST WORLD WAR Battle honours selected to appear on the Colours: Tigris, 1916 Kut el Amara, 1917 Baghdad Mesopotamia, 1915–18 Persia, 1918
1809	Oporto		
1810	Busaco		
1811	Fuentes d'Onor		
1812	Badajos		
1812	Salamanca		
1813	Vittoria		
1813	Pyrenees		
1814	Orthes		
1814	Toulouse		
1848–9	2nd Sikh War		

NICKNAMES

The Ramnuggur Boys   The Emperor's Chambermaids

October 1922	Amalgamated with the 20th Hussars to form: 14th/20th HUSSARS
December 1936	Title changed to: 14th/20th KING'S HUSSARS

see page 46 20th Hussars
see page 53 14th/20th King's Hussars

The 15th The King's Hussars

Raised near London during a strike of apprentice journey-men tailors many of whom joined, hence the nickname 'The Tabs'. Soon afterwards despatched to Germany where it began its active service.

TITLES

1759–66	The 15th Light Dragoons. Also known popularly as Eliott's Light Horse (from its Colonel's name).
1766–9	The 1st, or The King's Light Dragoons
1769–1806	The 15th, or The King's Light Dragoons
1806–1861	The 15th, The King's Hussars
1861–1921	The 15th (King's) Hussars
1921–2	The 15th The King's Hussars

PRINCIPAL CAMPAIGNS, BATTLES, etc.

1760–3	Germany	1914–18 1ST WORLD WAR
1760	Emsdorf	Battle honours
1794	Villers-en-Couches	selected to appear on
1794	Willems	the Guidon:
1793–5	Flanders	Retreat from Mons
1794	Cateau	Marne, 1914
1799	Egmont-op-Zee	Aisne, 1914
1808–14	Peninsula	Ypres, 1914, '15
1808	Sahagun	Bellewaarde
1809	Benevente	Somme, 1916, '18
1813	Vittoria	Cambrai, 1917, '18
1813	Nivelle	Rosières
1814	Orthes	Pursuit to Mons
1815	Waterloo	France & Flanders,
1878–1880	2nd Afghan War	1914–18
1881	Transvaal	

NICKNAMES

The Tabs *or* The Fighting Fifteenth

MOTTO

'Merebimur' (We will be worthy of our honours and title)

April 1922	Amalgamated with the 19th Royal Hussars (Queen Alexandra's Own) to form: THE 15th/19th THE KING'S ROYAL HUSSARS

see page 45   19th Royal Hussars (Queen Alexandra's Own)
see page 53   15th/19th The King's Royal Hussars

The 16th The Queen's Lancers

Raised near London during the Seven Years' War.

TITLES

1759–66	The 16th Light Dragoons. Also known popularly as Burgoyne's Light Horse, after its Colonel's name.
1766–9	The 2nd, Queen's Light Dragoons
1769–1815	The 16th, or The Queen's Light Dragoons
1815–1921	The 16th, (The Queen's) Lancers
1921–2	The 16th The Queen's Lancers

PRINCIPAL CAMPAIGNS, BATTLES, etc.

1761	Belle-Isle	1846	Sobraon
1775–8	American War of	1897	Dargai
	Independence	1900–2	South Africa
1776	Brooklyn	1900	Relief of Kimberley
1776	White Plains		
1777	Germantown	1914–18	1ST WORLD WAR
1793–6	Flanders		Battle honours
1794	Cateau		selected to appear on
1794	Tournay		the Guidon:
1809–14	Peninsula		Mons
1809	Talavera		Le Cateau
1811	Fuentes d'Onor		Marne, 1914
1812	Salamanca		Aisne, 1914
1813	Vittoria		Messines, 1914
1815	Waterloo		Ypres, 1914, '15
1826	Bhurtpore		Bellewaarde
1839	1st Afghan War		Arras, 1917
1839	Ghazni		Cambrai, 1917
1846	Aliwal		Somme, 1918

NICKNAME
The Scarlet Lancers

MOTTO
'Aut Cursu, aut Cominus Armis' (Either in the charge, or hand to hand)

April 1922	Amalgamated with the 5th Royal Irish Lancers to form: THE 16th/5th THE QUEEN'S ROYAL LANCERS

see page 25	5th Royal Irish Lancers
see page 54	16th/5th The Queen's Royal Lancers

The 17th Lancers
(Duke of Cambridge's Own)

TITLES

1759–63	The 18th Light Dragoons
1763–6	The 17th Light Dragoons
1766–9	The 3rd Light Dragoons
1769–1822	The 17th Light Dragoons
1822–76	The 17th Lancers
1876–1922	The 17th Lancers (Duke of Cambridge's Own)

PRINCIPAL CAMPAIGNS, BATTLES, etc.

1761	Germany	1914–18	IST WORLD WAR
1775–83	American War of		Battle honours
	Independence		selected to appear on
1775	Bunker's Hill		the Guidon:
1776	Brooklyn		Festubert, 1914
1806	Buenos Ayres		Somme, 1916, '18
1807	Monte Video		Morval
1814–20	Cutch		Cambrai, 1917, '18
1816–18	Pindaree War		St. Quentin
1854–5	Crimea		Avre
1854	Alma		Hazelbrouck
1854	Balaclava		Amiens
1854	Inkerman		Pursuit to Mons
1855	Sevastopol		France & Flanders,
1858	Indian Mutiny		1914–18
1879	South Africa		
1900–2	South Africa		

NICKNAMES

The Death or Glory Boys   The Tots
Bingham's Dandies   The Horse Marines

MOTTO

'Skull and Crossbones' (=Death) 'or Glory'

April 1922	Amalgamated with the 21st Lancers (The Empress of India's) to form: THE 17th/21st LANCERS

see page 47	21st Lancers (Empress of India's)
see page 54	17th/21st Lancers

The 18th Royal Hussars (Queen Mary's Own)

Raised in Leeds in 1759.

TITLES

1759–63	The 19th Light Dragoons. Popularly known as The Drogheda Light Horse.
1763–1805	The 18th Light Dragoons
1805–22	The 18th King's Irish Hussars (then disbanded but in 1858 reformed)
1858–1910	The 18th Hussars
1910–19	The 18th (Queen Mary's Own) Hussars
1919–22	The 18th Royal Hussars (Queen Mary's Own)

PRINCIPAL CAMPAIGNS, BATTLES, etc.

1808–14	Peninsula	1914–18	Mons
1808	Sahagun		Marne, 1914
1809	Corunna		Aisne, 1914
1813	Vittoria		Messines, 1914
1813	Nive		Ypres, 1914, '15
1814	Orthes		Somme, 1916, '18
1814	Toulouse		Cambrai, 1917, '18
1815	Waterloo		Amiens
1899–1902	South Africa		Hindenburg Line
1900	Defence of Ladysmith		France & Flanders, 1914–18
1914–18	1ST WORLD WAR Battle honours selected to appear on the Guidon:		

MOTTO

'Pro Rege, pro Lege, pro Patria Conamur' (We strive for King, Laws and Country)

April 1922	Amalgamated with the 13th Hussars to form: THE 13th/18th ROYAL HUSSARS (QUEEN MARY'S OWN)

see page 39	13th Hussars
see page 52	13th/18th Royal Hussars (Queen Mary's Own)

The 19th Royal Hussars (Queen Alexandra's Own)

TITLES

1759–63	The 19th Light Dragoons. Popularly known as the Drogheda Light Horse. Re-numbered as the 18th Dragoons in 1761, later designated the 18th Hussars and disbanded in 1821.
1779–83	Reformed as the 19th Light Dragoons, later disbanded.
1781–6	The 23rd Light Dragoons, then re-numbered.
1786–1817	The 19th Light Dragoons
1817–21	The 19th Lancers, then disbanded.
1858–62	The Hon. East India's Company's 1st Bengal European Cavalry
1862–1902	The 19th Hussars
1902–8	The 19th (Alexandra, Princess of Wales's Own Hussars)
1908–21	The 19th (Queen Alexandra's Own Royal) Hussars
1921–2	The 19th Royal Hussars (Queen Alexanda's Own)

PRINCIPAL CAMPAIGNS, BATTLES, etc.

1799	Mallavelly	1914–18	1ST WORLD WAR
1799	Seringapatam		Battle honours
1800–1	Deccan		selected to appear on
1800–1	Mysors		the Guidon:
1803	Assaye		Le Cateau
1813	Niagara		Retreat from Mons
1882–4	Egypt		Marne, 1914
1882	Tel-el-Kebir		Aisne, 1914
1883	El Teb		Armentieres, 1914
1884–5	Nile		Ypres, 1915
1885	Abu-Klea		Somme, 1916, '18
1889–1902	South Africa		Cambrai, 1917, '18
1900	Defence of Ladysmith		Amiens
			Pursuit to Mons

NICKNAMES

The Dumpies *or* The Droghedas

April 1922	Amalgamated with the 15th The King's Hussars to form: THE 15th/19th THE KING'S ROYAL HUSSARS

see page 41 15th The King's Hussars
see page 53 15th/19th The King's Royal Hussars

The 20th Hussars

TITLES

1759–63	The 20th Inniskilling Light Dragoons. Disbanded.
1778–83	The 20th Light Dragoons. Disbanded.
1791–1802	The 20th Jamaica Light Dragoons: renamed.
1802–19	The 20th Light Dragoons. Disbanded.
1858–60	The 2nd Bengal European Light Cavalry
1861–1922	The 20th Hussars

PRINCIPAL CAMPAIGNS, BATTLES, etc.

1795–6	Maroon War	1914 18	Mons
1806	Cape of Good Hope		Retreat from Mons
1806	Buenos Aires		Marne, 1914
1807	Monte Video		Aisne, 1914
1807	Egypt		Messines, 1914
1808	Peninsular		Ypres, 1914, '15
1808	Vimiera		Cambrai, 1917, '18
1809–12	Sicily		Somme, 1918
1812–13	Spain		Amiens
1885	Suakin		Sambre
1901–2	South Africa		

1914–18	1ST WORLD WAR Battle honours selected to appear on the Colours:
October 1922	Amalgamated with the 14th King's Hussars to form: 14th/20th HUSSARS
December 1936	Title became: 14th/20th KING'S HUSSARS

| see page 40 | 14th King's Hussars |
| see page 53 | 14th/20th King's Hussars |

46

The 21st Lancers
(Empress of India's)

TITLES

1759–63	The 21st Light Dragoons or Royal Windsor Foresters. Disbanded.
1779–83	The 21st Light Dragoons. Disbanded.
1794–1819	The 21st Light Dragoons. Disbanded.
1858	The East India Company's 3rd Bengal European Cavalry
1858–62	The 3rd Bengal European Cavalry
1862–97	The 21st Hussars
1897–9	The 21st Lancers
1899–1921	The 21st (Empress of India's) Lancers
1921–2	The 21st Lancers (Empress of India's)

PRINCIPAL CAMPAIGNS, BATTLES, etc.

1807	Monte Video	1914–18	1ST WORLD WAR
1812	Cape of Good Hope		Battle honours
1814–15	Kaffraria		selected to appear on
1899	Khartoum		the Colours:
	(Omdurman)		North-West Frontier, India, 1915, '16

NICKNAMES

Dumpies   Hooks and Eyes

April 1922	Amalgamated with the 17th (Duke of Cambridge's Own) Lancers to form: THE 17th/21st LANCERS

see page 43 17th (Duke of Cambridge's Own) Lancers
see page 54 17th/21st Lancers

The Life Guards

April 1922 Formed by an amalgamation of the 1st Life Guards and the 2nd Life Guards.

PRINCIPAL CAMPAIGNS, BATTLES, etc.

1914–18	1ST WORLD WAR	1939–45	2ND WORLD WAR
	Battle honours representing the service of the 1st and 2nd Life Guards, chosen to appear on the Guidon:		Battle honours chosen to appear on the Guidon:
	Mons		Souleuvre
	Le Cateau		Brussels
	Marne, 1914		Nederrijn
	Aisne, 1914		North-West Europe, 1944–5
	Messines, 1914		Iraq, 1941
	Ypres, 1914, '15, '17		Palmyra
	Somme, 1916, '18		Syria, 1941
	Arras, 1917, '18		El Alamein
	Hindenburg Line		North Africa, 1942–3
	France & Flanders, 1914–18		Italy, 1944

see page 3   1st Life Guards
see page 4   2nd Life Guards

The 3rd Carabiniers (Prince of Wales's Dragoon Guards)

April 1922 — Formed by an amalgamation of the 3rd Dragoon Guards (Prince of Wales's) and the Carabiniers (6th Dragoon Guards)

PRINCIPAL CAMPAIGNS, BATTLES, etc.

1914–18 — 1ST WORLD WAR Battle honours, representing the services of the 3rd Dragoon Guards (Prince of Wales's) and the Carabiniers (6th Dragoon Guards):
Retreat from Mons
Marne, 1914
Aisne, 1914
Messines, 1914
Ypres, 1914, '15
Arras, 1917
Cambrai, 1917, '18
Amiens
Hindenburg Line

1914–18 — France & Flanders, 1914–18

1939–45 — 2ND WORLD WAR Battle honours selected to appear on the Standard:
Imphal
Nunshigum
Bishenpur
Kangiatongbi
Kennedy Peak
Shwebo
Sagaing
Mandalay
Ava
Irrawaddy

July 1971
~~1972?~~
To be amalgamated with The Royal Scots Greys (2nd Dragoons) to form:
THE ROYAL SCOTS DRAGOON GUARDS (CARABINIERS AND GREYS)

see page 19 — Royal Scots Greys (2nd Dragoons)
see page 11 — 3rd Dragoon Guards (Prince of Wales's)
see page 14 — Carabiniers (6th Dragoon Guards)
see page 56 — The Royal Scots Dragoon Guards (Carabiniers and Greys)

The 4th/7th Royal Dragoon Guards

April 1922   Formed by an amalgamation of the 4th Royal Irish Dragoon Guards and the 7th Dragoon Guards (Princess Royal's)

PRINCIPAL CAMPAIGNS, BATTLES, etc.

1939–45

2ND WORLD WAR
Battle honours
selected to appear on
the Standard:
Dyle
Dunkirk, 1940
Normandy Landing

1939–45

Odon
Mont Pincon
Nederrijn
Geilenkirchen
Rhineland
Cleve
Rhine

see page 12   4th Royal Irish Dragoon Guards
see page 15   7th Dragoon Guards (Princess Royal's)

The 5th Royal Inniskilling Dragoon Guards

April 1922   Formed by an amalgamation of the 5th Dragoon Guards (Princess Charlotte of Wales's) and The Inniskillings (6th Dragoons).

PRINCIPAL CAMPAIGNS, BATTLES, etc.

1914–18	1ST WORLD WAR Battle honours representing the service of the 5th Dragoon Guards (Princess Charlotte of Wales's) and the Inniskillings (6th Dragoons), chosen to appear on the Guidon: Mons Le Cateau Marne, 1914 Messines, 1914 Ypres, 1914, '15 Somme, 1916, '18 Cambrai, 1917, '18	1914–18 Amiens Hindenburg Line Pursuit to Mons 1939–45 2ND WORLD WAR Battle honours selected to appear on the Guidon: Withdrawal to Escaut St. Omer-La-Bassée Dunkirk, 1940 Mont Pincon Lower Maas Roer 1951–53 KOREAN WAR The Hook, 1952 Korea, 1951–2

see page 13   5th Dragoon Guards (Princess Charlotte of Wales's)
see page 26   The Inniskillings (6th Dragoons)

51

The 13th/18th Royal Hussars (Queen Mary's Own)

April 1922 — Formed by an amalgamation of the 13th Hussars and the 18th Royal Hussars (Queen Mary's Own).

PRINCIPAL CAMPAIGNS, BATTLES, etc.

1939–45

2ND WORLD WAR
Battle honours
selected to appear on
the Guidon:
Ypres-Comines Canal
Normandy Landing
Caen

1939–45

Mont Pincon
Geilenkirchen
Roer
Rhineland
Goch
North-West Europe,
1940, '44–5

NICKNAMES

The Lilywhites

MOTTOES

'Viret in Aeternum' (It flourishes forever)
'Pro Rege, pro Lege, pro Patria Conamur' (We strive for King, Laws and Country)

see page 39 — 13th Hussars
see page 44 — 18th Royal Hussars (Queen Mary's Own)

The 14th/20th King's Hussars

October 1922	Formed by an amalgamation of the 14th King's Hussars and the 20th Hussars.

PRINCIPAL CAMPAIGNS, BATTLES, etc.

1939–45	2ND WORLD WAR Battle honours chosen to appear on the Guidon: Bologna Medicina	1939–45	Italy, 1945 The Regiment also took part in the invasion of Persia in 1941.

NICKNAME
The Hawks

see page 40   14th King's Hussars
see page 46   20th Hussars

The 15th/19th The King's Royal Hussars

April 1922	Formed by an amalgamation of the 15th The King's Hussars and the 19th Royal Hussars (Queen Alexandra's Own).

PRINCIPAL CAMPAIGNS, BATTLES, etc.

1939–45	2ND WORLD WAR Battle honours selected to appear on the Guidon: Withdrawal to Escaut Seine, 1944 Nederrijn	1939–45	Rhineland Hochwald Rhine Ibeenburen Aller North-West Europe, 1940, '44–5

NICKNAMES
The Tabs *or* The Five and Nines

see page 41   15th The King's Hussars
see page 45   19th Royal Hussars (Queen Alexandra's Own)

16th/5th The Queen's Royal Lancers

April 1922   Formed by an amalgamation of the 16th The Queen's Lancers and the 5th Royal Irish Lancers.

PRINCIPAL CAMPAIGNS, BATTLES, etc.

1939–45

2ND WORLD WAR   1939–45
Battle honours
selected to appear on
the Guidon:
Fondouk
Bordj
Djebel Kourninc

Tunis
North Africa, 1942–3
Cassino II
Liri Valley
Advance to Florence
Argenta Gap
Italy, 1944–5

see page 42   16th The Queen's Lancers
see page 25   5th Royal Irish Lancers

The 17th/21st Lancers

April 1922   Formed by an amalgamation of the 17th Lancers (Duke of Cambridge's Own) and the 21st Lancers (Empress of India's)

PRINCIPAL CAMPAIGNS, BATTLES, etc.

1939–45

2ND WORLD WAR   1939–45
Battle honours
selected to appear on
the Guidon:
Tebourba Gap
Kasserine
Foudouk

El Kourzia
Tunis
North Africa, 1942–3
Cassino II
Capture of Perugia
Argenta Gap
Italy, 1944–5

NICKNAMES
Death or Glory Boys   Tiny Tots

1969   H.R.H. Princess Alexandra appointed Colonel in Chief.

see page 43   17th Lancers (Duke of Cambridge's Own)
see page 47   21st Lancers (Empress of India's)

The Queen's Royal Irish Hussars

24 October 1958	Formed by amalgamation of the 4th Queen's Own Hussars and the 8th King's Royal Irish Hussars.

MOTTOES
'Mente et manu' (With heart and hand)
'Pristinae virtutis memores' (The memory of former valour)

see page 23   4th The Queen's Own Hussars
see page 29   8th The King's Royal Irish Hussars

The Queen's Own Hussars

3 November 1958	Formed by an amalgamation of the 3rd The King's Own Hussars and the 7th Queen's Own Hussars.

MOTTO
'Nec Aspera Terrent' (Nor do difficulties deter)

see page 21   3rd The King's Own Hussars
see page 27   7th Queen's Own Hussars

The 1st The Queen's Dragoon Guards

1 January 1959	Formed by the amalgamation of the 1st King's Dragoon Guards and The Queen's Bays (2nd Dragoon Guards).

PRINCIPAL CAMPAIGNS, BATTLES, etc.

1965–6	Borneo
1966–7	Aden
see page 7	1st King's Dragoon Guards
see page 9	The Queen's Bays (2nd Dragoon Guards)

The Royal Scots Dragoon Guards (Carabiniers and Greys)

~~July 1971~~ 197?	To be formed by an amalgamation of the 3rd Carabiniers (Prince of Wales's Dragoon Guards) and The Royal Scots Greys (2nd Dragoons)
see page 49	3rd Carbiniers (Prince of Wales's Dragoon Guards)
see page 19	The Royal Scots Greys (2nd Dragoons)

The 9th/12th Royal Lancers (Prince of Wales's)

11 September 1960	Formed by an amalgamation of the 9th Queen's Royal Lancers and the 12th Royal Lancers (Prince of Wales's).

MOTTO

There is no official motto, but beneath the Feather badge of the Prince of Wales on the cap badge and collar badges is his motto: 'Ich Dien' (I serve).

see page 31	9th Queen's Royal Lancers
see page 37	12th Royal Lancers (Prince of Wales's)

56

The Royal Hussars (Prince of Wales's Own)

1969 | Formed by an amalgamation of the 10th Royal Hussars (Prince of Wales's Own) and the 11th Hussars (Prince Albert's Own).

see page 33 | 10th Royal Hussars (Prince of Wales's Own)
see page 35 | 11th Hussars (Prince Albert's Own)

The Blues and Royals (Royal Horse Guards and 1st Dragoons)

1 April 1969 | Formed by an amalgamation of The Royal Horse Guards (The Blues) and The Royal Dragoons (1st Dragoons).

see page 5 | The Royal Horse Guards (The Blues)
see page 17 | The Royal Dragoons (1st Dragoons)

The Regiments of Foot Guards

The Grenadier Guards

The Royal Regiment of Guards was raised by Charles II in Bruges in 1656, with Lord Wentworth as Colonel. On his return to England Charles raised another regiment, The King's Royal Regiment of Foot Guards, with John Russel as its Colonel. On the death of Wentworth in 1665 these two regiments were amalgamated into the Royal Regiment of Foot Guards, renamed in 1685 The First Regiment of Foot Guards.

TITLES

1660–85	The King's Royal Regiment of Guards
1685–1815	The First Regiment of Foot Guards
from 1815	The 1st, or Grenadier Regiment of Foot Guards (The latter title was granted for having defeated the French Imperial Guards at Waterloo)

the Grenadiers 47 (handwritten)

PRINCIPAL CAMPAIGNS, BATTLES, etc.

1680–3	Tangier	1745	Fontenoy
1685	Sedgemoor	1745	Jacobite Rising
1691–7	Flanders	1747	Val
1692	Steenkirk	1758	Cherbourg
1693	Neer Landen	1759–62	Germany
1695	Namur	1762	Denkern
1702–13	Flanders & Germany	1762	Wilhelmstahl
1704	Schellenberg	1776–81	America
1704	Blenheim	1776	Brooklyn
1704–8	Spain	1777	Brandywine
1704–5	Gibraltar	1777	Germantown
1705–6	Barcelona	1778	Freehold
1706	Ramilies	1781	Guildford
1707	Almanza	1793	Famars
1708	Lisle	1793	Valenciennes
1708	Oudenarde	1793	Lincelles
1708	Ghent	1793–5	Flanders
1709	Tournay	1794	Cateau
1709	Malplaquet	1799	Helder
1710	Menin	1799	Crabbendam
1710	Douai	1799	Bergen
1729	Gibraltar	1799	Egmont-op-Zee
1742–7	Flanders	1799	Alkmaer
1743	Dettingen	1806–7	Sicily

continued overleaf

1808–14	Peninsula	1914–18	1ST WORLD WAR
1809	Flushing		Battle honours
1809	Corunna		selected to appear on
1811	Barossa		the Colours:
1813	St. Sebastian		Marne, 1914
1813	St. Marcial		Aisne, 1914
1813	Bidassoa		Ypres, 1914, '17
1813	Nive		Loos
1813	Nivelle		Somme, 1916, '18
1814	Bayonne		Cambrai, 1917, '18
1814–5	Netherlands		Arras, 1918
1814	Bergen-op-Zoom		Hazelbrouck
1815	Quatre Bras		Hindenburg Line
1815	Waterloo		France & Flanders,
1826–7	Portugal		1914–18
1838–42	Canada		
1854–5	Crimea	1939–45	2ND WORLD WAR
1854	Alma		Battle honours
1854	Inkerman		selected to appear on
1855	Sevastopol		the Colours:
1882	Egypt		Dunkirk, 1940
1882	Tel-el-Kebir		Mont Pincon
1885	Suakim		Nijmegen
1898	Khartoum		Rhine
1899–1902	South Africa		Mareth
1900	Modder River		Medjez Plain
			Salerno
			Monte Camino
			Anzio
			Gothic Line

NICKNAMES

The Sand Bags	The Coal-heavers	Old Eyes
The Bill Browns	The Bermuda Exiles	

The Coldstream Guards

The direct and only descendant of the Parliamentary Infantry, all other corps having been disbanded at the Restoration. The Regiment derives its name from Monck's march from Coldstream which resulted in the restoration of Charles II.

TITLES

1650–60	Colonel Monck's Regiment of Foot; also popularly known as Monck's Coldstreamers.
1660–1	The Lord General's Regiment of Foot
1661–70	The Lord General's Regiment of Foot Guards
1670–1817	The Coldstream Regiment of Footguards
from 1817	The Coldstream Guards

PRINCIPAL CAMPAIGNS, BATTLES, etc.

1660	Dunbar Restoration	1762	Amoneburg
1665–7	Dutch War	1776–81	America
1763 1673	Dutch War	1776	Brooklyn
1680–3	Tangier	1777	Brandywine
1689–97	Flanders	1777	Germantown
1689	Walcourt	1778	Freehold
1692	Steenkirk	1781	Guildford
1693	Neer Landen	1793–5	Flanders
1695	Namur	1793	St. Amand
1704–8	Spain & Portugal	1793	Valenciennes
1704	Gibraltar	1793	Lincelles
1705–6	Barcelona	1794	Tournay
1707	Almanza	1794	Cateau
1707–13	Germany	1799	Helder
1708	Oudenarde	1799	Crabbendam
1708	Ghent	1799	Bergen
1709	Malplaquet	1799	Egmont-op-Zee
1711	Bouchain	1799	Alkmaer
1742–5	Flanders	1801	Egypt
1743	Dettingen	1801	Aboukir
1745	Fontenoy	1801	Alexandria
1745	Jacobite Rising	1801	Marabout
1758	Cherbourg	1805	Hanover
1760–2	Westphalia	1807	Copenhagen
1761	Denkern	1809–14	Peninsula
1762	Wilhelmstahl	1809	Flushing

continued overleaf

63

1809	Douro	1914–18	1ST WORLD WAR
1809	Talavera		Battle honours
1810	Busaco		selected to appear on
1811	Fuentes d'Onor		the Colours:
1811	Barossa		Retreat from Mons
1812	Ciudad Rodrigo		Marne, 1914
1812	Badajos		Aisne, 1914
1812	Burgos		Ypres, 1914, '17
1812	Salamanca		Loos
1813	St. Sebastian		Somme, 1916, '18
1813	Vittoria		Cambrai, 1917, '18
1813	Pyrenees		Arras, 1918
1813	Bidassoa		Hazebrouck
1813	Nive		Hindenburg Line
1813	Nivelle		
1814	Bayonne	1939–45	2ND WORLD WAR
1814–15	Netherlands		Battle honours
1814	Bergen-op-Zoom		selected to appear on
1815	Quatre Bras		the Colours:
1815	Waterloo		Dunkirk, 1940
1827–8	Portugal		Mont Pincon
1838–42	Canada		Rhineland
1854–5	Crimea		North-West Europe,
1854	Alma		1940, '44–5
1854	Inkerman		Sidi Barrani
1855	Sevastopol		Tobruk, 1941, '42
1882	Egypt		Tunis
1882	Tel-el-Kebir		Salerno
1885	Suakim		Monte Ornito
1899–1902	South Africa		Italy, 1943–5
1899	Modder River		

NICKNAME
The Coldstreamers

MOTTO
'Nulli Secundus'

The Scots Guards

The original commission for the raising of a Scottish Regiment of Foot Guards was signed at Westminster by King Charles I and was issued to Archibald First Marquis and Eighth Earl of Argyll.

TITLES

1660–1712	The Scots Regiment of Guards
1712–1831	The 3rd Foot Guards
1831–77	The Scots Fusilier Guards
from 1877	The Scots Guards

PRINCIPAL CAMPAIGNS, BATTLES, etc.

1689–95	Flanders	1799	Alkmaer
1689	Walcourt	1801	Aboukir
1690	Boyne	1801	Egypt
1693	Neer Landen	1801	Alexandria
1695	Namur	1801	Marabout
1709–13	Spain	1807	Copenhagen
1710	Saragossa	1809–14	Peninsula
1742–8	Flanders	1809	Flushing
1743	Dettingen	1809	Douro
1745	Fontenoy	1809	Talavera
1747	Val	1811	Barossa
1758	Cherbourg	1812	Badajos
1759–62	Germany	1812	Burgos
1761	Denkern	1812	Ciudad Rodrigo
1762	Wilhelmstahl	1813	St. Sebastian
1776–83	America	1814–15	Netherlands
1776	Brooklyn	1814	Bayonne
1777	Brandywine	1814	Bergen-op-Zoom
1777	Germantown	1815	Quatre Bras
1778	Freehold	1815	Waterloo
1781	Guildford	1826–8	Portugal
1793	Valenciennes	1854–5	Crimea
1793–5	Flanders	1854	Alma
1793	Lincelles	1854	Inkerman
1799	Helder	1854	Sevastopol
1799	Crabbendam	1882	Egypt
1799	Bergen	1882	Tel-el-Kebir
1799	Egmont-op-Zee	1885	Suakim
		1900	South Africa

continued overleaf

1914–18	1ST WORLD WAR	1939–45	2ND WORLD WAR
	Battle honours selected to appear on the Colours:		Battle honours selected to appear on the Colours:
	Retreat from Mons		Quarry Hill
	Marne, 1914		Rhineland
	Aisne, 1914		North-West Europe, 1944–5
	Ypres, 1914, '17		Gazala
	Festubert, 1915		Medinine
	Loos		Djebel Bou Aoukaz, 1943, I
	Somme, 1916, '18		North Africa, 1941–3
	Cambrai, 1917, '18		Monte Camino
	Hindenburg Line		Anzio
	France & Flanders, 1914–18		Italy, 1943–5

NICKNAME
The Kiddies

MOTTO
'Nemo me impune lacessit' (No one provokes me with impunity)

The Irish Guards

Raised by an Army Order (No. 77, April 1900); 'Her Majesty the Queen, having deemed it desirable to commemorate the bravery shown by the Irish regiments in the recent operations in South Africa, has been graciously pleased to command that an Irish regiment of Foot Guards be formed. This regiment will be designated—"The Irish Guards".'

PRINCIPAL CAMPAIGNS, BATTLES, etc.

1914–18	1ST WORLD WAR	1939–45	2ND WORLD WAR
	Battle honours selected to appear on the Colours:		Battle honours selected to appear on the Colours:
	Retreat from Mons		Norway, 1940
	Marne, 1914		Boulogne, 1940
	Aisne, 1914		Mont Pincon
	Ypres, 1914, '17		Neerpelt
	Festubert, 1915		Nijmegen
	Loos		Rhineland
	Somme, 1916, '18		North-West Europe, 1944–5
	Cambrai, 1917, '18		Djebel Bou Aoukaz, 1943
	Hazebrouck		North Africa, 1943
	Hindenburg Line		Anzio

NICKNAME

The Micks

MOTTO

'Quis separabit?' (Who shall separate us?)

The Welsh Guards

The Regiment was raised in London in 1915 by the Royal Warrant of King George V.

PRINCIPAL CAMPAIGNS, BATTLES, etc.

1914–18	1ST WORLD WAR	1939–45	2ND WORLD WAR
	Battle honours		Battle honours
	selected to appear on		selected to appear on
	the Colours:		the Colours:
	Loos		Defence of Arras
	Ginchy		Boulogne, 1940
	Flers-Courcelette		Mont Pincon
	Morval		Brussels
	Pilckem		Hechtel
	Poelcappelle		Fondouk
	Cambrai, 1917, '18		Hammam Lif
	Bapaume, 1918		Monte Ornito
	Canal du Nord		Monte Piccolo
	Sambre		Battaglia

The Regiments of Foot from 1 to 25

Senior Foot Regiments

Details of Foot Regiments numbered from 1–25 will be found under the titles taken by these Regiments in 1881, or as subsequently varied.

continued overleaf

The 14th (Buckinghamshire– The Prince of Wales's Own) Regiment of Foot	The West Yorkshire Regiment (The Prince of Wales's Own)	99
The 15th (York, East Riding) Regiment of Foot	The East Yorkshire Regiment (Duke of York's Own)	101
The 16th (Bedfordshire) Regiment of Foot. (The County title was exchanged with the 14th Foot at the request of the Colonel of that Regiment)	The Bedfordshire and Hertfordshire Regiment	103
The 17th (Leicestershire) Regiment of Foot	The Royal Leicestershire Regiment	105
The 18th (The Royal Irish) Regiment of Foot	The Royal Irish Regiment	107
The 19th (1st Yorkshire, North Riding–Princess of Wales's Own) Regiment of Foot	The Green Howards (Alexandra, Princess of Wales's Own Yorkshire Regiment)	108
The 20th (East Devonshire) Regiment of Foot	The Lancashire Fusiliers	110
The 21st (Royal North British) Fusiliers Regiment of Foot	The Royal Scots Fusiliers	112
The 22nd (The Cheshire) Regiment of Foot	The Cheshire Regiment	114
The 23rd (Royal Welsh Fusiliers) Regiment of Foot	The Royal Welch Fusiliers	115
The 24th (2nd Warwickshire) Regiment of Foot	The South Wales Borderers	117
The 25th (The King's Own Borderers) Regiment of Foot	The King's Own Scottish Borderers	119

The Royal Scots
(The Royal Regiment)

Raised by a Royal Warrant dated 28 March 1633, when Charles I granted to Sir Charles Hepburn permission to raise in Scotland a regiment for French service. The Regiment served in France from 1633 to 1678 (except for short periods in 1661 and 1666–7) when it came to England. In the latter period it defended Chatham and other ports against the Dutch.

TITLES

1633–7	Le Regiment d'Hebron (Hepburn)
1637–78	Le Regiment de Douglas
1678–84	The Earl of Dumbarton's Regiment of Foot
1684–1751	The Royal Regiment of Foot
1751–1812	The 1st or The Royal Regiment of Foot
1812–21	The 1st Regiment of Foot or Royal Scots
1821–71	The 1st or The Royal Regiment of Foot
1871–81	The 1st or The Royal Scots Regiment
July 1881–July 1882	The Lothian Regiment (Royal Scots)
1882–1920	The Royal Scots (The Lothian Regiment)
from 1920	The Royal Scots (The Royal Regiment)

PRINCIPAL CAMPAIGNS, BATTLES, etc.

1673	Maestricht	1708	Oudenarde
1680–3	Tangier	1708	Wynedale
1685	Sedgemoor	1708	Lisle
1689–97	Flanders	1708	Ghent
1689	Walcourt	1709	Tournay
1692	Steenkirk	1709	Malplaquet
1693	Neer Landen	1710	Douay
1695	Namur	1743–9	Flanders
1701–14	Flanders & Germany	1745	Fontenoy
1702	Venloo	1746	Culloden
1704	Schellenberg	1747	Hulst
1704	Blenheim	1757–60	Canada
1706	Ramilies	1758	Louisbourg

continued overleaf

1758	Ticonderoga	1854	Inkerman
1761	Dominica	1855	Sevastopol
1762	Martinique	1860	Taku Forts
1762	Havannah	1860	Pekin
1793	Toulon	1900	South Africa
1794	Corsica	1914–18	1ST WORLD WAR
1799	Helder		Battle honours
1799	Krabbendam		selected to appear on
1799	Egmont-op-Zee		the Colours:
1801	Aboukir		Le Cateau
1801	Egypt		Marne, 1914, '18
1801	Mandora		Ypres, 1915, '17, '18
1801	Alexandria		Loos
1803	St. Lucia		Somme, 1916, '18
1809–14	Peninsula		Arras, 1917, '18
1809	Corunna		Lys
1809	Flushing		Struma
1810	Guadaloupe		Gallipoli, 1915–16
1810	Busaco		Palestine, 1917–18
1812	Salamanca		
1813	Vittoria	1939–45	2ND WORLD WAR
1813	St. Sebastian		Battle honours
1813	Nive		selected to appear on
1814–15	Netherlands		the Colours:
1814	Bayonne		Defence of Escaut
1814	Niagara		Odon
1814	Bergen-op-Zoom		Flushing
1815	Quatre Bras		Aart
1815	Waterloo		Rhine
1817	Nagpore		North-West Europe,
1817	Maheidpore		1940, '44–5
1824–6	Ava		Gothic Line
1838–9	Canada		Italy, 1944–5
1854–5	Crimea		Kohima
1854	Alma		Burma, 1943–5

NICKNAME

Pontius Pilate's Body-guard

MOTTO

'Nemo me impune lacessit' (No one provokes me with impunity)

The Queen's Royal Regiment (West Surrey)

TITLES

1661–84	Raised as The Tangier Regiment of Foot
1684–6	Regiment styled The Queen's Regiment
1686–1703	The Queen Dowager's Regiment
1703	Made a 'Royal' Regiment
1715–27	Her Royal Highness The Princess of Wales's Own Regiment of Foot
1727–51	The Queen's Own Royal Regiment of Foot
1751–1881	The 2nd or Queen's Royal Regiment of Foot
1881–1921	The Queen's Royal West Surrey Regiment
1921–59	The Queen's Royal Regiment (West Surrey)

PRINCIPAL CAMPAIGNS, BATTLES, etc.

1662–83	Tangier	1814	Toulouse
1690	Boyne	1839	1st Afghan War
1691	Augrhim	1839	Ghazni
1692–5	Flanders	1839	Khelat
1693	Neer Landen	1842	Kabul
1695	Namur	1851–3	South Africa
1702	Cadiz	1856–7	South Africa
1703–4	Germany	1860	Taku Forts
1703	Tongres	1860	Pekin
1704–8	Spain	1886–8	Burma
1707	Almanza	1897–8	Tirah
1711	Quebec	1899–1902	South Africa
1794	Glorious First of June		
1799	Helder	1914–18	IST WORLD WAR
1799	Bergen		Battle honours
1799	Egmont-op-Zee		selected to appear on
1801	Mandora		the Colours:
1801	Egypt		Retreat from Mons
1801	Alexandria		Ypres, 1914, '17, '18
1807	Rosetta		Somme, 1916, '18
1808–14	Peninsula		Messines, 1917
1809	Flushing		Vittoria Veneto
1809	Vimiera		Macedonia, 1916–17
1809	Corunna		Gallipoli, 1915
1809	Talavera		Palestine, 1917–18
1812	Salamanca		Mesopotamia,
1813	Vittoria		1915–18
1813	Pyrenees		North-West Frontier,
1813	Nivelle		1916–17

continued overleaf

1919	Afghanistan (3rd Afghan War)	1939–45	El Alamein Medinine Salerno Monte Camino Anzio Gemmano Ridge North Arakan Kohima
1939–45	2ND WORLD WAR Battle honours selected to appear on the Colours: Villers Bocage Tobruk, 1941		

NICKNAME

Kirke's Lambs

MOTTOES

'Pristinae Virtutis Memore' (Mindful of the Gallant Actions of the Past)
'Vex Exuviae Triumphant' (Even in defeat there can be Triumph)

14 October 1959	Amalgamated with the East Surrey Regiment to form: THE QUEEN'S ROYAL SURREY REGIMENT
31 December 1966	Redesignated: 1st Battalion THE QUEEN'S REGIMENT (QUEEN'S SURREYS)
1969	Redesignated: 1st Battalion THE QUEEN'S REGIMENT, and the County affiliation ceased.

see page 217 The East Surrey Regiment
see page 271 The Queen's Regiment

The Buffs (Royal East Kent Regiment)

The Regiment traces its ancestry from the Holland Regiment which served the throne of Holland from 1572 onwards.

TITLES

1665–89	The Holland Regiment
1689–1708	Prince George of Denmark's Regiment
1708–51	The Buffs
1751–82	The 3rd (or The Buffs) Regiment of Foot
1782–1881	The 3rd (East Kent—The Buffs) Regiment of Foot
1881–1935	The Buffs (East Kent) Regiment of Foot
1935–1961	The Buffs (Royal East Kent Regiment)

PRINCIPAL CAMPAIGNS, BATTLES, etc.

1689–97	Flanders	1813	Pyrenees
1689	Walcourt	1813	Nivelle
1693	Neer Landen	1813	Nive
1703–13	Flanders & Germany	1814	Orthes
1704	Schellenberg	1814	Toulouse
1704	Blenheim	1814	Plattsburg
1706	Ramilies	1843	Punniar
1708	Oudenarde	1854–5	Crimea
1708	Lisle	1855	Sevastopol
1709	Malplaquet	1860	Taku Forts
1715	Jacobite Rising	1879	South Africa
1742–9	Flanders	1895	Chitral
1709	Tournay	1900	South Africa
1743	Dettingen		
1745	Fontenoy	1914–18	1ST WORLD WAR
1747	Val		Battle honours selected to appear on the Colours:
1759	Guadaloupe		Aisne, 1914
1761	Belle Isle		Ypres, 1915, '17
1781	America		Loos
1782	Jamaica		Somme, 1916, '18
1794–5	Flanders		Arras, 1917
1794	Nimeguen		Amiens
1796	Grenada		Hindenburg Line
1809–14	Peninsula		Struma
1809	Douro		Jerusalem
1809	Talavera		Baghdad
1811	Albuera		
1813	Vittoria		

continued overleaf

77

The Buffs (Royal East Kent Regiment)

| 1939–45 | 2ND WORLD WAR
Battle honours
selected to appear on
the Colours:
North-West Europe
  1940
Alem Hamza
El Alamein | 1939–45 | Robaa Valley
Sicily, 1943
Trigno
Anzio
Argenta Gap
Leros
Shweli |

NICKNAMES

The Buff Howards   The Resurrectionists
The Nutcrackers   The Old Buffs

MOTTO
'Veteri frondescit honore' (With its ancient honour it is ever green.)

1 March 1961	Amalgamated with the Queen's Own Royal West Kent Regiment to form: THE QUEEN'S OWN BUFFS
31 December 1966	Redesignated: 2nd Battalion THE QUEEN'S REGIMENT (QUEEN'S OWN BUFFS)
1969	Redesignated: 2nd Battalion THE QUEEN'S REGIMENT and the County affiliation ceased.

see page 234 The Queen's Own Royal West Kent Regiment
see page 271 The Queen's Regiment

The King's Own Royal Regiment (Lancaster)

This Regiment was originally raised near London and the West of England, for the defence of Tangier.

TITLES

1680–4	The 2nd Tangier Regiment also The Tangierenes
1684–5	The Duchess of York and Albany's Regiment
1685–8	The Queen's Regiment
1688–1702	The Queen Consort's Regiment
1702–15	The Queen's Marines
1715–51	The King's Own Regiment
1751–1867	The 4th, or The King's Own Regiment
1867–1881	The 4th, (The King's Own Royal) Regiment
1881–1959	The King's Own (Royal Lancaster Regiment) later expressed as The King's Own Royal Regiment (Lancaster)

PRINCIPAL CAMPAIGNS, BATTLES, etc.

1685	Sedgemoor	1778	St. Lucia
1690	Boyne	1799	Egmont-op-Zee
1692–5	Flanders	1799	Alkmaer
1692	Steenkirk	1807	Copenhagen
1693	Neer Landen	1808–14	Peninsula
1695	Namur	1809	Corunna
1704–9	Spain	1809	Flushing
1704	Malaga	1812	Cadiz
1705	Gibraltar	1812	Badajos
1705	Barcelona	1812	Salamanca
1707	Almanza	1812	Burgos
1708	Minorca	1813	Bidassoa
1711	Quebec	1813	Vittoria
1746	Culloden	1813	St. Sebastian
1756	Minorca	1813	Nive
1759	Guadaloupe	1814	Bladensburg
1761	Dominica	1814	Washington
1762	Martinique	1815	New Orleans
1762	Havannah	1815	Waterloo
1775–8	America	1854–5	Crimea
1775	Lexington	1854	Alma
1775	Bunker's Hill	1854	Inkerman
1776	Brooklyn	1855	Sevastopol
1777	Germantown	1858	Indian Mutiny

continued overleaf

79

1868	Abyssinia	1939–45	2ND WORLD WAR
1879	South Africa		Battle honours
1899–1902	South Africa		selected to appear on
			the Colours:
1914–18	1ST WORLD WAR		Dunkirk, 1940

1ST WORLD WAR
Battle honours
selected to appear on
the Colours:
Marne, 1914
Ypres, 1915, '17
Somme, 1916, '18
Arras, 1917, '18
Messines, 1917
Lys
France & Flanders,
    1914–18
Macedonia
Gallipoli, 1915
Mesopotamia,
    1916–18

2ND WORLD WAR
Battle honours
selected to appear on
the Colours:
Dunkirk, 1940
North-West Europe,
    1940
Defence of Habbaniya
Merjayun
Tobruk Sortie
North Africa, 1940–2
Montone
Lamone Bridgehead
Malta, 1941–2
Chindits, 1944

NICKNAMES

Barrell's Blues   The Lions

1 October   Amalgamated with The Border Regiment to form:
1959   THE KING'S OWN ROYAL BORDER
            REGIMENT

see page 220 The Border Regiment
see page 268 The King's Own Royal Border Regiment

The Royal Northumberland Fusiliers

The Regiment was granted the privilege of wearing Fusilier caps for defeating a French division of Grenadiers at Wilhelmstahl. The territorial title was bestowed in 1782 as a compliment to its Colonel, Earl Percy.

TITLES

1674–88	The Irish Regiment, and later a Holland Regiment. (At this time the Regiment was in the service of the Prince of Orange.)
1688–1751	The title changed with the Colonel's name
1751–82	The 5th Regiment of Foot
1782–1836	The 5th or Northumberland Regiment of Foot
1836–81	The 5th or Northumberland Fusiliers
1881–1935	The Northumberland Fusiliers
1935–68	The Royal Northumberland Fusiliers

PRINCIPAL CAMPAIGNS, BATTLES, etc.

1690	Boyne	1787–97	Canada
1691	Athlone	1799	Bergen
1691	Limerick	1799	Egmont-op-Zee
1692–7	Flanders	1799	Crabbendam
1695	Namur	1799	Alkmaer
1707–13	Spain	1806	Buenos Ayres
1709	Caya	1808–14	Peninsula
1727	Gibraltar	1808	Roleia
1758	Cherbourg	1808	Vimiera
1760–3	Germany	1809	Corunna
1760	Corbach	1809	Flushing
1760	Warburg	1809	Talavera
1761	Denkern	1810	Busaco
1762	Wilhelmstahl	1811	El Bodon
1775–8	America	1812	Ciudad Rodrigo
1775	Lexington	1812	Badajos
1775	Bunker's Hill	1812	Salamanca
1776	Brooklyn	1813	Vittoria
1776	Long Island	1813	Nivelle
1776	White plains	1814	Orthes
1776	Brunx	1814	Toulouse
1777	Brandywine	1814	Plattsburg
1777	Germantown	1857–8	Indian Mutiny
1778	St. Lucia (La Vigie)	1857	Lucknow

continued overleaf

1878–80	2nd Afghan War	1914–18	Struma
1898	Khartoum		Suvia
1899–1902	South Africa		
1902	Modder River	1939–45	2ND WORLD WAR
			Battle honours
1914–18	1ST WORLD WAR		selected to appear on
	Battle honours		the Colours:
	selected to appear on		Dunkirk, 1940
	the Colours:		Caen
	Mons		Rhineland
	Marne, 1914		Sidi Barrani
	Ypres, 1914, '15, '17,		Defence of Tobruk
	'18		Tobruk, 1941
	St. Julien		Cauldron
	Somme, 1916, '18		El Alamein
	Scarpe, 1917, '18		Salerno
	Selle		Cassino II
	Piave	1950–1	Imjin
		1950–1	Korea

NICKNAMES

The Shiners   The Fighting Fifth

The Old Bold Fifth   Lord Wellington's Body-guard

MOTTO

'Quo fata vocant' (Where fate calls)

23 April 1968	Amalgamated with The Royal Warwickshire Fusiliers, The Royal Fusiliers, and The Lancashire Fusiliers to form: **THE ROYAL REGIMENT OF FUSILIERS**

see page 83 The Royal Warwickshire Fusiliers
see page 110 The Lancashire Fusiliers
see page 85 The Royal Fusiliers
see page 272 The Royal Regiment of Fusiliers

The Royal Warwickshire Fusiliers

Raised in 1673 from Irish troops in the Dutch service, the Regiment came to England in 1688 with William of Orange.

TITLES

1688–1751	The title changed with the Colonel's name
1751–82	The 6th Regiment of Foot (Ranked as the 6th Regiment in 1747.)
1782–1832	The 6th (1st Warwickshire) Regiment of Foot
1832–81	The 6th (Royal Warwickshire) Regiment of Foot
1881–1963	The Royal Warwickshire Regiment
1963–8	The Royal Warwickshire Fusiliers

PRINCIPAL CAMPAIGNS, BATTLES, etc.

1690	Boyne	1846–7	South Africa
1690–6	Flanders	1851–3	South Africa
1702	Cadiz	1856–7	South Africa
1704–10	Spain	1857–8	Indian Mutiny
1707	Almanza	1860	Sikkim
1710	Saragossa	1865	Jamaica
1741	Carthagena	1868	Hazara
1745	Jacobite Rising	1869	Punjaub
1772	St. Vincent	1898	Atbara
1776–7	America	1898	Khartoum
1794	Martinique	1899–1902	South Africa
1794	Guadaloupe		
1796–8	Ireland	1914–18	1ST WORLD WAR
1799–1806	Canada		Battle honours
1808–14	Peninsula		selected to appear on
1808	Roleia		the Colours:
1808	Vimiera		Le Cateau
1809	Corunna		Marne, 1914
1809	Walcherun		Ypres, 1914, '15, '17
1813	Vittoria		Somme, 1916, '18
1813	Pyrenees (Eschalar)		Arras, 1917, '18
1813	Nivelle		Lys
1813	Niagara		Hindenburg Line
1814	Orthes		Piave
1832	Scinde		Sari Bar
1832	Baloochistan		Baghdad
1840–1	Aden		

continued overleaf

1939–45	2ND WORLD WAR	1939–45	Caen
	Battle honours		Mont Pincon
	selected to appear on		Venraij
	the Colours:		Bremen
	Defence of Escaut		North-West Europe,
	Wormhoudt		1940, '44–5
	Ypres-Comines Canal		Burma, 1945
	Normandy Landing		

NICKNAMES

Guise's Geese   The Warwickshire Lads
The Saucy Sixth

23 April 1968   Amalgamated with The Royal Northumberland Fusiliers, The Royal Fusiliers, and The Lancashire Fusiliers to form:

THE ROYAL REGIMENT OF FUSILIERS

see page 81   The Royal Northumberland Fusiliers
see page 85   The Royal Fusiliers
see page 110   The Lancashire Fusiliers
see page 272   The Royal Regiment of Fusiliers

The Royal Fusiliers
(City of London Regiment)

Raised at the time of the Monmouth Rebellion.

TITLES

1685–9	Our Royal Regiment of Fuziliers, also **Our Ordnance** Regiment
1689–1881	The 7th (Royal Fusiliers)
1881–1968	The Royal Fusiliers (City of London) Regiment

PRINCIPAL CAMPAIGNS, BATTLES, etc.

1689–90	Flanders	1879–80	Afghanistan
1690	Cork	1880	Kandahar
1690	Kinsale	1899–1902	South Africa
1692–6	Flanders	1900	Relief of Ladysmith
1693	Neer Landen	1904	Tibet Expedition
1695	Namur		
1702	Cadiz	1914–18	1ST WORLD WAR
1704–9	Spain		Battle honours
1705–6	Barcelona		selected to appear on
1707	Lerida		the Colours:
1773–82	America		Mons
1775	Quebec		Ypres, 1914, '15, '17,
1807	Copenhagen		'18
1809	Peninsula		Nonne Bosschen
1809	Talavera		Somme, 1916, '18
1809	Martinique		Arras, 1917, '18
1810	Busaco		Cambrai, 1917, '18
1811	Albuera		Hindenburg Line
1812	Badajos		Struma
1812	Salamanca		Landing at Helles
1813	Vittoria		Egypt, 1916
1813	Pyrenees		
1813	Bidassoa	1939–45	2ND WORLD WAR
1814	Orthes		Battle honours
1814	Toulouse		selected to appear on
1814	Bordeaux		the Colours:
1814	America		Dunkirk, 1940
1815	New Orleans		Keren
1854–5	Crimea		North Africa, 1940, '43
1854	Alma		Mozzagrogna
1854	Inkerman		Salerno
1855	Sevastopol		Garigliano Crossing
1857–8	Indian Mutiny		Anzio

continued overleaf

IRR

1939–45	Cassino II	1952–3	KOREAN WAR
	Gothic Line		Korea, 1952–3
	Coriano		

NICKNAME

The Elegant Extracts

23 April 1968   Amalgamated with The Royal Northumberland Fusiliers, The Royal Warwickshire Fusiliers, and The Lancashire Fusiliers to form:

THE ROYAL REGIMENT OF FUSILIERS

see page 81   The Royal Northumberland Fusiliers
see page 83   The Royal Warwickshire Fusiliers
see page 110   The Lancashire Fusiliers
see page 272   The Royal Regiment of Fusiliers

The King's Regiment (Liverpool)

Raised chiefly in Derbyshire at the time of the Monmouth Rebellion.

TITLES

1685–1702	The Princess Anne of Denmark's Regiment
1702–16	The Queen's Regiment
1716–51	The King's Regiment of Foot (White Horse of Hanover worn as Regimental Badge)
1751–1881	The 8th (The King's Regiment)
1881–1921	The King's (Liverpool Regiment)
1921–58	The King's Regiment (Liverpool)

PRINCIPAL CAMPAIGNS, BATTLES, etc.

1690	Boyne	1762	Wilhelmstahl
1691	Limerick	1794	Martinique
1696–7	Flanders	1794	Guadaloupe
1701–14	Flanders & Germany	1794–5	Flanders
1702	Venlo	1794	Nimuegen
1702	Liege	1796	Grenada
1704	The Schellenberg	1801	Egypt
1704	Blenheim	1801	Mandora
1706	Ramillies	1801	Alexandria
1708	Oudenarde	1807	Copenhagen
1708	Lille	1809	Martinique
1709	Tournai	1809	Flushing
1709	Malplaquet	1812–14	North America
1710	Douai	1813	Ogdensburg
1711	Ne plus ultra lines	1813	York
1715	Sheriffmuir	1813	Sackets Harbour
1742–9	Flanders & Germany	1813–14	Niagara
1743	Dettingen	1814	Plattsburg
1745	Fontenoy	1857–8	Indian Mutiny
1745–6	Jacobite Rising	1857	Delhi
1746	Falkirk	1857	Agra
1746	Culloden	1857	Lucknow
1746	Roucoux	1857	Cawnpore
1747	Laffeld	1878–80	2nd Afghan War
1760–3	Germany	1878	Peiwar Kotal
1760	Warburg	1885–7	Burma
1760	Zierenberg	1899–1902	South Africa
1760	Kloster Kampen	1899–1900	Defence of Ladysmith
1761	Kirsch Dunkern		

continued overleaf

1914–18	1ST WORLD WAR	1939–45	2ND WORLD WAR
	Battle honours		Battle honours
	selected to appear on		selected to appear on
	the Colours:		the Colours:
	Retreat from Mons		Normandy Landing
	Marne, 1914		Cassino II
	Aisne, 1914		Trasimene Line
	Ypres, 1914, '15, '17		Tuori
	Festubert, 1915		Capture of Forli
	Loos		Rimini Line
	Somme, 1916, '18		Athens
	Arras, 1917, '18		Chindits, 1943
	Scarpe, 1917, '18		Chindits, 1944
	Cambrai, 1917, '18	1952–3	KOREAN WAR
			The Hook, 1953
			Korea, 1952–3

NICKNAME

The Leather Hats

MOTTO

'Nec aspera terrent' (Nor do difficulties deter)

1 September 1958	Amalgamated with The Manchester Regiment to form: THE KING'S REGIMENT (MANCHESTER & LIVERPOOL)
1969	Title was changed to: THE KING'S REGIMENT, and the County affiliation ceased.

see page 240 The Manchester Regiment
see page 266 The King's Regiment

The Royal Norfolk Regiment

TITLES

1685–8	Colonel Henry Cornwell's Regiment of Foot
1688–1751	The title changed with the Colonel's name
1751–81	The 9th Regiment of Foot
1782–1881	The 9th (East Norfolk) Regiment of Foot
1881–1935	The Norfolk Regiment
1935–59	The Royal Norfolk Regiment

PRINCIPAL CAMPAIGNS, BATTLES, etc.

1689	Londonderry	1811	Barossa
1690	Boyne	1811	Fuentes d'Onor
1691	Aughrim	1812	Salamanca
1701–4	Holland	1813	Vittoria
1702	Liege	1813	St. Sebastian
1702	Kaiserswerth	1813	Nive
1702	Venloo	1842	1st Afghan War
1702	Huy	1842	Kabul
1704–8	Spain	1845–6	1st Sikh War
1707	Almanza	1845	Moodkee
1707	Valencia d'Alcantara	1845	Ferozeshah
1707	Alburquerque	1846	Sobraon
1710	Badajos	1854–5	Crimea
1761	Belle Isle	1855	Sevastopol
1762	Havannah	1879–80	2nd Afghan War
1765–9	America	1879	Kabul
1777–82	America	1889	Burma
1777	Saratoga	1900	South Africa
1794	Martinique	1914–18	1ST WORLD WAR
1794	St. Lucia		Battle honours
1796	Guadaloupe		selected to appear on
1796	Grenada		the Colours:
1799	Bergen		Mons
1799	Egmont-op-Zee		Le Cateau
1799	Alkanaer		Marne, 1914
1808–14	Peninsula		Ypres, 1914, '15, '17, '18
1808	Roleia		Somme, 1916, '18
1808	Vimiera		Hindenburg Line
1809	Corunna		Landing at Suvia
1809	Flushing		Gaza
1809	Douro		Shaiba
1810	Busaco		
1811	Tarifa		

continued overleaf

1914–18	Kut al Amara, 1915, '17	1939–45	Venraij
			Rhineland
1919–21	Waziristan		North West Europe
1936–7	North-West Frontier		1940, '44–5
			Singapore Island
1939–45	2ND WORLD WAR Battle honours selected to appear on the Colours:		Kohima
			Aradura
			Burma, 1944–5
	St. Omer-La Bassee	1951–2	KOREAN WAR
	Normandy Landing		Korea, 1951–2
	Brieux Bridgehead	1955–6	Cyprus

NICKNAMES

The Holy Boys   The Fighting Ninth
The Norfolk Howards

25 August 1959	Amalgamated with the Suffolk Regiment to form: THE 1st EAST ANGLIAN REGIMENT (ROYAL NORFOLK AND SUFFOLK)
1 September 1964	The above unit was re-designated: THE 1st (NORFOLK AND SUFFOLK) BATTALION THE ROYAL ANGLIAN REGIMENT
1 July 1968	The County affiliation ceased—(Norfolk and Suffolk) being deleted from the title

see page 95   The Suffolk Regiment
see page 270 The Royal Anglian Regiment

The Royal Lincolnshire Regiment

TITLES

1685–95	Colonel Sir John Granville's (The Earl of Bath) Regiment of Foot
1695–1751	The title changed with the Colonel's name
1751–82	The 10th Regiment of Foot
1782–1881	The 10th (North Lincoln) Regiment of Foot
1881–1946	The Lincolnshire Regiment
1946–60	The Royal Lincolnshire Regiment

PRINCIPAL CAMPAIGNS, BATTLES, etc.

1690–6	Flanders	1848–9	2nd Sikh War
1692	Steenkirk	1849	Mooltan
1701–13	Flanders & Germany	1849	Gujerat
1702	Kaiserwerth	1857–8	Indian Mutiny
1702	Liege	1857	Lucknow
1704	Schellenberg	1875–6	Perak
1704	Blenheim	1888	Burma
1705	Neer Hespen	1898	Atbara
1706	Ramillies	1898	Khartoum
1708	Oudenarde	1900–2	South Africa
1708	Lisle	1914–18	1ST WORLD WAR
1708	Ghent		Battle honours
1709	Tournay		selected to appear on
1709	Malplaquet		the Colours:
1711	Bouchain		Mons
1712	Quesnoy		Marne, 1914
1767–78	America		Messines, 1914, '17, '18
1775	Lexington		Ypres, 1914, '15, '17
1775	Bunker's Hill		Neuve Chapelle
1776	Long Island		Loos
1776	White Plains		Somme, 1915, '18
1776	Brunx		Lys
1777	Brandywine		Hindenburg Line
1777	Germantown		Suvla
1778	Freehold		
1798	Grenada		
1801	Egypt	1939–45	2ND WORLD WAR
1809	Flushing		Battle honours
1809	Ionian Islands		selected to appear on
1812–14	Peninsula		the Colours:
1845–6	1st Sikh War		Dunkirk, 1940
1846	Sobraon		Normandy Landing

continued overleaf

1939–45	Fontenay le Pesmil	1939–45	Salerno
	Antwerp-Turnhout		Gothic Line
	Canal		Ngakyedauk Pass
	Rhineland		Burma, 1943–5
	North Africa, 1943		

NICKNAMES

The Springers   The Poachers

1 June 1960   Amalgamated with the Northamptonshire Regiment to form:
THE 2nd EAST ANGLIAN REGIMENT (DUCHESS OF GLOUCESTER'S OWN ROYAL LINCOLNSHIRE AND NORTHAMPTONSHIRE)

1 September 1964   The above unit was redesignated:
THE 2nd (DUCHESS OF GLOUCESTER'S OWN LINCOLNSHIRE AND NORTHAMPTONSHIRE) BATTALION THE ROYAL ANGLIAN REGIMENT

1 July 1968   Redesignated:
THE 2nd BATTALION THE ROYAL ANGLIAN REGIMENT
and the County affiliation ceased.

see page 232   The Northamptonshire Regiment
see page 270   The Royal Anglian Regiment

The Devonshire Regiment

TITLES

1685–7	Colonel the Duke of Beaufort's Musketeers
1687–1751	The title changed with the Colonel's name
1751–82	The 11th Regiment of Foot
1782–1881	The 11th (North Devonshire) Regiment of Foot
1881–1958	The Devonshire Regiment

PRINCIPAL CAMPAIGNS, BATTLES, etc.

1690	Boyne	1811	Sabugal
1690	Athlone	1812	Salamanca
1690	Limerick	1812	Burgos
1690–6	Flanders	1813	Vittoria
1692	Steenkirk	1813	Pyrenees
1703–4	Germany	1813	Nivelle
1706–8	Spain	1813	Nive
1707	Almanza	1814	Orthes
1708–11	Germany	1814	Toulouse
1709	Malplaquet	1837–8	Ionian Islands
1709	Mons	1838–9	Canada
1709	Pont-a-Vendin	1879–80	2nd Afghan War
1710	Douay	1895	Chitral
1710	Bethune	1897–8	Tirah
1710	Aire	1899–1902	South Africa
1710	St. Venant	1900	Defence of Ladysmith
1711	Quebec	1900	Relief of Ladysmith
1715	Jacobite Rising		
1715	Dunblane	1914–18	IST WORLD WAR
1742–8	Flanders		Battle honours
1743	Dettingen		selected to appear on
1745	Fontenoy		the Colours:
1745	Jacobite Rising		La Bassee, 1914
1746	Roucoux		Ypres, 1915, '17
1760–3	Germany		Loos
1760	Corbach		Somme, 1916, '18
1760	Warburg		Bois des Buttes
1760	Campen		Hindenburg Line
1762	Wilhemstahl		Vittoria Veneto
1793	Toulon		Doiran, 1917, '18
1794	Corsica		Palestine, 1917–18
1809	Flushing		Mesopotamia,
1809–14	Peninsula		1916–18
1810	Busaco		

continued overleaf

| 1939–45 | 2ND WORLD WAR
Battle honours
selected to appear on
the Colours:
Normandy Landing
Caen
Rhine
North-West Europe,
  1944–5 | 1939–45 | Landing in Sicily
Regalbuto
Malta, 1940–2
Imphal
Myinmu Bridgehead
Burma, 1943–4 |

NICKNAME

The Bloody Eleventh

MOTTO

'Semper Fidelis' (Ever faithful)

| 17 May
1958 | Amalgamated with the Dorset Regiment to form:
THE DEVONSHIRE AND DORSET
REGIMENT |

see page 224 The Dorset Regiment
see page 265 The Devonshire and Dorset Regiment

The Suffolk Regiment

TITLES

1685–	Colonel the Duke of Norfolk's Regiment of Foot
1685–6	Colonel The Earl of Lichfield's Regiment of Foot
1685–1751	The title changed with the Colonel's name
1751–82	The 12th Regiment of Foot
1782–1881	The 12th (East Suffolk) Regiment of Foot
1881–1959	The Suffolk Regiment

PRINCIPAL CAMPAIGNS, BATTLES, etc.

1690	Boyne	1914–18	1ST WORLD WAR
1691	Aughrim		Battle honours
1694–7	Flanders		selected to appear on
1719	Messina		the Colours:
1742–5	Flanders		Le Cateau
1743	Dettingen		Neuve Chapelle
1745	Fontenoy		Ypres, 1915, '17, '18
1758–63	Germany		Somme, 1916, '18
1759	Minden		Arras, 1917, '18
1761	Denkern		Cambrai, 1917, '18
1762	Wilhelmstahl		Hindenburg Line
1779–83	Gibraltar		Macedonia, 1915–18
1794	Martinique		Landing at Suvla
1794	Guadaloupe		Gaza
1794–5	Flanders		
1794	Nimeguen	1939–45	2ND WORLD WAR
1795	Guildermalsen		Battle honours
1798–1807	India		selected to appear on
1799	Mallavelly		the Colours:
1799	Seringapatam		Dunkirk, 1940
1810	Bourbon		Normandy Landing
1810	Mauritius		Odon
1851–3	South Africa		Falaise
1863–6	New Zealand		Venraij
1878–80	2nd Afghan War		Brinkum
1888	Hazara		Singapore Island
1899–1902	South Africa		North Arakan
			Imphal
			Burma, 1943–5

NICKNAME

The Old Dozen

continued overleaf

MOTTO
'Montis insignia calpe' (Arms of the rock of Gibraltar)

25 August 1959	Amalgamated with the Royal Norfolk Regiment to form: THE 1st EAST ANGLIAN REGIMENT (ROYAL NORFOLK AND SUFFOLK)
1 September 1964	The above unit was redesignated: THE 1st (NORFOLK AND SUFFOLK) BATTALION THE ROYAL ANGLIAN REGIMENT
1 July 1968	The County affiliation ceased—(Norfolk and Suffolk) being deleted from the title

see page 89   The Royal Norfolk Regiment
see page 270   The Royal Anglian Regiment

The Somerset Light Infantry (Prince Albert's)

Chiefly raised in Buckinghamshire.

TITLES

1685–8	Colonel The Earl of Huntingdon's Regiment of Foot
1688–1751	The title changed with its Colonel's name
1751–82	The 13th Regiment of Foot
1782–1822	The 13th (1st Somersetshire) Regiment of Foot
1822–42	The 13th (1st Somersetshire Light Infantry) Regiment
1842–81	The 13th (1st Somersetshire) (Prince Albert's Light Infantry) Regiment
1881–1959	The Prince Albert's (Somerset Light Infantry), later expressed as The Somerset Light Infantry (Prince Albert's)

PRINCIPAL CAMPAIGNS BATTLES, etc.

1689	Killicrankie	1801	Mandora
1690	Boyne	1801	Alexandria
1690	Cork	1809	Martinique
1690	Kinsale	1810	Guadaloupe
1701–3	Flanders	1813–15	America
1702	Kaiserwerth	1814	Plattsburg
1702	Venloo	1824–6	Ava
1702	Ruremonde	1825–7	1st Burma War
1702	Huy	1839	1st Afghan War
1702	Limberg	1839	Ghazni
1702	Liege	1842	Jellalabad
1704–11	Spain	1842	Kabul
1704–5	Gibraltar	1854–5	Crimea
1705	Barcelona	1855	Sevastopol
1707	Almanza	1858	Indian Mutiny
1709	Caya	1878–9	South Africa
1711	Tortosa	1885–7	Burma
1711	St. Matheo	1899–1902	South Africa
1727	Gibraltar	1900	Relief of Ladysmith
1742–8	Flanders		
1743	Dettingen	1914–18	1ST WORLD WAR
1745	Fontenoy		Battle honours
1745	Jacobite Rising		selected to appear on
1746	Roucoux		the Colours:
1747	Val		Marne, 1914, '18
1793–5	San Domingo		Aisne, 1914
1801	Egypt		Ypres, 1915, '17, '18

continued overleaf

The Somerset Light Infantry (Prince Albert's)

1914–18	Somme, 1916, '18	1939–45	Hill 112
	Albert, 1916, '18		Mont Pincon
	Arras, 1917, '18		Rhineland
	Cambrai, 1917, '18		Rhine
	Hindenburg Line		North-West Europe,
	Palestine, 1917–18		1944–5
	Tigris, 1916		Cassino II
			Cosina Canal Crossing
1939–45	2ND WORLD WAR		Italy, 1944–5
	Battle honours		North Arakan
	selected to appear on		Ngakyedauk Pass
	the Colours:		

NICKNAMES

The Bleeders   The Illustrious Garrison
The Jellalabad Heroes

| 6 October 1959 | Amalgamated with The Duke of Cornwall's Light Infantry to form:
 THE SOMERSET AND CORNWALL LIGHT INFANTRY |

see page 218 The Duke of Cornwall's Light Infantry
see page 268 The Somerset and Cornwall Light Infantry
see page 272 The Light Infantry

The West Yorkshire Regiment (The Prince of Wales's Own)

The Regiment was first raised in Kent

TITLES

1685–8	Colonel Sir Edward Hales's Regiment of Foot
1688–1751	The title changed with the Colonel's name
1751–82	The 14th Regiment of Foot
1782–1809	The 14th (Bedfordshire) Regiment of Foot
1809–76	The 14th (Buckinghamshire) Regiment of Foot
1876–81	The 14th (Buckinghamshire—The Prince of Wales's Own) Regiment of Foot
1881–1920	The Prince of Wales's Own (West Yorkshire Regiment)
1920–58	The West Yorkshire Regiment (The Prince of Wales's Own)

PRINCIPAL CAMPAIGNS, BATTLES, etc.

1690	Scotland	1809	Walcheren (2nd Bn)
1692–6	Flanders	1810	Mauritius
1693	Neer Landen	1810–14	Gibraltar, Malta, Sicily &
1695	Kenogue, Namur		Lampedusa
1715	Scotland (Sheriffmuir)	1811	Java
1719	Scotland (Glenshiel)	1813	North-West Borneo
1727	Gibraltar	1814	Genoa (2nd Bn)
1745	Flanders	1815	Toulon (2nd Bn)
1746	Falkirk	1815	Waterloo (3rd Bn)
1746	Culloden	1815	Cambray (3rd Bn)
1766–71	America	1815	1st Nepal War
1772	St. Vincent	1817	Pindaree War
1773–6	America	1826	Bhurtpore (1st Bn)
1793–5	Flanders	1854–5	Crimea
1793	Famars	1855	Sevastopol
1793	Valenciennes	1860–6	New Zealand (2nd Bn)
1793	Dunkirk		
1794	Tournay	1879–80	2nd Afghan War (2nd Bn)
1795	Guildermalsen		
1796	St. Lucia	1895	Ashanti (2nd Bn)
1797	Trinidad, Port Rico	1899–1902	South Africa (2nd Bn)
1807–31	India	1900	Relief of Ladysmith
1808–9	Peninsula (2nd Bn)	1908	Mohmand Field Force
1809	Corunna (2nd Bn)		

continued overleaf

1914–18	1ST WORLD WAR	1939–45	2ND WORLD WAR
	Battle honours		Battle honours
	selected to appear on		selected to appear on
	the Colours:		the Colours:
	Armentieres, 1914		Keren
	Neuve Chapelle		Defence of Alamein
	Somme, 1916, '18		Line
	Ypres, 1917, '18		Pegu, 1942
	Cambrai, 1917, '18		Yenangyanung, 1942
	Villers Bretonneaux		Maungdaw
	Lys		Defence of Sinzweya
	Tardenois		Imphal
	Piave		Bishenpur
	Suvia		Meiktila
1922–4	Kurdistan		Sittang, 1945
1936	Palestine		
1938	Palestine		

NICKNAMES

The Old and Bold   Calvert's Entire
The Rugged and Tough

MOTTO

'Nec aspera terrent' (Nor do difficulties deter)

25 April 1958	Amalgamated with The East Yorkshire Regiment (The Duke of York's Own) to form: THE PRINCE OF WALES'S OWN REGIMENT OF YORKSHIRE

see page 101 The East Yorkshire Regiment (The Duke of York's Own)
see page 264 The Prince of Wales's Own Regiment of Yorkshire

The East Yorkshire Regiment
(The Duke of York's Own)

TITLES

1685–6	Colonel Sir William Clifton's Regiment
1686–1751	The title changed with the Colonel's name
1751–82	The 15th Regiment of Foot
1782–1881	The 15th (York, East Riding) Regiment of Foot
1881–1958	The East Yorkshire Regiment (The Duke of York's Own)

PRINCIPAL CAMPAIGNS, BATTLES, etc.

1694–7	Flanders	1879–80	2nd Afghan War
1695	Namur	1900–2	South Africa
1702–12	Flanders & Germany	1914–18	1ST WORLD WAR
1702	Liege		Battle honours
1704	Schellenberg		selected to appear on
1704	Blenheim		the Colours:
1706	Ramilies		Aisne, 1914, '18
1708	Oudenarde		Armentieres, 1914
1708	Lisle		Ypres, 1915, '17, '18
1709	Tournay		Loos
1709	Malplaquet		Somme, 1916, '18
1709	Mons		Arras, 1917, '18
1710	Douai		Cambrai, 1917, '18
1711	Bouchain		Selle
1741	Carthagena		Doiran, 1917
1745	Jacobite Rising		Gallipoli, 1915
1758–60	Canada		
1758	Louisburg	1939–45	2ND WORLD WAR
1759	Quebec		Battle honours
1760	Sillery		selected to appear on
1762	Martinque		the Colours:
1762	Havannah		Dunkirk, 1940
1776–8	America		Normandy Landing
1776	Brooklyn		Odon
1777	Brandywine		Schaddenhof
1777	Germantown		North-West Europe,
1778	St. Lucia		1940, '44–5
1794	Martinique		Gazala
1794	Guadaloupe		El Alamein
1809	Martinique		Mareth
1810	Guadaloupe		Sicily, 1943
1815	Martinique		Burma, 1945

continued overleaf

The East Yorkshire Regiment (The Duke of York's Own)

NICKNAMES

The Snappers   The Poona Guards

25 April   Amalgamated with The West Yorkshire Regiment (The
1958   Prince of Wales's Own) to form:
            THE PRINCE OF WALES'S OWN
            REGIMENT OF YORKSHIRE

see page 99 The West Yorkshire Regiment (The Prince of Wales's Own)
see page 264 The Prince of Wales's Own Regiment of Yorkshire

The Bedfordshire and Hertfordshire Regiment

With the 17th Foot was the sole survivor of twelve Regiments raised in 1688.

TITLES

1688–1751	When raised was known as Colonel Archibald Douglas's Regiment of Foot. In 1689 as Colonel James Stanley's Regiment of Foot. Later the title changed with the Colonel's name.
1751–82	The 16th Regiment of Foot
1782–1809	The 16th (Buckinghamshire) Regiment of Foot
1809–81	The 16th (Bedfordshire) Regiment of Foot. (The County title was exchanged with the 14th Foot at the request of the Colonel of that Regiment.)
1881–1919	The Bedfordshire Regiment
1919–1958	The Bedfordshire and Hertfordshire Regiment

PRINCIPAL CAMPAIGNS, BATTLES, etc.

1689–97	Flanders	1900–2	South Africa
1689	Walcourt	1914–18	1ST WORLD WAR
1692	Steenkirk		Battle honours selected to appear on the Colours:
1693	Neer Landen		
1695	Namur		
1702–12	Germany		Mons
1702	Liege		Marne, 1914
1704	Schellenberg		Ypres, 1914, '15, '17
1704	Blenheim		Loos
1706	Ramillies		Somme, 1916, '18
1708	Oudenarde		Arras, 1917, '18
1708	Lisle		Cambrai, 1917, '18
1709	Tournay		Suvla
1709	Malplaquet		Sambre
1741	Carthagena		Gaza
1742	Cuba		
1745	Melle	1939–45	2ND WORLD WAR
1778	Baton Rouge		Battle honours selected to appear on the Colours:
1779–81	America		
1781	Pensacola		
1793–4	San Domingo		Dunkirk, 1940
1795	Jamaica		North-West Europe, 1940
1804	Surinam		
1895	Chitral		Tobruk Sortie

continued overleaf

1939–45	Belhamed	1939–45	Trasimene Line
	Tunis		Italy, 1944–5
	North Africa, 1941,' 43		Chindits, 1944
	Cassino II		

NICKNAMES

The Old Bucks   The Peacemakers

The Featherbeds

2 June 1958   Amalgamated with the Essex Regiment to form:
THE 3rd EAST ANGLIAN REGIMENT
(16th/44th FOOT (Soubriquet—'Pompadours'))

1 September 1964   The regiment was re-designated:
THE 3rd (16th/44th FOOT) BATTALION
THE ROYAL ANGLIAN REGIMENT

1 July 1968   '(16th/44th)' dropped from title. County affiliation ceased.

see page 229 The Essex Regiment
see page 270 The Royal Anglian Regiment

The Royal Leicestershire Regiment

Mainly raised near London. Was one of the only two regiments to survive out of twelve formed in 1688.

TITLES

1688–9	Colonel Solomon Richard's Regiment of Foot
1689–1751	The title changed with the Colonel's name
1751–82	The 17th Regiment of Foot
1782–1881	The 17th (Leicestershire) Regiment of Foot
1881–1946	The Leicestershire Regiment
1946–64	The Royal Leicestershire Regiment

PRINCIPAL CAMPAIGNS, BATTLES, etc.

1693–7	Flanders	1855	Sevastopol
1693	Neer Landen	1878–9	2nd Afghan War
1695	Namur	1878	Ali Kasjid
1702–4	Germany	1899–1902	South Africa
1702	Venloo	1900	Defence of Ladysmith
1702	Huy		
1702	Liege	1914–18	1ST WORLD WAR
1704–9	Spain		Battle honours
1707	Almanza		selected to appear on
1715	Jacobite Rising		the Colours:
1757–60	Canada		Aisne, 1914, '18
1758	Louisbourg		Neuve Chapelle
1762	Martinique		Somme, 1916, '18
1762	Havannah		Ypres, 1917
1775–81	America		Cambrai, 1917, '18
1776	Brooklyn		Lys
1777	Brandywine		St. Quentin Canal
1777	Germantown		France & Flanders,
1778	Freehold		1914–18
1796	San Domingo		Palestine, 1918
1799	Helder		Mesopotamia,
1799	Crabbendam		1915–18
1799	Bergen	1939–45	2ND WORLD WAR
1799	Egmont-op-Zee		Battle honours
1804–23	Hindoostan		selected to appear on
1813–14	Gurkha War		the Colours:
1839	1st Afghan War		Scheldt
1839	Ghazni		North-West Europe,
1839	Khelat		1944–5
1854–5	Crimea		

continued overleaf

| 1939–45 | Sidi Barrani
North Africa, 1940–1,
   '43
Salerno
Gothic Line
Italy, 1943–5 | 1939–45 | Crete
Malaya, 1941–2
Chindits, 1944 |
| | | 1951–2 | KOREAN WAR
Korea, 1951–2 |

NICKNAMES

The Lily-whites   The Bengal Tigers

1 September 1964	Redesignated: 4th (LEICESTERSHIRE) BATTALION THE ROYAL ANGLIAN REGIMENT
1 July 1968	Redesignated: 4th BATTALION THE ROYAL ANGLIAN REGIMENT and the County affiliation ceased.
1970	The battalion reduced to an independent Company of the Royal Anglian Regiment, 'Tiger Company'.

see page 270 The Royal Anglian Regiment

The Royal Irish Regiment

The only regiment out of nineteen raised in Ireland from Independent Garrison Companies to survive into the 20th century.

TITLES

1684–6	Colonel the Earl of Granard's Regiment of Foot
1686–95	The title changed with the Colonel's name
1695–1751	The Royal Regiment of Ireland
1751–1881	The 18th (The Royal Irish) Regiment of Foot
1881–1922	The Royal Irish Regiment

PRINCIPAL CAMPAIGNS, BATTLES, etc.

1690	Boyne	1801	Alexandria
1691	Limerick	1809	San Domingo
1691	Aughrim	1840–2	China
1693–7	Flanders	1852	Rangoon
1695	Namur	1852–3	Pegu
1702–15	Flanders & Germany	1855	Sevastopol
1702	Venloo	1863–6	New Zealand
1702	Liege	1879–80	2nd Afghan War
1704	Schellenberg	1882	Egypt
1704	Blenheim	1882	Kassassin
1705	Neer Hespen	1882	Tel-el-Kebir
1706	Ramillies	1884–5	Nile
1708	Oudenarde	1900–2	South Africa
1708	Lisle	1914–18	1ST WORLD WAR
1709	Tournay		Battle honours
1709	Malplaquet		selected to appear on
1711	Bouchain		the Colours:
1715	Aire		Mons
1727	Gibraltar		Le Cateau
1745	Flanders		Marne, 1914
1775–6	America		Ypres, 1915, '17, '18
1775	Lexington		Somme, 1916, '18
1775	Bunker's Hill		Messines, 1917
1793	Toulon		Hindenburg Line
1794	Corsica		Struma
1801	Egypt		Suvla
1801	Mandora		Gaza

NICKNAMES

Paddy's Blackguards   The Namurs

31 July 1922	The Regiment was disbanded

The Green Howards
(Alexandra, Princess of Wales's
Own Yorkshire Regiment)

Raised from independent companies of pikemen and musketeers in Devonshire.

TITLES

1688–91	Colonel Francis Luttrell's Regiment of Foot
1691–1751	The title changed with the Colonel's name
1751–82	The 19th Regiment of Foot
1782–1875	The 19th (1st Yorkshire, North Riding) Regiment of Foot
1875–81	The 19th (1st Yorkshire, North Riding—Princess of Wales's Own) Regiment of Foot
1881–1921	The Princess of Wales's Own (Yorkshire) Regiment
from 1921	The Green Howards (Alexandra, Princess of Wales's Own Yorkshire Regiment)

PRINCIPAL CAMPAIGNS, BATTLES, etc.

1689–91	The Irish War	1761	Siege of Belle Isle
	Battles of the Boyne and Aughrim	1781	Campaign in South Carolina
	Sieges of Athlone, Sligo and Limerick	1793–5	Flanders Attack on Tuyl
1692	Flanders		Geldermalsen
	Battle of Steenkirke		Retreat through
1693	Battle of Landen		Holland and
1694	Expedition to Brest		Germany
1694–7	Flanders	1796	Five companies at the
	Siege of Namur		capture of the Cape
1702–3	Expedition to Cadiz and the West Indies	1799	of Good Hope Five companies in the
1707–9	Flanders		campaign against
	Battle of Malplaquet		the Southern
1710–14	Flanders		Polygars, India
	Sieges of Douai, Bethune and	1803	Expedition to Kandy
	Bouchain	1809	The War in Travancore
1719	Expedition to Vigo	1815	The capture of Kandy
1744–8	War of the Austrian	1817–18	Rebellion in Ceylon
	Succession	1854–5	Crimea
	Battles of Fontenoy, Roucoux and		Battles of the Alma and Inkerman
	Lauffeldt		Siege of Sebastopol

1854–5	Attacks on the Redan, 18 June and 8 September 1855	1914–18	Somme, 1916, '18
			Arras, 1917, '18
			Messines, 1917, '18
1857–8	The Indian Mutiny		Valenciennes
1868	Hazara Campaign and Expedition against the tribes on the Black Mountain		Sambre
			France & Flanders, 1914–18
			Vittorio Veneto
1885	The Nile Expedition		Suvla
1885–6	Soudan Expedition Action at Ginnis	1919	3rd Afghan War
1897–8	The Tirah War	1939–45	2ND WORLD WAR
1899–1902	South Africa Relief of Kimberley Battles of Paardeberg, Driefontein, Johannesburg, Diamond Hill and Belfast		Battle honours selected to appear on the Colours: Norway. 1940 Normandy Landing North-West Europe, 1940, '44–5 Gazala El Alamein Mareth Akarit Sicily, 1943 Mintruno Anzio
1914–18	1ST WORLD WAR Battle honours selected to appear on the Colours: Ypres, 1914, '15, '17 Loos		

NICKNAME
The Green Howards

The Lancashire Fusiliers

Raised in Devonshire on the landing of William of Orange, afterwards William III.

TITLES

1688–9	Colonel Sir Robert Peyton's Regiment of Foot
1689–1751	The title changed with the Colonel's name
1751–82	The 20th Regiment of Foot
1782–1881	The 20th (East Devonshire) Regiment of Foot
1881–1968	The Lancashire Fusiliers

PRINCIPAL CAMPAIGNS, BATTLES, etc.

1690	Boyne	1814	Orthes
1691	Athlone	1814	Toulouse
1691	Aughrim	1854–5	Crimea
1707–12	Spain	1854	Alma
1709	Caya	1854	Inkerman
1727	Gibraltar	1855	Sevastopol
1742–5	Flanders	1857–8	Indian Mutiny
1743	Dettingen	1858	Lucknow
1745	Fontenoy	1898	Khartoum
1745	Culloden	1899–1902	South Africa
1758	Cherbourg	1900	Relief of Ladysmith
1758–63	Germany		
1759	Minden	1914–18	1ST WORLD WAR
1760	Warburg		Battle honours
1760	Campen		selected to appear on
1761	Denkern		the Colours:
1762	Wilhemstahl		Retreat from Mons
1776–81	America		Aisne, 1914, '18
1777	Stillwater		Ypres, 1915, '17, '18
1799	Crabbenham		Somme, 1916, '18
1799	Bergen		Arras, 1917, '18
1799	Egmont-op-Zee		Passchendaele
1799	Alkmaer		Cambrai, 1917, '18
1800	Quiberon		Hindenburg Line
1801	Egypt		Macedonia, 1915–18
1806	Maida		Landing at Helles
1808–14	Peninsula	1939–45	2ND WORLD WAR
1808	Vimiera		Battle honours
1809	Corunna		selected to appear on
1809	Flushing		the Colours:
1813	Vittoria		Defence of Escaut
1813	Pyrenees		Caen

1939–45	Medjez el Bab	1939–45	Malta, 1941–2
	Sangro		Kohima
	Cassino II		Chindits, 1944
	Argenta Gap		Burma, 1943–5

NICKNAMES

The Two Tens   The Minden Boys
Kingsley's Stand

MOTTO

'Omnia audax' (Daring everything)

23 April 1968	Amalgamated with The Royal Northumberland and The Royal Warwickshire Fusiliers, and The Royal Fusiliers (City of London Regiment) to form: THE ROYAL REGIMENT OF FUSILIERS

see page 81   The Royal Northumberland Fusiliers
see page 83   The Royal Warwickshire Fusiliers
see page 85   The Royal Fusiliers (City of London Regiment)
see page 272   The Royal Regiment of Fusiliers

Disbanded 1972

The Royal Scots Fusiliers

When first raised was armed with fusils instead of muskets and hence its title.

TITLES

1678–86	Colonel The Earl of Mar's Regiment of Foot
1686–1707	The title changed with the Colonel's name, but the unit became a regiment of Fusiliers. Also popularly known as The Scots Fusiliers Regiment of Foot.
1707–12	The Scots Fusiliers Regiment of Foot
1712–51	The Royal North British Fusiliers Regiment of Foot
1751–1877	The 21st (Royal North British) Fusiliers Regiment of Foot
1877–81	The 21st (Royal Scots Fusiliers) Regiment of Foot
1881–1959	The Royal Scots Fusiliers

PRINCIPAL CAMPAIGNS, BATTLES, etc.

1689–97	Flanders	1814	Netherlands
1689	Walcourt	1814	Bladensburg
1692	Steenkirk	1815	New Orleans
1693	Neer Landen	1854–5	Crimea
1702–12	Flanders & Germany	1854	Alma
1704	Schellenberg	1854	Inkerman
1704	Blenheim	1855	Sevastopol
1705	Neer Hespen	1879	South Africa
1706	Ramilies	1885–7	Burma
1708	Oudenarde	1897–8	Tirah
1708	Lisle	1899–1902	South Africa
1709	Mlplaquet	1900	Relief of Ladysmith
1710	Douay		
1711	Bouchain	1914–18	1ST WORLD WAR
1742–8	Flanders		Battle honours
1743	Dettingen		selected to appear on
1745	Fontenoy		the Colours:
1747	Val		Mons
1761	Belle-Isle		Marne, 1914
1776–8	America		Ypres, 1914, '17, '18
1777	Stillwater		Somme, 1916, '18
1794	Martinique		Arras, 1917, '18
1794	St. Lucia		Lys
1794	Guadaloupe		Hindenburg Line
1809	Ionian Islands		Doiran, 1917, '18
1809	Scylla		Gallipoli, 1915–16
1814	Bergen-op-Zoom		Palestine, 1917–18

1939–45	2ND WORLD WAR	1939–45	Scheldt
	Battle honours		Rhine
	selected to appear on		Bremen
	the Colours:		Landing in Sicily
	Ypres-Comines Canal		Garigliano Crossing
	Odon		North Arakan
	Falaise		Pinwe

NICKNAME

The Earl of Mar's Grey-breeks

MOTTO

'Nemo me impune lacessit' (No one provokes me with impunity)

20 January 1959   Amalgamated with The Highland Light Infantry to form: THE ROYAL HIGHLAND FUSILIERS (PRINCESS MARGARET'S OWN GLASGOW AND AYRSHIRE REGIMENT)

see page 244   The Highland Light Infantry (City of Glasgow Regiment)
see page 266   The Royal Highland Fusiliers (Princess Margaret's Own Glasgow and Ayrshire Regiment)

The Cheshire Regiment

First raised at Chester.

TITLES

1689	Colonel the Duke of Norfolk's Regiment of Foot
1689–1751	The title changed with the Colonel's name
1751–82	The 22nd Regiment of Foot
1782–1881	The 22nd (The Cheshire) Regiment of Foot
from 1881	The Cheshire Regiment (Within the Regiment the title used is The 22nd (Cheshire) Regiment)

PRINCIPAL CAMPAIGNS, BATTLES, etc.

1690	Boyne	1914–18	Mons
1691	Athlone		Ypres, 1914, '15, '17,
1691	Limerick		'18
1691	Aughrim		Somme, 1916, '18
1727	Gibraltar		Arras, 1917, '18
1757–60	Canada		Messines, 1917, '18
1758	Louisberg		Bapaume, 1918
1759	Quebec		Dorian, 1917, '18
1761	Dominica		Suvla
1762	Martinique,		Gaza
	Havannah		Kut al Amara, 1717
1775–9	American War of		
	Independence	1939–45	2ND WORLD WAR
1775	Bunker's Hill		Battle honours
1776	Brooklyn		selected to appear on
1794	Guadaloupe		the Colours:
1794	St. Lucia		St. Omer-La Bassee
1800	Cape of Good Hope		Normandy Landing
1805	Bhurtpore		Capture of Tobruk
1843	Meeanee		El Alamein
1843	Hyderabad		Mareth
1843	Scinde		Sicily, 1943
1887	Burma		Salerno
1900–2	South Africa		Rome
			Gothic Line
1914–18	1ST WORLD WAR		Malta, 1941–2
	Battle honours		
	selected to appear on		
	the Colours:		

NICKNAMES

The Old Two Twos   The Red Knights
The Lightning Conductors

The Royal Welch Fusiliers

TITLES

1688–9	Colonel Lord Herbert's Regiment of Foot
1689–1712	The title changed with the Colonel's name
1712–14	The Royal Regiment of Welch Fuzileers
1714–27	The Prince of Wales's Own Royal Regiment Welch Fusiliers
1727–51	The Royal Welch Fusiliers
1751–1881	The 23rd (Royal Welch Fusiliers) Regiment of Foot
1881–1920	The Royal Welsh Fusiliers
from 1920	The Royal Welch Fusiliers

PRINCIPAL CAMPAIGNS, BATTLES, etc.

1690	Boyne	1813	Pyrenees
1691	Aughrim	1813	Nivelle
1692–7	Flanders	1814	Orthes
1695	Namur	1814	Toulouse
1702–12	Flanders & Germany	1815	Quatre Bras & Waterloo
1704	Blenheim		
1706	Ramillies	1854–5	Crimea
1708	Oudenarde	1854	Alma
1709	Malplaquet	1854	Inkerman
1742–8	Flanders	1855	Sevastopol
1743	Dettingen	1857–8	Indian Mutiny
1745	Fontenoy	1858	Lucknow
1756	Minorca	1874	Ashantee
1758–62	Germany	1885–7	Burma
1759	Minden	1899–1902	South Africa
1760	Warburg	1900	Relief of Ladysmith
1775–81	American War of Independence	1900	Pekin
1775	Bunker's Hill	1914–18	1ST WORLD WAR
1776	Brooklyn		Battle honours
1801	Aboukir		selected to appear on
1807	Copenhagen		the Colours:
1808–14	Peninsula		Marne, 1914
1809	Corunna		Ypres, 1914, '17, '18
1809	Martinique		Somme, 1916, '18
1811	Albuera		Hindenburg Line
1812	Badajoz		Vittorio Veneto
1812	Salamanca		Doiran, 1917, '18
1813	Vittoria		Gallipoli, 1915–16

continued overleaf

1914–18	Egypt, 1915–17	1939–45	Caen
	Gaza		Lower Maas
	Baghdad		Reichswald
			Weeze
1939–45	2ND WORLD WAR		Rhine
	Battle honours		Madagascar
	selected to appear on		Donbaik
	the Colours:		North Arakan
	St. Omer-La Bassee		Kohima

MOTTO

'Nec aspera terrent' (Difficulties do not dismay us)

The South Wales Borderers

TITLES

1689–1751	Colonel Sir Edward Dering's Regiment of Foot. Later the title changed with the Colonel's name. (In 1702 the Duke of Marlborough was Colonel.)
1751–82	The 24th Regiment of Foot
1782–1881	The 24th (2nd Warwickshire) Regiment of Foot
1881–1969	The South Wales Borderers

PRINCIPAL CAMPAIGNS, BATTLES, etc.

1690–1	Ireland	1867	Andaman Islands
1697	Flanders	1877–9	South Africa (Kaffir
1702–13	Germany &		& Zulu Wars)
	Netherlands	1879	Defence of Rorke's
1704	Blenheim		Drift
1706	Ramilies	1885–7	Burma
1708	Oudenarde	1900–2	South African War
1709	Malplaquet		
1740–2	West Indies	1914–18	1ST WORLD WAR
1756	Minorca		Battle honours
1759	Guadaloupe		selected to appear on
1760–2	Germany		the Colours:
1760	Warburg		Mons
1762	Wilhemstahl		Marne, 1914
1776–81	American War of		Ypres, 1914, '17, '18
	Independence		Gheluvelt
1777	Saratoga		Somme, 1916, '18
1801	Egypt		Cambrai, 1917, '18
1801	Alexandria		Doiran, 1917, '18
1806	Cape of Good Hope		Landing at Helles
1809–14	Peninsula		Baghdad
1809	Talavera		Tsingtao
1811	Fuentes d'Onor	1939–45	2ND WORLD WAR
1812	Salamanca		Battle honours
1813	Vittoria, Pyrenees,		selected to appear on
	Nivelle		the Colours:
1814	Orthes		Norway, 1940
1814–16	Nepal		Normandy Landing
1848–9	2nd Sikh War		Sully
1849	Chillianwallah		Caen
1849	Gujerat		Le Havre
1857–8	Indian Mutiny		North-West Europe,
1865–7	2nd Burma War		1944–5

continued overleaf

| 1939–45 | North Africa, 1942 | 1939–45 | Pinwe |
| | Mayu Tunnels | | Burma, 1944–5 |

NICKNAMES

| Howard's Green | The Bengal Tigers |

June 1969   Amalgamated with The Welch Regiment to form:
THE ROYAL REGIMENT OF WALES
(24th/41st FOOT)

see page 226   The Welch Regiment
see page 274   The Royal Regiment of Wales (24th/41st Foot)

The King's Own Scottish Borderers

PRINCIPAL CAMPAIGNS, BATTLES, etc.

1689	Killiecrankie	1914–18	Aisne, 1914
1691	Limerick		Ypres, 1914, '15, '17, '18
1692–7	Flanders		
1695	Namur		Loos
1715	Jacobite Rising		Somme, 1916, '18
1743–7	Flanders		Arras, 1917, '18
1745	Fontenoy		Soissonnais-Ourcq
1745	Jacobite Rising		Hindenburg Line
1758–63	Germany		Gallipoli, 1915–16
1759	Minden		Gaza
1760	Warburg & Campen		
1762	Wilhelmstahl	1939–45	2ND WORLD WAR Battle honours selected to appear on the Colours:
1794	The Glorious 1st of June		Dunkirk, 1940
1799	Egmont-op-Zee		Odon
1801	Alexandria		Caen
1809	Martinique		Arnhem, 1944
1815	Guadaloupe		Flushing
1878–80	2nd Afghan War		Rhine
1889	Sudan		Bremen
1895	Chitral		Ngakyedauk Pass
1897–8	Tirah		Imphal
1900–2	South Africa		Irrawaddy
1914–18	1ST WORLD WAR Battle honours selected to appear on the Colours: Mons	1951–2	KOREAN WAR Korea, 1951–2 Kowang-San

NICKNAMES

Kosbees   The Botherers   The Kokky-Olly Birds

MOTTO

'In veritate Religionis confido' (I trust in the truth of religion)

The Regiments of Foot from 26 onwards

The following section deals with the regiments of infantry of the line numbered 26–109 which (with the exception of the 60th Rifles and the 79th Highlanders) were linked in pairs in 1871 (the 'Cardwell system'), thus becoming either the first or second battalions of a series of new regiments which, in 1881, were given territorial titles.

The 26th Cameronian Regiment

The Regiment traced its descent from the much persecuted Puritans, the Scottish Covenanters, of whom it was originally composed, and for the protection of whose freedom of worship and way of life it had primarily been raised. It is believed to be the only regiment to have been founded upon a religious cause. It was raised in Lanarkshire 'all in one day, and without tuck of drum, nor expense of levy money' on 14 May 1689 by the young Earl of Angus, and bore his name until three years later when he was killed at the battle of Steinkirk.

TITLES

1689–92	The Earl of Angus's Regiment
1692–1751	The title changed with the Colonel's name
1751–86	26th Regiment of Foot. (By 1751 the Regiment had long been known unofficially as 'The Cameronians', in memory of Richard Cameron, the preacher, who had been killed in 1680 by the Moss Troopers of Claverhouse, the 'Bonny Dundee' of the song.)
1786–1881	26th Cameronian Regiment

PRINCIPAL CAMPAIGNS, BATTLES, etc.

1689	Dunkeld	1715	Preston
1691–5	Netherlands	1775–81	American War of
1692	Steinkirk		Independence
1702–13	Flanders & Germany	1801	Egypt
1704	Blenheim		Alexandria
1706	Ramillies	1808–9	Peninsula
1708	Oudenarde	1841–3	China War
1709	Malplaquet	1868	Abyssinia
1715	Jacobite Rebellion		

1881	Linked to the 90th Perthshire Light Infantry to form: THE CAMERONIANS (SCOTTISH RIFLES)

see page 192 90th Perthshire Light Infantry
see page 212 The Cameronians (Scottish Rifles)

The 27th (Inniskilling) Regiment of Foot

TITLES

1689–1761 Colonel Zachariah Tiffin's Regiment of Foot. Later the title changed with the Colonel's name.

1751–1881 The 27th (Inniskilling) Regiment of Foot

PRINCIPAL CAMPAIGNS, BATTLES, etc.

1690	Boyne	1777	Germantown
1691	Aughrim	1796	Lucia
1695	Namur	1801	Egypt
1715	Jacobite Rising	1808–14	Peninsula
1739	Porto Bello	1811	Albuera
1745	Jacobite Rising	1812	Badajos
1756–60	Canada	1812	Salamanca
1758	Ticonderoga	1813	Vittoria
1762	Martinique	1814	Orthes
1775–8	American War of	1815	Waterloo
	Independence	1834–5	South Africa
1776	Brooklyn	1846–7	South Africa

MOTTO

'Nec aspero terrent' (Nor do difficulties deter)

NICKNAME

The Lumps

1881 Linked to The 108th (Madras Infantry) Regiment of Foot to form:
THE ROYAL INNISKILLING FUSILIERS

see page 210 108th (Madras Infantry) Regiment
see page 213 The Royal Inniskilling Fusiliers
see page 273 The Royal Irish Rangers (27th (Inniskilling) 83rd and 87th)

The 28th (North Gloucestershire) Regiment of Foot

TITLES

1694–1751	Colonel Sir John Gibson's Regiment of Foot. Later the title changed with the Colonel's name.
1751–82	The 28th Regiment of Foot
1782–1881	The 28th (North Gloucestershire) Regiment of Foot

PRINCIPAL CAMPAIGNS, BATTLES, *etc.*

1704–6	Flanders	1809–14	Peninsula
1706	Ramilies	1809	Corunna
1706–12	Spain	1811	Barossa
1707	Almanza		Albuhera
1743–7	Flanders	1812	Badajos
1745	Fontenoy	1813	Vittoria
1757–60	America	1814	Orthes
1758	Louisburg		Toulouse
1759	Quebec	1815	Quatre Bras &
1761–2	Martinique		Waterloo
1774–8	American War of	1854–5	Crimea
	Independence	1854	Alma
1778	St. Lucia	1854	Inkerman
1796	Grenada	1855	Sevastopol
1801	Egypt		

NICKNAMES

The Old Braggs   The Slashers   The Fore and Afts

1881	Linked to the 61st (South Gloucestershire) Regiment of Foot to form: THE GLOUCESTERSHIRE REGIMENT

see page 161 61st (South Gloucestershire) Regiment
see page 214 The Gloucestershire Regiment

The 29th (Worcestershire) Regiment of Foot

TITLES

1694–1751   Colonel Thomas Farington's Regiment of Foot. Later the title changed with the Colonel's name.

1751–82   The 29th Regiment of Foot

1782–1881   The 29th (Worcestershire) Regiment of Foot

PRINCIPAL CAMPAIGNS, BATTLES, etc.

1704–6	Holland & Flanders	1809	Talavera
1706	Ramillics	1811	Albuera
1715	Jacobite Rising	1845–6	1st Sikh War
1776–81	America (War of Independence)	1845	Ferozeshah
		1846	Sobraon
1794	Glorious 1st of June	1848–9	2nd Sikh War
1808–14	Peninsula	1848	Chenab
1808	Roleira	1849	Chillianwalah
1808	Vimiera	1849	Gujerat

NICKNAMES

The Ever-Sworded 29th   The Old and Bold

The Vein-Openers   The Guards of the Line

MOTTO

Firm

1881   Linked to the 36th (Herefordshire) Regiment of Foot to form:

THE WORCESTERSHIRE REGIMENT

see page 133   36th (Herefordshire) Regiment of Foot

see page 215   The Worcestershire Regiment

see page 274   The Worcestershire and Sherwood Foresters Regiment (29th/54th Foot)

The 30th (Cambridgeshire) Regiment of Foot

TITLES

1689–94	Colonel Lord Castleton's Regiment of Foot
1694–8	Colonel Thomas Sanderson's Regiment of Foot. Disbanded 4 March 1698.
1702–4	Colonel Thomas Sanderson's Regiment of Marines. Later the title changed with the Colonel's name.
1714–51	Colonel Charles Willis's Regiment of Foot. Later the title changed with the Colonel's name.
1751–82	The 30th Regiment of Foot
1782–1881	The 30th (Cambridgeshire) Regiment of Foot

PRINCIPAL CAMPAIGNS, BATTLES, etc.

1704–5	Gibraltar	1815	Waterloo
1761	Belleisle	1854–5	Crimea
1808–13	Peninsula	1854	Alma
1812	Badajoz	1854	Inkerman
1812	Salamanca	1858	Sevastopol

NICKNAMES

The Triple X's   The Three Tens

1881	Linked to the 59th (2nd Nottinghamshire) Regiment of Foot to form: THE EAST LANCASHIRE REGIMENT

see page 158 59th (2nd Nottinghamshire) Regiment of Foot
see page 216 The East Lancashire Regiment
see page 276 The Queen's Lancashire Regiment

The 31st (Huntingdonshire) Regiment

TITLES

1702–11	Colonel George Villier's Regiment of Marines. Later the title changed with the Colonel's name.
1711–14	Goring's Marines
1714–82	The 31st Regiment of Foot
1782–1881	The 31st (Huntingdonshire) Regiment

PRINCIPAL CAMPAIGNS, BATTLES, etc.

1702	Cadiz	1813	Nivelle
1704–6	Spain	1814	Orthes
1705	Barcelona	1839–42	1st Afghan War
1706	Majorca	1842	Kabul
1742–5	Flanders	1845–6	1st Sikh War
1743	Dettingen	1845	Mudki
1745	Fontenoy	1845	Ferozeshah
1776–81	America	1846	Aliwal
1809–14	Peninsula	1846	Sobraon
1809	Talavera	1854–5	Crimea
1811	Albuera	1855	Sevastopol
1813	Vittoria	1860	Taku Forts

NICKNAME

The Young Buffs

1881	Linked with the 70th (Surrey) Regiment of Foot to form: THE EAST SURREY REGIMENT

see page 170 70th (Surrey) Regiment of Foot
see page 217 The East Surrey Regiment
see page 271 The Queen's Regiment

The 32nd (Cornwall) Light Infantry

TITLES

1702–4	Colonel Edward Fox's Regiment of Marines. Later the title changed with the Colonel's name.
1704–13	Colonel Jacob Borr's Regiment of Marines
1715–82	32nd Regiment of Foot
1782–1858	The 32nd (The Cornwall) Regiment of Foot
1858–81	The 32nd (Cornwall) Light Infantry

PRINCIPAL CAMPAIGNS, BATTLES, etc.

1702	Cadiz	1812	Salamanca
1704–5	Gibraltar	1813	Nivelle, Nive,
1704–6	Spain		Pyrenees
1705	Barcelona	1814	Orthes
1742–7	Flanders	1815	Quatre Bras
1743	Dettingen	1815	Waterloo
1745	Fontenoy	1848–9	2nd Sikh War
1808–9	1st Peninsular	1849	Multan
1808	Roleia	1849	Gujerat
1808	Vimiera	1857–8	Indian Mutiny
1809	Corunna	1857	Lucknow (Defence)
1811–14	2nd Peninsular		

1881	Linked to The 46th (South Devonshire) Regiment of Foot to form:
	THE DUKE OF CORNWALL'S LIGHT INFANTRY

see page 145 46th (South Devonshire) Regiment of Foot
see page 218 The Duke of Cornwall's Light Infantry
see page 272 The Light Infantry

The 33rd (Duke of Wellington's) Regiment of Foot

TITLES

1702–51	Colonel The Earl of Huntingdon's Regiment of Foot. Later the title changed with the Colonel's name.
1751–82	The 33rd Regiment of Foot
1782–1853	The 33rd (1st York, West Riding) Regiment of Foot
1853–81	The 33rd (Duke of Wellington's) Regiment of Foot

PRINCIPAL CAMPAIGNS, BATTLES, etc.

1702–4	Germany	1799	Seringapatam
1704–10	Spain	1815	Waterloo
1742–7	Flanders	1854–5	Crimea
1743	Dettingen	1854	Alma
1745	Fontenoy	1854	Inkerman
1745	Jacobite Rising	1855	Sevastopol
1760–3	Germany	1868	Abyssinia
1776–81	America		

NICKNAME

Havercake Lads

MOTTO

'Virtutis fortuna comes' (Fortune accompanies honour)

1881	Linked to the 76th Regiment of Foot to form: THE DUKE OF WELLINGTON'S REGIMENT

see page 176 76th Regiment of Foot
see page 219 The Duke of Wellington's Regiment

The 34th (Cumberland) Regiment of Foot

TITLES

1702–51   Colonel Lord Lucas's Regiment of Foot. Later the title changed with the Colonel's name.
1751–82   The 34th Regiment of Foot
1782–1881   The 34th (Cumberland) Regiment of Foot

PRINCIPAL CAMPAIGNS, BATTLES, etc.

1705–7	Spain	1809–14	Peninsula
1705	Barcelona	1811	Arrroyo-dos-Molinos
1709–12	Flanders & Germany	1811	Albuera
1710	Douay	1813	Vittoria
1727	Gibraltar	1813	Nivelle
1744	Flanders	1814	Orthes
1745	Fontenoy	1854–5	Crimea
1757–60	Canada	1855	Sevastopol
1758	Ticonderoga	1857–8	Indian Mutiny
1775–8	America	1858	Lucknow
1776	Brooklyn		

1881   Linked with The 55th (Westmoreland) Regiment of Foot, to form:
           THE BORDER REGIMENT

see page 154   55th (Westmoreland) Regiment of Foot
see page 220   The Border Regiment
see page 268   The King's Own Royal Border Regiment

The 35th (Royal Sussex) Regiment of Foot

TITLES

1701–51   Colonel The Earl of Donegall's Regiment of Foot. Later the title changed with the Colonel's name.

1751–82   The 35th Regiment of Foot

1782–1805   The 35th (Dorsetshire) Regiment of Foot

1805–32   The 35th (Sussex) Regiment of Foot

1832–81   The 35th (Royal Sussex) Regiment of Foot

PRINCIPAL CAMPAIGNS, BATTLES, etc.

1702	Cadiz	1775–8	America
1704–5	Gibraltar	1775	Bunker's Hill
1704–8	Spain	1776	Brooklyn
1757–60	Canada	1794	Martinique
1758	Louisbourg	1800	Malta
1759	Quebec	1806	Maida
1762	Martinique	1807	Egypt
	Havannah	1857–8	Indian Mutiny

1881   Linked with the 107th (Bengal Infantry) Regiment to form:

THE ROYAL SUSSEX REGIMENT

see page 209   107th (Bengal Infantry) Regiment

see page 221   The Royal Sussex Regiment

see page 271   The Queen's Regiment

The 36th (Herefordshire) Regiment of Foot

TITLES

1701–51	Colonel Viscount Charlemont's Regiment. Later the title changed with the Colonel's name.
1751–82	The 36th Regiment of Foot
1782–1881	The 36th (Herefordshire) Regiment of Foot

PRINCIPAL CAMPAIGNS, BATTLES, etc.

1702	Spain	1809–14	Peninsula
1705–7	Spain	1809	Corunna
1707	Almanza	1812	Salamanca
1746	Culloden	1813	Pyrenees
1783–98	India	1813	Nivelle
1791	Bangalore	1813	Nive
1792	Seringapatam	1814	Orthes
1793	Pondicherry	1814	Toulouse

NICKNAME
The Saucy Greens

1881	Linked with The 29th (Worcestershire) Regiment of Foot to form:
	THE WORCESTERSHIRE REGIMENT

see page 126 The 29th (Worcestershire) Regiment of Foot
see page 215 The Worcestershire Regiment
see page 274 The Worcestershire and Sherwood Foresters Regiment (29th/54th Foot)

The 37th (North Hampshire) Regiment of Foot

TITLES

1702–51	Colonel Thomas Meredith's Regiment of Foot. Later the title changed with the Colonel's name.
1751–82	The 37th Regiment of Foot
1782–1881	The 37th (North Hampshire) Regiment of Foot

PRINCIPAL CAMPAIGNS, BATTLES, etc.

1702–12	Germany	1745	Jacobite Rising
1704	Blenheim	1746	Culloden
1705	Neer-Hespen	1758–62	Germany
1706	Ramillies	1759	Minden
1708	Oudenarde	1761	Wilhelmstahl
1709	Malplaquet	1776–80	America
1742–7	Flanders	1794	Tournay
1743	Dettingen	1794	Nimeguen

1881	Linked to the 67th (South Hampshire) Regiment of Foot to form: THE HAMPSHIRE REGIMENT (later THE ROYAL HAMPSHIRE REGIMENT)

see page 167   67th (South Hampshire) Regiment of Foot
see page 222   The Royal Hampshire Regiment

The 38th (1st Staffordshire) Regiment of Foot

TITLES

1705–51	Colonel Luke Lillingstone's Regiment of Foot. Later the title changed with the Colonel's name.
1751–82	The 38th Regiment of Foot
1782–1881	The 38th (1st Staffordshire) Regiment of Foot

PRINCIPAL CAMPAIGNS, BATTLES, etc.

1759	Guadaloupe	1809	Walcheren
1762	Martinique	1810	Busaco
1775–83	America	1812	Badajos
1775	Bunker's Hill	1812	Salamanca
1776	Brooklyn	1813	Vittoria
	Fort Washington	1813	San Sebastian
	(New York)	1813	Nive
1778	Newport	1814	Bayonne
1794–5	Flanders	1824–6	1st Burma War
1806	Cape of Good Hope	1826	Ava
1807	Monte Video	1854–5	Crimea
	Buenos Aires	1854	Alma
1808–14	Peninsula	1854	Inkerman
1808	Roleia	1855	Sevastopol
1808	Vimiera	1857–8	Indian Mutiny
1809	Corunna	1858	Lucknow

NICKNAME

The Pump and Tortoise

1881	Linked to the 80th (Staffordshire Volunteers) Regiment of Foot to form: THE SOUTH STAFFORDSHIRE REGIMENT

see page 181   80th (Staffordshire Volunteers) Regiment of Foot
see page 223   The South Staffordshire Regiment
see page 267   The Staffordshire Regiment (The Prince of Wales's)

135

The 39th (Dorsetshire) Regiment of Foot

TITLES

1702–51	Colonel Richard Coote's Regiment of Foot. Later the title changed with the Colonel's name.
1751–82	The 39th Regiment of Foot
1782–1807	The 39th (East Middlesex) Regiment of Foot
1807–81	The 39th (Dorsetshire) Regiment of Foot

PRINCIPAL CAMPAIGNS, BATTLES, etc.

1707–12	Spain & Portugal	1810	Busaco
1718	Cape Passaro (as Marines)	1811	Albuera
		1812	Badajos
1727	Gibraltar	1813	Vittoria
1757	Plassey	1813	Nivelle
1779–83	Gibraltar	1813	Pyrenees (Colours)
1794	West Indies, e.g.	1813	Nive
	Martinique (on	1814	Orthes
	Colours) and	1843	Maharajpore
	Guadaloupe	1854–5	Crimea
1796	St. Vincent	1855	Sevastopol
1809–14	Peninsula		

MOTTO

'Primus in Indis' (First in India)

NICKNAMES

Sankey's Horse   The Green Linnets

1881	Linked to the 54th (West Norfolk) Regiment of Foot to form: THE DORSETSHIRE REGIMENT
1951	The title varied to: THE DORSET REGIMENT

see page 153 The 54th (West Norfolk) Regiment of Foot
see page 224 The Dorset Regiment
see page 265 The Devon and Dorset Regiment

The 40th (2nd Somersetshire) Regiment of Foot

Formed in 1717 from companies of Infantry, which had been on duty in the West Indies for many years.

TITLES

1717–51	Colonel Richard Philip's Regiment of Foot
1751–82	The 40th Regiment of Foot
1782–1881	The 40th (2nd Somersetshire) Regiment of Foot

PRINCIPAL CAMPAIGNS, BATTLES, etc.

1757–60	Canada	1812	Salamanca
1758	Louisbourg	1813	Vittoria
1762	Martinique	1813	Pyrenees
1762	Havannah	1813	Nivelle
1778	St. Lucia	1814	Orthes
1807	Monte Video	1815	Waterloo
1808–14	Peninsula	1839–42	1st Afghan War
1808	Roliea	1842	Candahar
1808	Vimiera	1842	Ghazni
1809	Talavera	1842	Kabul
1811	Albuera	1843	Maharajpore
1812	Badajoz	1860–5	New Zealand

NICKNAMES

The Excellers   The Fighting Fortieth

1881	Linked to the 82nd (The Prince of Wales's Volunteers) Regiment of Foot to form: **THE SOUTH LANCASHIRE REGIMENT (THE PRINCE OF WALES'S VOLUNTEERS)**

see page 183 82nd (Prince of Wales's Volunteers) Regiment of Foot

see page 225 The South Lancashire Regiment of Foot (Prince of Wales's Volunteers)

see page 276 The Queen's Lancashire Regiment

The 41st (The Welsh) Regiment of Foot

Raised in 1719 as a regiment of invalids and was for a long time known as '1st Invalids', appearing as such in the old army lists.

TITLES

1719–87	Independent Companies of Invalids subsequently known as The 41st (Royal Invalids) Regiment
1787–1822	The 41st Regiment of Foot
1822–81	The 41st (The Welsh) Regiment of Foot

PRINCIPAL CAMPAIGNS, BATTLES, etc.

1761	Belle Isle	1839–42	1st Afghan War
1778	St. Lucia	1842	Candahar
1794	Corsica	1842	Ghazni
1796	Genoa	1842	Kabul
1812	Detroit	1854–5	Crimea
1812	Queenstown	1854	Alma
1813	Niagara	1854	Inkerman
1824–6	Ava	1855	Sevastopol

MOTTO

'Gwell angau na Chywilydd '(Death rather than dishonour)

1881	Linked to the 69th (South Lincolnshire) Regiment of Foot to form: THE WELSH REGIMENT
1920	Title varied to: THE WELCH REGIMENT

see page 169 69th (South Lincolnshire) Regiment of Foot
see page 226 The Welch Regiment
see page 274 The Royal Regiment of Wales (24th/41st Foot)

The 42nd (Royal Highland-Black Watch)

The oldest Highland Regiment in the British Army raised circa 1725 from six Independent companies of Highlanders.

TITLES

1725–39	Independent Companies—Am Freiceadan Dubh—The Black Watch
1739–51	The Highland Regiment of Foot; also known by the Colonel's name
1751–8	The 42nd Foot
1758–1861	42nd (The Royal Highland) Regiment of Foot
1861–81	42nd (The Royal Highland) Regiment of Foot (The Black Watch)

PRINCIPAL CAMPAIGNS, BATTLES, etc.

1743–7	Flanders	1809	Corunna
1745	Fontenoy	1810	Busaco
1745	Jacobite Rising	1811	Fuentes d'Onor
1757–60	Canada	1812	Salamanca
1758	Ticonderoga	1813	Pyrenees
1759	Guadaloupe	1813	Nivelle
1762	Martinique	1813	Nive
	Havannah	1814	Orthes
1763–4	North America	1814	Toulouse
1775–81	America	1815	Quatre Bras
1793–5	Flanders	1815	Waterloo
1793	Nieuport	1854–5	Crimea
1794	Nimeguen	1854	Alma
1801	Egypt	1855	Sevastopol
1808–14	Peninsula	1857–8	Indian Mutiny
1808	Roleia	1858	Lucknow
1808	Vimiera	1873–4	Ashantee

MOTTO

'Nemo me impune lacessit' (No one provokes me with impunity)

NICKNAME

The Forty-twas

continued overleaf

The 42nd (Royal Highland-Black Watch)

1881   Linked to the 73rd (Perthshire) Regiment of Foot to form:
THE BLACK WATCH (ROYAL HIGHLANDERS)

1934   The title was changed to:
THE BLACK WATCH (ROYAL HIGHLAND) REGIMENT

see page 173 73rd (Perthshire) Regiment of Foot
see page 227 The Black Watch (Royal Highland Regiment)

The 43rd (Monmouthshire Light Infantry) Regiment

TITLES

1741–8	The 54th Regiment of Foot
1748–82	The 43rd Regiment of Foot
1782–1803	The 43rd (Monmouthshire) Regiment of Foot
1803–81	The 43rd (Monmouthshire Light Infantry) Regiment

PRINCIPAL CAMPAIGNS, BATTLES, etc.

1759–60	Canada	1811	Fuentes d'Onor
1759	Quebec	1812	Ciudad Rodrigo
1762–4	West Indies	1812	Badajos
1762	Martinique	1812	Salamanca
1775–82	America	1813	Vittoria
1794–5	West Indies	1813	Nivelle
1794	Martinique	1813	Nive
1808–14	Peninsula	1815	New Orleans
1808	Vimiera	1851–3	South Africa
1809	Corunna	1857–8	Indian Mutiny
1810	Busaco	1864–6	New Zealand

1881	Linked to the 52nd (Oxfordshire Light Infantry) Regiment to form:

THE OXFORDSHIRE LIGHT INFANTRY

Later known as:

THE OXFORDSHIRE AND
BUCKINGHAMSHIRE LIGHT INFANTRY

see page 151 52nd (Oxfordshire Light Infantry) Regiment
see page 228 The Oxfordshire and Buckinghamshire Light Infantry
see page 275 The Royal Green Jackets

The 44th (East Essex) Regiment of Foot

Previous Unit with which the Regiment claims no connection

1740–8   The 44th Regiment of Foot. Disbanded.

TITLES

1741   55th Regiment of Foot (commanded by Colonel James Long, 1741–3)
1748   55th Regiment of Foot was renumbered 44th (commanded by Colonel John Lee, 1743–51)
1751–82   44th Regiment of Foot
1782–1881 44th (East Essex) Regiment of Foot

PRINCIPAL CAMPAIGNS, BATTLES, etc.

1741	Carthagena	1812	Salamanca
1745	Jacobite Rising	1814	Bladensburg
1746	Culloden	1815	Quatre Bras
1755–60	Canada	1815	Waterloo
1758	Ticonderoga	1824–6	1st Burma War
1775–80	America	1826	Ava
1776	Brooklyn	1839–42	1st Afghan War
1777	Brandywine	1841–2	Kabul
1794	St. Lucia	1854–5	Crimea
1801	Egypt	1854	Alma
1801	Alexandria	1854	Inkerman
1810–13	Peninsula	1855	Sevastopol
1812	Badajos	1860	Taku Forts

NICKNAMES

The Two Fours   The Little Fighting Fours

1881   Linked with the 56th (West Essex) Regiment of Foot to form:
THE ESSEX REGIMENT

see page 155 56th (West Essex) Regiment of Foot
see page 229 The Essex Regiment
see page 270 The Royal Anglian Regiment

The 45th (Nottinghamshire Regiment) Sherwood Foresters

TITLES

1741–5	Colonel D. Houghton's Regiment (numbered 56)
1745–8	Colonel Warburton's Regiment (numbered 56)
1748–51	Colonel Warburton's Regiment re-numbered 45 on the disbandment of the ten Marine Regiments)
1751–79	The 45th Regiment of Foot
1779–1866	The 45th (The 1st Nottinghamshire Regiment)
1866–81	The 45th (Nottinghamshire Regiment) Sherwood Foresters

PRINCIPAL CAMPAIGNS, BATTLES, etc.

1755–8	Canada	1812	Ciudad Rodrigo
1758	Louisburg		Badajos Retreat from
1759	Quebec (two		Burgos
	Grenadier		Capture of Madrid
	companies only)	1813	Nive
1762	Relief of Halifax		Pyrenees
1776	New York	1824–6	1st Burma War
	Long Island	1826	Ava
	(from 1804 to 1814 a		(In 1840 a Reserve
	2nd Bn was serving)		Bn was raised. In
1805	Buenos Ayres		1850 it was amal-
1807	Monte Video		gamated with the 1st
1808–14	Peninsula		Bn in South Africa)
1808	Roleia	1843	South Africa
	Vimiera	1847–8	Kaffir Wars
1809	Talavera	1848	1st Boer War
1810	Busaco	1868	Abyssinian Campaign
1811	Fuentes d'Onor		Magdala

NICKNAME

The Old Stubborns

May 1881	Linked to the 95th or Derbyshire Regiment of Foot to form The Derbyshire Regiment (Sherwood Foresters)
July 1881	Title varied to: **THE SHERWOOD FORESTERS (DERBYSHIRE REGIMENT)**

continued overleaf

1902   Title changed to:
              THE SHERWOOD FORESTERS
              (NOTTINGHAMSHIRE AND
              DERBYSHIRE REGIMENT)

see page 197 95th (Derbyshire) Regiment of Foot
see page 230 The Sherwood Foresters (Nottingham and Derbyshire Regiment)
see page 274 The Worcestershire and Sherwood Foresters Regiment (29th/54th Foot)

The 46th (South Devonshire) Regiment of Foot

TITLES

1741–8	57th Regiment of Foot—on its formation it was commanded by Colonel John Price. In 1743 the Regiment was commanded by Colonel The Honourable Thomas Murray.
1748–82	Renumbered the 46th Regiment of Foot
1782–1881	The 46th (South Devonshire) Regiment of Foot

PRINCIPAL CAMPAIGNS, BATTLES etc.,

1757–60	Nova Scotia, Canada	1805	Dominica
1758	Ticonderoga	1854–5	Crimea
1776–8	America	1854	Alma
1778	West Indies	1854	Inkerman
1776	Brooklyn	1854	Balaclava
1777	Brandywine	1858	Sevastopol
1778	St. Lucia		

NICKNAMES

Murray's Bucks   The Surprisers

The Lacedemonians   The Red Feathers

1881	Linked to the 32nd (Cornwall) Light Infantry to form: THE DUKE OF CORNWALL'S LIGHT INFANTRY

see page 129   32nd (Cornwall) Light Infantry

see page 218   The Duke of Cornwall's Light Infantry

see page 272   The Light Infantry

The 47th (Lancashire) Regiment of Foot

TITLES

1740–8	The 47th (4th Marines) Regiment of Foot; disbanded.
1741–51	Colonel John Mordaunt's Regiment of Foot. The title changed with the Colonel's name.
1751–82	The 47th Regiment of Foot
1782–1881	The 47th (Lancashire) Regiment of Foot

PRINCIPAL CAMPAIGNS, BATTLES, etc.

1745	Jacobite Rising	1811	Tarifa
1757–60	Canada	1813	Vittoria
1758	Louisbourg	1813	St. Sebastian
1759	Quebec	1824–6	1st Burma War
1760	Montreal	1826	Ava
1762	Martinique	1854–5	Crimea
1775–81	America	1854	Alma
1775	Lexington	1854	Inkerman
1775	Bunker's Hill	1855	Sevastopol
1810–14	Peninsula		

NICKNAMES

Wolfe's Own   The Cauliflowers
The Lancashire Lads

1881	Linked to the 81st (Loyal Lincoln Volunteers) Regiment of Foot to form: THE LOYAL NORTH LANCASHIRE REGIMENT
1921	The title was varied to: THE LOYAL REGIMENT (NORTH LANCASHIRE)

see page 182 81st (Loyal Lincoln Volunteers) Regiment of Foot
see page 231 The Loyal Regiment (North Lancashire)
see page 276 The Queen's Lancashire Regiment

The 48th (Northamptonshire) Regiment of Foot

PRINCIPAL CAMPAIGNS, BATTLES, etc.

1744–7	Flanders	1809	Talavera
1745	Fontenoy	1811	Albuera
1745	Jacobite Rising	1812	Badajos
1746	Culloden	1812	Salamanca
1758–62	Canada	1813	Vittoria
1758	Louisbourg	1813	Pyrenees
1759	Quebec	1813	Nivelle
1762	Martinique	1814	Orthes
1762	Havannah	1814	Toulouse
1809–14	Peninsula	1854–5	Crimea
1809	Douro	1855	Sevastopol

1881   Linked to the 58th (Rutlandshire) Regiment of Foot to form:

THE NORTHAMPTONSHIRE REGIMENT

See page 157 58th (Rutlandshire) Regiment of Foot
See page 232 The Northamptonshire Regiment
See page 270 The Royal Anglian Regiment

The 49th Princess Charlotte of Wales's Hertfordshire Regiment of Foot

Raised in Jamaica from Volunteer Companies left in the Island in 1714.

TITLES

1742–8	The 49th (The 6th or Cotterell's Marines) Regiment; disbanded.
1743–8	Colonel Edward Trelawney's Regiment of Foot. Later the title changed with the Colonel's name.
1748–82	The 49th Regiment of Foot
1782–1816	The 49th (Hertfordshire) Regiment of Foot
1816–81	The 49th Princess of Wales's Hertfordshire Regiment of Foot

PRINCIPAL CAMPAIGNS, BATTLES, etc.

1775–8	America	1813	Chrystler's Farm
1777	Brandywine Creek	1840–2	China
1799	Egmont-op-Zee	1854–5	Crimea
1801	Copenhagen	1854	Alma
1812–14	America	1854	Inkerman
1812	Queenstown	1855	Sevastopol

1881	Linked to the 66th (Berkshire) Regiment of Foot to form: PRINCESS CHARLOTTE OF WALES'S BERKSHIRE REGIMENT
1885	The title 'Royal' was conferred
1921	The titled varied to: THE ROYAL BERKSHIRE REGIMENT (PRINCESS CHARLOTTE OF WALES'S)

see page 166 66th (Berkshire) Regiment of Foot
see page 233 The Royal Berkshire Regiment (Princess Charlotte of Wales's)
see page 267 The Duke of Edinburgh's Royal Regiment

The 50th (The Queen's Own) Regiment of Foot

TITLES

1757–82	The 50th (raised in 1751 as the 52nd) Regiment of Foot
1782–1827	The 50th (West Kent) Regiment of Foot
1827–31	The 50th (The Duke of Clarence's) Regiment of Foot
1831–81	The 50th (The Queen's Own) Regiment of Foot

PRINCIPAL CAMPAIGNS, BATTLES, etc.

1760–2	Germany	1813	Pyrenees
1760	Warburg	1813	Nive
1761	Belle Isle	1814	Orthes
1761	Kirk Denkern	1843	Punniar (Gwalior
1762	Wilhemstahl		Campaign)
1778	Ushant	1845–6	1st Sikh War
1794	Corsica	1845	Mudki
1798–9	Portugal	1845	Ferozeshah
1801	Egypt	1845	Aliwal
1807	Copenhagen	1846	Sobraon
1808–14	Peninsula	1854–5	Crimea
1808	Vimiera	1854	Alma
1809	Corunna	1854	Inkerman
1812	Almaraj	1855	Sevastopol
1812	Badajos	1863–6	New Zealand (Maori
1813	Vittoria		Wars)

NICKNAMES

The Blind Half-Hundred   The Dirty Half-Hundred
The Devil's Royals   The Gallant Fiftieth

1881   Linked to the 97th (The Earl of Ulster's) Regiment of Foot to form:

THE QUEEN'S OWN (ROYAL WEST KENT) REGIMENT

see page 199   97th (Earl of Ulster's) Regiment of Foot
see page 234   The Queen's Own (Royal West Kent) Regiment
see page 271   The Queen's Regiment

The 51st (2nd Yorkshire, West Riding, The King's Own Light Infantry) Regiment

Previous Units to which the Regiment claims no connection

1740–8	The 51st (The 8th or Sir Thomas Hammer's Marines) Regiment; disbanded.
1745–9	The 51st Regiment of Foot
1754–6	The 51st Regiment of Foot

TITLES

1755–7	The 53rd Regiment of Foot; renumbered.
1757–82	The 51st Regiment of Foot
1782–1809	The 51st (2nd Yorkshire West Riding) Regiment of Foot
1809–21	The 51st (2nd Yorkshire, West Riding, Light Infantry) Regiment
1821–81	The 51st (2nd Yorkshire, West Riding, The King's Own Light Infantry) Regiment

PRINCIPAL CAMPAIGNS, BATTLES, etc.

1758–62	Germany	1813	Vittoria
1759	Minden	1813	Nivelle
1760	Warburg	1814	Orthes
1793	Nieuport	1815	Waterloo
1808–14	Peninsula	1852–3	Pegu
1809	Corunna	1878–80	2nd Afghan War
1811	Fuentes d'Onor	1878	Ali Masjid
1812	Badajos	1885–7	Burma
1812	Salamanca		

NICKNAME

The Koylis

1881   Linked to the 105th (Madras Light Infantry) Regiment to form:

THE KING'S OWN YORKSHIRE LIGHT INFANTRY

see page 207   105th (Madras Light Infantry) Regiment
see page 233   The King's Own Yorkshire Light Infantry
see page 272   The Light Infantry

The 52nd (Oxfordshire Light Infantry) Regiment

TITLES

1755–7	The 54th Regiment of Foot
1757–82	The 52nd Regiment of Foot
1782–1803	The 52nd (Oxfordshire) Regiment of Foot
1803–81	The 52nd (Oxfordshire Light Infantry) Regiment

PRINCIPAL CAMPAIGNS, BATTLES, etc.

1775–82	America	1812	Badajos
1783	Mysore	1812	Salamanca
1790–3	India	1813	Vittoria
1792	Seringapatam	1813	Nivelle
1793	Pondicherry	1813	Nive
1795–96	Ceylon	1814	Orthes
1808–14	Peninsula		Toulouse
1808	Vimiera	1814–15	Netherlands
1809	Corunna	1815	Waterloo
1810	Busaco	1857–8	Indian Mutiny
1811	Fuentes d'Onor	1857	Delhi
1812	Ciudad Rodrigo		

1881	Linked to the 43rd (Monmouthshire Light Infantry) Regiment to form The Oxfordshire Light Infantry, later known as: THE OXFORDSHIRE AND BUCKINGHAMSHIRE LIGHT INFANTRY

see page *141* 43rd (Monmouthshire Light Infantry) Regiment
see page *228* The Oxfordshire and Buckinghamshire Light Infantry
see page *275* The Royal Green Jackets

The 53rd (Shropshire) Regiment of Foot

TITLES

1755–7	The 55th Regiment of Foot; renumbered.
1757–82	The 53rd Regiment of Foot
1782–1881	The 53rd (Shropshire) Regiment of Foot

PRINCIPAL CAMPAIGNS, BATTLES, etc.

1756	Gibraltar	1815–17*	St. Helena
1776–81	America	1805–23	India
	Ticonderoga	1812	Callinger
1793 5	Flanders	1814–15	Nepaul
	Famars, Valenciennes		Kalunga
	& Dunkirk	1816–19	Pindaree War
1793	Nieuport	1845–6	1st Sikh War
1794	Tournay	1846	Aliwal
1796	West Indies	1846	Sobraon
	St. Lucia	1849	Gujerat
1809–14	Peninsula	1848–9	2nd Sikh War
1809	Talavera	1857–8	Indian Mutiny
1812	Salamanca	1857	Chutra
1813	Vittoria	1857	Lucknow
1813	Pyrenees		Relief of Lucknow
1813	Nivelle	1857	Cawnpore
1814	Toulouse	1860–8	Canada

NICKNAMES

The Brickdusts   The Old Five and Threepennies
The Honeysuckers

1881	Linked to the 85th (Bucks) Volunteers (King's Light Infantry) Regiment to form: The Shropshire Regiment (King's Light Infantry) A few weeks later the title was changed to: The King's Light Infantry (Shropshire Regiment) And soon afterwards changed again to: The King's (Shropshire Light Infantry)
1920	The title became: THE KING'S SHROPSHIRE LIGHT INFANTRY

see page 186 85th (Bucks Volunteers) (King's Light Infantry) Regiment
see page 236 The King's Shropshire Light Infantry
see page 272 The Light Infantry

*Denotes service of 2nd Bn 53rd.

The 54th (West Norfolk) Regiment of Foot

TITLES

1755–7	The 56th Regiment of Foot; renumbered.
1757–82	The 54th Regiment of Foot
1782–1881	The 54th (West Norfolk) Regiment of Foot

PRINCIPAL CAMPAIGNS, BATTLES, etc.

1776–81	America	1815	Waterloo. (In reserve but received Medal and had Waterloo wreath on cap badge)
1777	Brooklyn		
1778	Rhode Island		
1781	New London		
1801	Egypt		
1801	Aboukir	1824–6	1st Burma War
1801	Marabout	1826	Ava
1813	Netherlands, e.g. Merxem	1857	Epic of Sarah Sands Troopship—Fire at sea
		1858	Indian Mutiny

NICKNAME

The Flamers

1881	Linked to the 39th (Dorsetshire) Regiment of Foot to form: THE DORSETSHIRE REGIMENT
1951	Title varied to: THE DORSET REGIMENT

see page 136 39th (Dorsetshire) Regiment of Foot
see page 224 The Dorset Regiment
see page 265 The Devon and Dorset Regiment

The 55th (Westmorland) Regiment of Foot

TITLES

1742–8	The 55th Regiment of Foot
1756–8	The 55th Regiment of Foot
1755–7	The 57th Regiment of Foot
1757–82	The 55th Regiment of Foot
1782–1881	The 55th (Westmoreland) Regiment of Foot

PRINCIPAL CAMPAIGNS, BATTLES, etc.

1775–8	America	1854–5	Crimea
1840 2	China	1854	Alma
1842	Chusan	1854	Inkerman
1842	Chinghai	1855	Sevastopol

NICKNAME

The Two Fives

1881   Linked with the 34th (Cumberland) Regiment of Foot to form:
THE BORDER REGIMENT

see page 131   34th (Cumberland) Regiment of Foot
see page 220   The Border Regiment
see page 268   The King's Own Royal Border Regiment

The 56th (West Essex) Regiment of Foot

PRINCIPAL CAMPAIGNS, BATTLES, etc.

1762	Havana	1842	Canada
1762	Moro		Maine, New
1779–83	Gibraltar		Brunswick
1794	Martinique	1853	Bermuda
1799	Egmont-op-Zee	1854–5	Crimea
1809	Rodriguez	1855	Sevastopol
	Mauritius		

NICKNAMES

The Pompadours   Saucy Pompeys

MOTTO

'Montis Insignia Calpe' (By the sign of the rock of Gibraltar)

1881	Linked to the 44th (East Essex) Regiment of Foot to form: THE ESSEX REGIMENT

see page 142 44th (East Essex) Regiment of Foot
see page 229 The Essex Regiment
see page 270 The Royal Anglian Regiment

The 57th (West Middlesex) Regiment of Foot

TITLES

1741–8	The 57th Regiment of Foot; renumbered the 46th.
1755–7	The 57th Regiment of Foot; renumbered the 55th.
1755–7	The 59th Regiment of Foot; renumbered the 57th.
1757–82	The 57th Regiment of Foot
1782–1881	The 57th (West Middlesex) Regiment of Foot

PRINCIPAL CAMPAIGNS, BATTLES, etc.

1756–63	Gibraltar	1813	Pyrenees
1763	Minorca	1813	Nivelle
1776–82	America		Nive
1776	Brooklyn	1814–15	Canada
1777	Brandywine	1854–5	Crimea
1781	York Town	1854	Balaclava
1785–91	Canada	1854	Alma
1793–5	Flanders	1854	Inkerman
1793	Nieuport	1855	Sevastopol
1809–14	Peninsula	1858	Indian Mutiny
1811	Albuera	1861–6	New Zealand
1813	Vittoria	1879	South Africa

NICKNAMES

The Die-Hards   The Steel Backs

1881	Linked to the 77th (East Middlesex) Regiment of Foot to form:
	The Duke of Cambridge's Own (Middlesex Regiment)
1921	The title varied to: REGIMENT
	THE MIDDLESEX (DUKE OF CAMBRIDGE'S OWN)

see page 177 77th (East Middlesex) Regiment of Foot
see page 238 The Middlesex Regiment (Duke of Cambridge's Own)
see page 271 The Queen's Regiment

The 58th (Rutlandshire) Regiment of Foot

TITLES

1740–8	The 58th Regiment of Foot; renumbered the 47th, and later to become The 1st Battalion Loyal North Lancashire.
1756–7	The 58th Regiment of Foot; renumbered The 56th.
1755–7	The 60th Regiment of Foot; renumbered The 58th.
1757–82	The 58th Regiment of Foot
1782–1881	The 58th (Rutlandshire) Regiment of Foot

PRINCIPAL CAMPAIGNS, BATTLES, etc.

1758–62	Canada	1813	Vittoria
1758	Louisbourg	1813	Pyrenees
1759	Quebec	1813	Nivelle
1779–83	Gibraltar	1814	Orthes
1801	Egypt	1849–56	New Zealand
1806	Maida	1879	South Africa (Zulu
1809–14	Peninsula		War)
1812	Salamanca		

NICKNAME

The Steelbacks

1881	Linked to the 48th (Northamptonshire) Regiment of Foot to form: THE NORTHAMPTONSHIRE REGIMENT

see page 147 48th (Northamptonshire) Regiment of Foot
see page 232 The Northamptonshire Regiment
see page 270 The Royal Anglian Regiment

The 59th (2nd Nottinghamshire) Regiment of Foot

TITLES

1741–8	The 59th Regiment of Foot; renumbered The 48th Foot.
1755	The 59th Regiment of Foot; renumbered The 56th Foot.
1755–7	The 61st Regiment of Foot; renumbered The 59th Foot.
1757–82	The 59th Regiment of Foot
1782–1881	The 59th (2nd Nottinghamshire) Regiment of Foot

PRINCIPAL CAMPAIGNS, BATTLES, etc.

1806	Cape of Good Hope	1813	Nive
1808–9	Peninsula	1826	Bhurtpore
1809	Corunna	1857–8	China
1811	Java	1857	Canton
1810–13	Peninsula	1878–80	2nd Afghan War
1813	Vittoria	1879	Ahmed Khel
1813	St. Sebastien		

NICKNAME

The Lily-whites

1881	Linked to the 30th (Cambridgeshire) Regiment of Foot to form:
	THE EAST LANCASHIRE REGIMENT

see page 127   30th (Cambridgeshire) Regiment of Foot
see page 216   East Lancashire Regiment
see page 276   The Queen's Lancashire Regiment

The King's Royal Rifle Corps

Previous Unit to which the Regiment claims no connection

1741–8   The 60th Regiment of Foot

TITLES

1755–6   The 62nd (Royal American) Regiment of Foot; renumbered
1756–1824   The 60th (Royal American) Regiment of Foot
1824   The 60th (Duke of York's Rifle Corps)
1824–30   The 60th or The Duke of York's Own Rifle Corps
1830–81   The 60th or The King's Royal Rifle Corps
1881–1958   The King's Royal Rifle Corps

PRINCIPAL CAMPAIGNS, BATTLES, *etc.*

1757–60	Canada	1814	Bayonne
1758	Ticonderoga	1848–9	2nd Sikh War
1758	Louisbourg	1849	Mooltan
1759–60	Quebec	1849	Gujerat
1760	Sillery	1850–3	South Africa
1762	Martinique	1857–8	Indian Mutiny
1762	Havannah	1857	Delhi
1763–4	North America	1860	China
1796	Grenada	1860	Taku Forts
1799	Surinam	1860	Pekin
1808–14	Peninsula	1878–80	2nd Afghan War
1808	Roleia	1879	Ahmed Khel
1808	Vimiera	1880	Kandahar
1809	Duoro	1879–81	South Africa
1809	Martinique	1882–4	Egypt
1809	Talavera	1882	Tel-el-Kebir
1810	Guadaloupe	1884–5	Nile
1810	Busaco	1884	El Teb
1811	Fuentes d'Onoro	1884	Tamai
1811	Albuera	1885	Abu Klea
1812	Ciudad Rodrigo	1890–2	Burma
1812	Badajos	1895	Chitral
1812	Salamanca	1899–1902	South Africa
1813	Vittoria	1900	Defence of Ladysmith
1813	Pyrenees	1900	Relief of Ladysmith
1813	Nivelle		
1813	Nive		
1814	Orthes		
1814	Toulouse		

continued overleaf

1914–18	1ST WORLD WAR	1939–45	2ND WORLD WAR
	The principal battle honours were as follows:		Principal battle honours were as follows:
	Mons		Calais, 1940
	Marne, 1914		Rhineland
	Ypres, 1914, '15, '17 '18		North-West Europe, 1940, '44–5
	Somme, 1916, '18		Egyptian Frontier, 1940
	Arras, 1917, '18		Sidi Rezezh, 1941
	Messine, 1917, '18		Alam el Halfa
	Epehy		El Alamein
	Canal du Nord		North Africa, 1940–3
	Selle		Italy, 1943–5
	Sambre		Greece, 1941, '44–5

MOTTO

'Celer et Audax' (Swift and Bold)

7 November 1958	Redesignated 2nd Green Jackets The King's Royal Rifle Corps, so becoming part of: THE GREEN JACKETS BRIGADE
1 January 1966	Further redesignated The 2nd Battalion, The Royal Green Jackets (The King's Royal Rifle Corps), thus becoming a battalion of: THE ROYAL GREEN JACKETS
June 1968	Sub-title (The King's Royal Rifle Corps) was dropped.

see page 275 The Royal Green Jackets

The 61st (South Gloucestershire) Regiment of Foot

Previous Units with which the Regiment claims no connection

1742–8 The 61st Regiment of Foot; disbanded.
1755–9 The 61st Regiment of Foot; renumbered as the 59th Foot which in 1881 became the 2nd Battalion The East Lancashire Regiment.

TITLES

1756   2nd Battalion 3rd Foot raised
1758   Reconstituted as 61st Foot
1758–82   The 61st Regiment of Foot
1782–1881   The 61st (South Gloucestershire) Regiment of Foot

PRINCIPAL CAMPAIGNS, BATTLES, etc.

1759	Guadeloupe	1814	Orthes
1801	Egypt	1848–9	2nd Sikh War
1806	Maida	1849	Chillianwallah
1810	Busaco	1849	Gujerat
1809–14	Peninsula	1857–8	Indian Mutiny
1809	Talavera	1857	Delhi
1812	Salamanca		
1813	Pyrenees, Nivelles, Nive		

NICKNAMES

The Silver Tailed Dandies   The Flowers of Toulouse

1881   Linked to the 28th (North Gloucestershire) Regiment of Foot to form:
            THE GLOUCESTERSHIRE REGIMENT

see page 125 28th (North Gloucestershire) Regiment of Foot
see page 214 The Gloucestershire Regiment

The 62nd (Wiltshire) Regiment of Foot

TITLES

1743–8	The 62nd Regiment of Foot; disbanded.
1755–7	The 62nd (Royal American) Regiment of Foot; renumbered The 60th.
1756–7	The 62nd Regiment of Foot; renumbered The 77th.
1756–8	The 4th King's Own (2nd Batt.); separately constituted as The 62nd Foot.
1758–82	The 62nd Regiment of Foot
1782–1881	The 62nd (Wiltshire) Regiment of Foot

PRINCIPAL CAMPAIGNS, BATTLES, etc.

1743	Dettingen	1813	Nive (2nd Bn)
1745	Fontenoy	1814–15	America (1st Bn)
1745	Jacobite Rising	1845–6	1st Sikh War
1746	Culloden	1845	Ferozeshah
1758	Carrickfergus	1846	Sobraon
1776–80	America	1854–5	Crimea
1813–14	Peninsula	1855	Sevastopol

NICKNAME

The Springers

1881	Linked to the 99th (Duke of Edinburgh's) Regiment of Foot to form: THE WILTSHIRE REGIMENT (DUKE OF EDINBURGH'S)

see page 201 99th (Duke of Edinburgh's) Regiment of Foot
see page 239 The Wiltshire Regiment (Duke of Edinburgh's)
see page 267 The Duke of Edinburgh's Royal Regiment (Berkshire and Wiltshire)

The 63rd (West Suffolk) Regiment of Foot

PRINCIPAL CAMPAIGNS, BATTLES, etc.

1759	Guadaloupe	1809	Martinique
1775–81	America	1810	Guadaloupe
1775	Bunker's Hill	1854–5	Crimea
1776	Long Island	1854	Alma
1777	Brandywine	1854	Inkerman
1777	Germantown	1855	Sevastopol
1794–5	Flanders	1879–80	2nd Afghan War
1799	Egmont-op-Zee		

NICKNAME

The Bloodsuckers

1881   Linked to the 96th Regiment of Foot to form:
THE MANCHESTER REGIMENT

see page 198 6th Regiment of Foot
see page 240 The Manchester Regiment
see page 266 The King's Regiment

The 64th (2nd Staffordshire) Regiment of Foot

Previous Unit with which the Regiment claims no connection

1740–8   The 64th (Irish) Regiment of Foot; disbanded.

TITLES

1756–8   The 11th (2nd Batt.) Regiment of Foot; regimented in
1758–82   The 64th Regiment of Foot
1782–1881 The 64th (2nd Staffordshire) Regiment of Foot

PRINCIPAL CAMPAIGNS, BATTLES, etc.

1759	Guadaloupe	1801	Virgin Islands
1762	Martinique	1803	St. Lucia
1776–81	America	1804	Surinam
1775	Bunker's Hill	1856–7	Persia
1776	Brooklyn	1856	Bushire
1777	Brandywine		Reshire
1777	Germantown	1857	Koosh-ab
1780	Charleston	1857–8	Indian Mutiny
1781	Eutaw Springs	1857	Lucknow
1794	Martinique		Cawnpore

NICKNAME

The Black Knots

1881   Linked to the 98th (Prince of Wales's) Regiment of Foot
to form:
THE NORTH STAFFORDSHIRE
REGIMENT (THE PRINCE OF WALES'S)

see page 200 98th (Prince of Wales's) Regiment of Foot
see page 241 The North Staffordshire Regiment (The Prince of Wales's)
see page 267 The Staffordshire Regiment (The Prince of Wales's)

The 65th (2nd Yorkshire, North Riding) Regiment of Foot

TITLES

1756–8	Raised as 2nd Bn to the 12th Regiment of Foot
1758–82	Renumbered 65th Regiment of Foot
1782–1881	The 65th (2nd Yorkshire, North Riding) Regiment of Foot

PRINCIPAL CAMPAIGNS, BATTLES, etc.

1759	Martinique	1801	Cape of Good Hope
	Guadaloupe	1802	Ceylon
1762	Cuba	1803	India
1768–75	North America	1810	Mauritius
1775	Bunker's Hill	1819–21	Arabia
1776	Nova Scotia	1846–65	New Zealand (Maori
1784–94	Canada		Wars)
	West Indies		
1794	Martinique		
	Guadaloupe		

NICKNAME

The Royal Tigers

1881	Linked to the 84th (York and Lancaster) Regiment of Foot to form: THE YORK AND LANCASTER REGIMENT

see page 185 84th (York and Lancaster) Regiment of Foot
see page 242 The York and Lancaster Regiment

The 66th (Berkshire) Regiment of Foot

TITLES

1755–8	The 19th (2nd Battalion) Regiment of Foot; renumbered.
1758–82	The 66th Regiment of Foot
1782–1881	The 66th (Berkshire) Regiment of Foot

PRINCIPAL CAMPAIGNS, BATTLES, etc.

1809–14	Peninsula	1816	Nepalese War
1809	Douro	1879–80	2nd Afghan War
1809	Talavera	1880	Maiwand
1811	Albuera	1880	Kandahar
1813	Vittoria		Note: Peninsular War honours
1813	Nivelle		were gained by the 2nd/66th. In
1813	Nive		1817 the 1st and 2nd/66th were
1814	Orthes		merged at St. Helena.

1881	Linked to the 49th Princess Charlotte of Wales's Hertfordshire Regiment of Foot to form: **PRINCESS OF CHARLOTTE OF WALES'S BERKSHIRE REGIMENT**
1885	The title 'Royal' was conferred
1921	The title was varied to: **THE ROYAL BERKSHIRE REGIMENT (PRINCESS CHARLOTTE OF WALES'S)**

see page 148 49th Princess Charlotte of Wales's Hertfordshire Regiment of Foot

see page 233 The Royal Berkshire Regiment (Princess Charlotte of Wales's)

see page 267 The Duke of Edinburgh's Royal Regiment (Berkshire and Wiltshire)

The 67th (South Hampshire) Regiment of Foot

PRINCIPAL CAMPAIGNS, BATTLES, etc.

1805	India	1860	Taku Forts
1810–14	Peninsula	1860	Pekin
1811	Barossa	1878–80	2nd Afghan War
1857–8	Indian Mutiny	1879	Charasiah
1860–2	China	1879	Kabul

NICKNAME

The Hampshire Tigers

The 68th (Durham-Light Infantry) Regiment of Foot

PRINCIPAL CAMPAIGNS, BATTLES, etc.

1758	Cherbourg	1813	Pyrenees
1795	St. Lucia	1813	Nivelle
1796	St. Vincent	1814	Orthes
1796	Grenada	1814	Bordeaux
1803	St. Lucia	1854–5	Crimea
1809	Walcheren	1854	Alma
1811–14	Peninsula	1854	Inkerman
1812	Salamanca	1855	Sevastopol
1812	Burgos	1864–6	New Zealand
1813	Vittoria		

NICKNAME

The Faithful Durhams

1881	Linked to the 106th (Bombay Light Infantry) Regiment to form:
	THE DURHAM LIGHT INFANTRY

see page 208 106th (Bombay Light Infantry) Regiment
see page 243 The Durham Light Infantry
see page 272 The Light Infantry

The 69th (South Lincolnshire) Regiment of Foot

PRINCIPAL CAMPAIGNS BATTLES, etc.

1797	St. Vincent	1815	Waterloo
1809	Bourbon	1815–26	India
1811	Java		

NICKNAMES

Old Agamemnons   The Ups and Downs
Wardour's Horse

1881	Linked to the 41st (The Welsh) Regiment of Foot to form: THE WELSH REGIMENT
1920	Title varied to: THE WELCH REGIMENT

see page 138   41st (The Welsh) Regiment of Foot
see page 226   The Welch Regiment
see page 274   The Royal Regiment of Wales (24th/41st Foot)

The 70th (Surrey) Regiment of Foot

TITLES

1756–8	The 31st Regiment of Foot
1758–82	The 70th Regiment of Foot
1782–1812	The 70th (Surrey) Regiment
1812–25	The 70th Glasgow Lowland Regiment
1825–81	The 70th (Surrey) Regiment of Foot

PRINCIPAL CAMPAIGNS, BATTLES, etc.

1778–81	American War of Independence	1857–8	Indian Mutiny
		1863 5	New Zealand
1794	Martinique	1878–9	2nd Afghan War
1794	Guadaloupe		

NICKNAME

The Glasgow Greys

1881	Linked with the 31st (Huntingdonshire) Regiment of Foot to form: THE EAST SURREY REGIMENT

see page 128 31st (Huntingdonshire) Regiment of Foot
see page 217 The East Surrey Regiment
see page 271 The Queen's Regiment

The 71st (Highland Light Infantry) Regiment

TITLES

1777–86   The 1st Bn 73rd (Highland) Regiment of Foot
1786–1808   The 71st (Highland) Regiment of Foot
1808–9   The 71st (Glasgow Highland) Regiment of Foot
1809–10   The 71st (Glasgow Highland Light Infantry) Regiment
1810–81   The 71st (Highland) Light Infantry

PRINCIPAL CAMPAIGNS, BATTLES, etc.

1780–83	Siege of Gibraltar	1809	Corunna
1780–97	India	1811	Fuentes d'Onor
1780	Carnatic	1812	Almaraj
1780	Arcot	1812	Vittoria
1781	Sholingur	1813	Pyrenees
1783	Mysore		Nive
1792	Seringapatam	1814	Orthes
1793	Pondicherry	1815	Quatre Bras
1806	Cape of Good Hope	1815	Waterloo
1808–14	Peninsula	1854–5	Crimea
1808	Roleia	1855	Sevastopol
1808	Vimiera	1858	Indian Mutiny

NICKNAMES

The Pig and Whistle Light Infantry   Glesca Keelies

1881   Linked to the 74th (Highlanders) Regiment to form:
THE HIGHLAND LIGHT INFANTRY

see page 174   74th (Highlanders) Regiment
see page 244   The Highland Light Infantry
see page 266   The Royal Highland Fusiliers (Princess Margaret's Own Glasgow and Ayrshire Regiment)

The 72nd Duke of Albany's Own Highlanders

TITLES

1778	Seaforth's Highlanders, after establishment obtained the numerical title of the 78th Regiment (of Highland Foot).
1786	Many senior regiments having been disbanded, the Regiment was numbered on 12 September 1786, the 72nd (Highland) Regiment of Foot.
1823	The 72nd (or The Duke of Albany's Own Highlanders) Regiment of Foot

PRINCIPAL CAMPAIGNS, BATTLES, etc.

1779 & 1781	In Action against French in Jersey	1835	South Africa
		1854–5	Crimea
1782–97	India	1855	Sevastopol
1782	Carnatic	1858	Indian Mutiny
1783	Mysore	1858	Kotah
1783	Bangalore	1858	Central India
1783	Savendroog	1878–80	2nd Afghan War
1783	Oootradong	1878	Peiwar Kotal
1791 & 1792	Seringapatam	1879	Charasiah
1793	Pondicherry	1879	Kabul
1795	Ceylon	1880	Kandahar
1806	Cape of Good Hope		

MOTTO

Cabar Feidh (The Horns of the Deer)

1881	Amalgamated with the 78th Highlanders (Ross-shire Buffs) to form: SEAFORTH HIGHLANDERS (ROSS-SHIRE BUFFS, THE DUKE OF ALBANY'S)

73rd (Perthshire) Regiment of Foot

As may be seen from titles the unit was raised originally in Perthshire as 2nd Battalion of the 42nd Royal Highlanders and was later renumbered.

TITLES

1758–62 ⎱ 1779–86 ⎰	The 2nd Battalion 42nd (The Royal Highland) Regiment of Foot
1786–1809	The 73rd Highland Regiment of Foot
1809—62	The 73rd Regiment of Foot
1862–81	The 73rd (Perthshire) Regiment of Foot

PRINCIPAL CAMPAIGNS, BATTLES, etc.

1762–7	Canada	1815	Quatre Bras
1783	Mysore	1815	Waterloo
1783	Mangalore	1846–53	South Africa (Kaffir
1793	Pondicherry		War)
1799	Seringapatam		

1881	Linked to the 42nd (Royal Highland—The Black Watch) to form: THE BLACK WATCH (ROYAL HIGHLANDERS)
1934	The title was changed to: THE BLACK WATCH (ROYAL HIGHLAND) REGIMENT

see page 139 42nd (Royal Highland—The Black Watch)
see page 227 The Black Watch (Royal Highland Regiment)

The 74th (Highlanders) Regiment

TITLES

1787–1816	The 74th (Highland) Regiment of Foot; also 'The Assaye Regiment' (1803)
1816–45	The 74th Regiment of Foot
1845–81	The 74th (Highlanders) Regiment of Foot

PRINCIPAL CAMPAIGNS, BATTLES, etc.

1799	Seringapatam	1812	Salamanca
1803	Assaye	1813	Nivelle
1808–14	Peninsula	1813	Vittoria
1810	Busaco	1813	Pyrenees
1811	Fuentes d'Onor	1814	Orthes
1812	Ciudad Rodrigo	1814	Toulouse
1812	Badajos	1851–3	South Africa

1881	Linked to the 71st (Highland Light Infantry) Regiment to form:

THE HIGHLAND LIGHT INFANTRY

see page 171 71st (Highland Light Infantry) Regiment
see page 244 The Highland Light Infantry
see page 266 The Royal Highland Fusiliers (Princess Margaret's Own Glasgow and Ayrshire Regiment)

The 75th (Stirlingshire) Regiment of Foot

TITLES

1758–63	The 75th Regiment of Foot; raised in 1756 as 2nd Bn 37th Foot, separately constituted as 75th in 1757, and disbanded in 1765.
1764–5	The 75th (Invalids) Regiment of Foot; formerly (1760) The 118th Invalids; dispersed for garrison service.
1778–83	The 75th (Prince of Wales's) Regiment of Foot; disbanded at the close of the American War of Independence.
1787–1809	The 75th (Highland) Regiment of Foot; also 'Abercrombie's Highlanders'.
1809–62	The 75th Regiment of Foot
1862–81	The 75th (Stirlingshire) Regiment of Foot

PRINCIPAL CAMPAIGNS, BATTLES, etc.

1778–83	America	1835	South Africa
1791–1806	India	1857–8	Indian Mutiny
1792	Seringapatam	1857	Delhi
1799	Mysore	1858	Lucknow
1799	Seringapatam		

1881	Linked to the 92nd (Gordon Highlanders) Regiment of Foot to form :
	THE GORDON HIGHLANDERS

see page 194 92nd (Gordon Highlanders) Regiment of Foot
see page 246 The Gordon Highlanders

76th Regiment of Foot

TITLES

1756–63	The 76th Regiment of Foot; disbanded.
1777–84	The 76th (Macdonald's Highlanders) Regiment of Foot; disbanded.
1787–1812	The 76th (Hindoostan) Regiment of Foot
1812–81	The 76th Regiment of Foot

PRINCIPAL CAMPAIGNS, BATTLES, etc.

1780–1806	India	1808–9	Peninsula
1792	Seringapatam	1809	Corunna
1800	Mysore	1813	Nive
1803	Allyghur	1813	Nivelle
1803	Delhi	1813–14	Peninsula
1803	Leswarree		

NICKNAMES

The Immortals   The Pigs
The Old Seven and Sixpennies

MOTTO

'Virtutis fortuna comes' (Fortune accompanies honour)

1881	Linked to the 33rd (Duke of Wellington's) Regiment of Foot to form: THE DUKE OF WELLINGTON'S REGIMENT (WEST RIDING)

see page 130 33rd (Duke of Wellington's) Regiment of Foot
see page 219 The Duke of Wellington's Regiment (West Riding)

The 77th (East Middlesex) Regiment of Foot

TITLES

1756–63	The 77th (Montgomery Highlanders) Regiment; disbanded.
1775–83	The 77th (Atholl Highlanders) Regiment; disbanded.
1787–1807	The 77th Regiment of Foot
1807–76	The 77th (East Middlesex) Regiment of Foot
1876–81	The 77th (East Middlesex) (Duke of Cambridge's Own) Regiment of Foot

PRINCIPAL CAMPAIGNS, BATTLES, etc.

1788–1807	India	1812	Badajos
1790	Mysore	1854–5	Crimea
1799	Seringaptam	1854	Inkerman
1809	Flushing		Alma
	Walcheren	1855	Sevastopol
1811–14	Peninsula	1858	Indian Mutiny
1812	Ciudad Rodrigo		

NICKNAME

The Pot Hooks

1881	Linked to the 57th (West Middlesex) Regiment of Foot to form: THE DUKE OF CAMBRIDGE'S OWN (MIDDLESEX REGIMENT)
1921	The title varied to: THE MIDDLESEX REGIMENT (DUKE OF CAMBRIDGE'S OWN)

see page 156 57th (West Middlesex) Regiment of Foot
see page 238 The Middlesex Regiment (Duke of Cambridge's Own)
see page 271 The Queen's Regiment

The 78th Highlanders
(The Ross-shire Buffs)

Previous Unit to which the Regiment claims no connection

1756–63   Fraser's Highlanders or 78th Regiment of Foot (This unit served at Louisberg and Quebec)

TITLE

1793–1881   The 78th (Highland) Regiment of Foot or The Ross-shire Buffs

(*Note:* from 1778 to 1786 the 78th was represented in the Seaforth Highlanders by the 1st Battalion)

PRINCIPAL CAMPAIGNS, BATTLES, etc.

1794–5	Flanders	1814	Flanders
1794	Nijmegen	1814	Merxem
1795	Cape of Good Hope	1857	Persia
1803	Assaye	1857	Koosh-Ab
1803	Ahmednuggar	1857–8	Indian Mutiny
1803	Argaum	1857	Cawnpore
1806	Maida	1857	Lucknow
1807	Egypt	1878–80	2nd Afghan War
1811	Java		

MOTTO

Cuidich 'n Righ (Save The King)

1881   Amalgamated with the 72nd Duke of Albany's Own Highlanders to form:
SEAFORTH HIGHLANDERS (ROSS-SHIRE BUFFS, THE DUKE OF ALBANY'S)

see page 172   72nd Duke of Albany's Own Highlanders
see page 245   Seaforth Highlanders (Ross-shire Buffs, The Duke of Albany's)
see page 269   Queen's Own Highlanders (Seaforth and Camerons)

The Queen's Own Cameron Highlanders

For many years the Regiment was the only single battalion regiment in the Army, the 2nd Battalion being re-raised in 1897.

continued overleaf

179

1914–18	Ypres, 1914, '15, '17, '18	1939–45	St. Omer-La-Basse
	Neuve Chapelle		Reichswald
	Loos		Rhine
	Somme, 1916, '18		Keren
	Delville Wood		Sidi Barrani
	Arras, 1917, '18		El Alamein
	Sambre		Akarit
	Macedonia, 1915, '18		Gothic Line
			Kohima
			Mandalay
1939–45	2ND WORLD WAR Battle honours selected to appear on the Colours:	1956	Aden

| 7 February 1961 | Linked to the Seaforth Highlanders (Ross-shire Buffs, The Duke of Albany's) to form: QUEEN'S OWN HIGHLANDERS (SEAFORTH AND CAMERONS) |

see page 245 Seaforth Highlanders (Ross-shire Buffs, The Duke of Albany's)

see page 269 Queen's Own Highlanders (Seaforth and Camerons)

The 80th (Staffordshire Volunteers) Regiment of Foot

TITLES

1758–64	The 80th (Light-armed) Regiment of Foot; disbanded.
1778–84	The 80th (Royal Edinburgh Volunteers) Regiment of Foot; disbanded.
1793–1881	The 80th (Staffordshire Volunteers) Regiment of Foot

PRINCIPAL CAMPAIGNS, BATTLES, etc.

1794–5	Flanders	1846	Sobraon
1795	Isle Dieu	1852–3	2nd Burma War
1801	Egypt	1853	Pegu
1845–6	1st Sikh War	1858	Indian Mutiny
1845	Ferozeshah	1875	Perak
1845	Mudki	1878–9	South Africa (Zulu War)

NICKNAMES

Gage's Light Infantry   The Staffordshire Knots

1881	Linked to the 38th (1st Staffordshire) Regiment of Foot to form: THE SOUTH STAFFORDSHIRE REGIMENT

see page 135	38th (1st Staffordshire) Regiment of Foot
see page 223	The South Staffordshire Regiment
see page 267	The Staffordshire Regiment (The Prince of Wales's)

The 81st (Loyal Lincoln Volunteers) Regiment of Foot

TITLES

1759–63	The 81st (Invalids) Regiment; dispersed as Independent Companies.
1778–83	The 81st (Aberdeen Highlanders) Regiment of Foot; disbanded.
1793–4	The 81st (Loyal Lincoln Volunteers) Regiment
1794–1833	The 81st Regiment of Foot
1833–81	The 81st (Loyal Lincoln Volunteers) Regiment of Foot. (When the Regiment was re-formed in 1793, the Lincoln Militia volunteered in a body, and the unit had the unique honour of being entitled 'Loyal'. From 1881 this term became embodied in the title of The Loyal Regiment.)

PRINCIPAL CAMPAIGNS, BATTLES, etc.

1806	Maida	1857–8	Indian Mutiny
1809	Corunna	1878–9	2nd Afghan War
1810–14	Peninsula	1878	Ali Masjid

1881	Linked to the 47th (Lancashire) Regiment of Foot to form: THE LOYAL NORTH LANCASHIRE REGIMENT
1921	The title varied to: THE LOYAL REGIMENT (NORTH LANCASHIRE)

see page 146 47th (Lancashire) Regiment of Foot
see page 231 The Loyal Regiment (North Lancashire)
see page 276 The Queen's Lancashire Regiment

The 82nd (The Prince of Wales's Volunteers) Regiment of Foot

TITLE

1793–1881   The 82nd (The Prince of Wales's Volunteers) Regiment of Foot

PRINCIPAL CAMPAIGNS, BATTLES, etc.

1808–9	Peninsula	1813	Nivelle
1808	Roliea	1813	Orthes
1808	Vimiera	1814	Niagara
1809	Corunna	1854–5	Crimea
1813–14	Peninsula	1855	Sevastopol
1813	Vittoria	1857–8	Indian Mutiny
1813	Pyrenees	1857	Lucknow

1881   Linked to the 40th (2nd Somersetshire) Regiment of Foot to form:
THE SOUTH LANCASHIRE REGIMENT (THE PRINCE OF WALES'S VOLUNTEERS)

see page 137   40th (2nd Somersetshire) Regiment of Foot
see page 225   The South Lancashire Regiment (The Prince of Wales's Volunteers)
see page 276   The Queen's Lancashire Regiment

The 83rd (County of Dublin) Regiment of Foot

TITLES

1793–4	Lieut.-Colonel Commandant Fitch's Corps
1794–1859	The 83rd Regiment of Foot
1859–81	The 83rd (County of Dublin) Regiment of Foot

PRINCIPAL CAMPAIGNS, BATTLES, etc.

1795	Jamaica	1812	Badajos
1797–8	San Domingo	1812	Salamanca
1806	Cape of Good Hope	1813	Vittoria
1809–14	Peninsula	1813	Nivelle
1809	Talavera	1813	Orthes
1810	Busaco	1814	Toulouse
1811	Fuentes d'Onor	1842–59	Central India
1813	Ciudad Rodrigo	1857–8	Indian Mutiny

NICKNAME

Fitch's Grenadiers

MOTTO

'Quis separabit' (Who shall separate us?)

1881	Linked to the 86th (Royal County Down) Regiment of Foot to form: THE ROYAL IRISH RIFLES
1921	The title was changed to: THE ROYAL ULSTER RIFLES

see page 188 86th (Royal County Down) Regiment of Foot
see page 247 The Royal Ulster Rifles
see page 273 The Royal Irish Rangers (27th (Inniskilling) 83rd and 87th)

The 84th (York and Lancaster) Regiment of Foot

Previous Units with which the Regiment claims no connection

1758–64   Eyre Coote's 84th Regiment of Foot; disbanded.
1775–8   The Royal Highland Emigrant Corps
1778–83   The above numbered: 84th (Royal Highland Emigrants) Regiment of Foot (two bns); disbanded.
          (*Note:* Eyre Coote's Regiment of Foot served at Wandewash, Arcot, Pondicherry, and Patna between 1759 and 1762. In 1775 the Royal Highland Emigrants Corps served in North America.)

TITLES

1783–1809   The 84th Regiment of Foot
1809–81   The 84th (York and Lancaster) Regiment of Foot

PRINCIPAL CAMPAIGNS, BATTLES, etc.

1794	Flanders	1810	Mauritius (1st Bn)
	Flushing (1st Bn)	1811–19	India (1st Bn)
1794	Cape of Good Hope (2nd Bn)	1811	Spain & France (2nd Bn)
1796	Cape of Good Hope (1st Bn)	1813	Nive
			Nivelle (2nd Bn)
	(In this year the 2nd Bn was absorbed by the 1st)		(In 1818 the 2nd Bn was absorbed by the 1st)
1799–1819	India	1854	Burma
1799	Gujerat, Bhurtpore	1857–9	Indian Mutiny
1809	Flanders (re-raised 2nd Bn)	1857	Lucknow

1881   Linked to the 65th (2nd Yorkshire, North Riding) Regiment to form:
THE YORK AND LANCASTER
REGIMENT

see page 165 65th (2nd Yorkshire, North Riding) Regiment of Foot
see page 242 The York and Lancaster Regiment

The 85th (Bucks Volunteers) (The King's Light Infantry) Regiment

TITLES

1759–63   The 85th Light Infantry Regiment or Royal Volonters. Crauford's Regiment of Foot.

1778–83   The 85th (Westminster Volontiers) Regiment of Foot, mostly lost at sea returning from Jamaica in 1782; disbanded in 1783.

1794–1808   The 85th (Bucks Volunteers) Regiment of Foot

1808 15   The 85th (Bucks Volunteers) (Light Infantry) Regiment

1815–21   The 85th (Bucks Volunteers) (Duke of York's Own Light Infantry) Regiment

1821–81   The 85th (Bucks Volunteers) (The King's Light Infantry) Regiment
(On 28 August 1827 the Regiment received permission to discontinue the title 'Bucks Volunteers' but it appeared in the Army List till 1881.)

PRINCIPAL CAMPAIGNS, BATTLES, etc.

The Royal Volunteers

1761	Belleisle
1762–3	Portugal

Westminster Volunteers

1780	Jamaica

The King's Light Infantry

1794	Walcheren
1795	Gibraltar
1799	Holland
1800	Madeira
1802	Jamaica
1811–14	Peninsula
1811	Fuentes d'Onor
1811	Badajos (San Christobal)

1813	San Sebastian
1813	Bidassoa
1813	Nivelle
1814	Nive
1814	Bayonne
1814–15	America
	Washington, New Orleans
1827	Gibraltar
1828	Malta
1836	Nova Scotia
1837	New Brunswick
1838	Canada
1853	Mauritius
1856–63	Cape of Good Hope
1868–78	India
1878–80	2nd Afghan War

NICKNAMES

The Elegant Extracts   The Young Bucks

1881	Linked to the 53rd (Shropshire) Regiment of Foot to form:
	The Shropshire Regiment (King's Light Infantry)
	a few weeks later the title was changed to:
	The King's Light Infantry (Shropshire Regiment)
	and soon afterward changed again to:
	THE KING'S (SHROPSHIRE) LIGHT INFANTRY
1920	The titled became:
	THE KING'S SHROPSHIRE LIGHT INFANTRY

see page 152 53rd (Shropshire) Regiment of Foot
see page 236 The King's Shropshire Light Infantry
see page 272 The Light Infantry

The 86th (Royal County Down) Regiment of Foot

Previous Units with which the Regiment claims no connection

1759–63	The 86th Regiment of Foot, formerly 2nd Bn the 76th Foot; disbanded.
1779–83	The 86th Regiment of Foot; disbanded.

TITLES

1793–4	General Cuylers Shropshire Volunteers
1794–1809	The 86th Regiment of Foot
1809–12	The 86th (The Leinster) Regiment of Foot
1812–81	The 86th (Royal County Down) Regiment of Foot

PRINCIPAL CAMPAIGNS, BATTLES, etc.

1799–1819	India	1842–59	Central India
1801	Egypt	1857–8	Indian Mutiny
1810	Boubon		

NICKNAME

The Irish Giants

1881	Linked to the 83rd (County of Dublin) Regiment of Foot to form: THE ROYAL IRISH RIFLES
1921	The title changed to: THE ROYAL ULSTER RIFLES

see page 184   83rd (County of Dublin) Regiment of Foot
see page 247   The Royal Ulster Rifles
see page 273   The Royal Irish Rangers (27th (Inniskilling) 83rd and 87th)

The 87th (The Royal Irish Fusiliers) Regiment of Foot

Previous Units with which the Regiment claims no connection

1759–63 The 87th (Highland Volunteers) Regiment of Foot; also 'Keith's Highlanders'; disbanded.

1779–83 The 87th Regiment of Foot; disbanded.

TITLES

1793–1811 The 87th (The Prince of Wales's Irish) Regiment of Foot

1811–27 The 87th (The Prince of Wales's Own Irish) Regiment of Foot

1827–81 The 87th (The Royal Irish Fusiliers) Regiment of Foot for a short period of six months The Prince of Wales's Own Irish Fusiliers)

PRINCIPAL CAMPAIGNS, BATTLES, etc.

1794–5	Flanders	1813	Vittoria (2nd Bn)
1807	Monte Video	1813	Nivelle (2nd Bn)
1809–14	Peninsula (2nd Bn)	1814	Orthes (2nd Bn)
1809	Talavera (2nd Bn)	1814	Toulouse (2nd Bn)
1811	Barosa (2nd Bn)r	1816	Nepaul (1st Bn)
1811	Tarifa (2nd Bn)	1824–6	Burma (1st Bn)
1810–11	Mauritius (1st Bn)	1857–8	Indian Mutiny

MOTTO (Unofficial)

'Faugh-a-Ballagh' (Clear the way)

NICKNAMES

Faugh-a-Ballagh Boys   The Faughs

1881 Linked to the 89th (Princess Victoria's) Regiment of Foot to form:
PRINCESS VICTORIA'S (THE ROYAL IRISH FUSILIERS)

1920 The title was changed to:
THE ROYAL IRISH FUSILIERS (PRINCESS VICTORIA'S)

see page 191 89th (Princess Victoria's) Regiment of Foot
see page 248 The Royal Irish Fusiliers (Princess Victoria's)
see page 273 The Royal Irish Rangers (27th (Inniskilling) 83rd and 87th)

The 88th (Connaught Rangers) Regiment of Foot

PRINCIPAL CAMPAIGNS, BATTLES, *etc.*

1760–2	Germany	1813	Vittoria
1760	Warburg	1813	Nivelle
1762	Wilhemstahl	1814	Orthes
1794–5	Flanders	1814	Toulouse
1801	Egypt	1854–5	Crimea
1809–14	Peninsula	1854	Alma
1809	Talavera	1854	Inkerman
1810	Busaco	1855	Sevastopol
1811	Fuentes d'Onor	1857–8	Indian Mutiny
1812	Cuidad Rodrigo	1858	Central India
1812	Badajos	1877–9	South Africa
1812	Salamanca		

NICKNAME

The Devil's Own

1881	Linked to the 94th Regiment of Foot to form: THE CONNAUGHT RANGERS

see page 196 94th Regiment of Foot
see page 249 The Connaught Rangers

The 89th (Princess Victoria's) Regiment of Foot

Previous Units with which the Regiment claims no connection

1759–65	The 89th (Gordon Highlanders) Regiment of Foot; disbanded.
1779–83	The 89th Regiment of Foot; disbanded.

TITLES

1793–1866	The 89th Regiment of Foot
1866–81	The 89th (Princess Victoria's) Regiment of Foot

PRINCIPAL CAMPAIGNS, BATTLES, *etc.*

1801	Egypt	1824–6	1st Burma War
1810	Mauritius (1st Bn)	1826	Ava
1811	Java (1st Bn)	1854–5	Crimea
1813–14	Canada (2nd Bn)	1855	Sevastopol
1813	Niagara (2nd Bn)		

NICKNAME

Blaney's Bloodhounds, circa 1800

1881	Linked to the 87th (Royal Irish Fusiliers) Regiment of Foot to form: PRINCESS VICTORIA'S (THE ROYAL IRISH FUSILIERS)
1920	The title was changed to: THE ROYAL IRISH FUSILIERS (PRINCESS VICTORIA'S)

see page 189 87th (The Royal Irish Fusiliers) Regiment of Foot
see page 248 The Royal Irish Fusiliers (Princess Victoria's)
see page 273 The Royal Irish Rangers (27th (Inniskilling) 83rd and 87th)

The 90th Perthshire
Light Infantry

The Regiment owed its existence to most unusual circumstances. In 1792 a Scottish Laird, Mr Thomas Graham, was cruising in the Mediterranean when his wife, the Hon. Mary died of tuberculosis. In Toulouse her coffin was desecrated by some drunken revolutionaries, and although he was 42 years of age and with no military service, Graham offered his services to the Army, hoping to raise a regiment to fight the French. In a distinguished career Graham became Lieutenant-General Lord Lynedoch.

Previous Units with which the Regiment claims no connection

1759–63	The 90th (Irish Light Infantry) Regiment; disbanded.
1775–83	The 90th Regiment of Foot; disbanded.

TITLES

1794–1815	The 90th Perthshire Volunteers
1815–81	The 90th Perthshire Light Infantry

PRINCIPAL CAMPAIGNS, BATTLES, *etc.*

1801	Egypt	1854–5	Crimea
	Mandora	1855	Sevastopol
	Alexandria	1857–8	Indian Mutiny
1809	Martinique	1857	Relief of Lucknow
1810	Guadaloupe	1877–9	South Africa (Zulu
1846–7	South Africa (Kaffir		War)
	War)		

1881   Linked to the 26th Cameronian Regiment to form:
THE CAMERONIANS (SCOTTISH RIFLES)

see page 123 26th Cameronian Regiment
see page 212 The Cameronians (Scottish Rifles)

The 91st (Princess Louise's Argyllshire) Highlanders

Raised by Duncan Campbell of Lochnell: embodied at Stirling in 1794.

TITLES

1794–6	The 98th (Argyllshire Highlanders) Regiment of Foot; renumbered.
1796–1809	The 91st (Argyllshire Highlanders) Regiment of Foot. Three other corps had previously borne this number; none had been retained longer than four years.
1809–21	The 91st Regiment of Foot; its distinctive title was probably dropped for the same reason that the Highland dress was for a time discarded, because of its supposed impediment to recruiting.
1821–64	The 91st (Argyllshire) Regiment of Foot
1864–72	The 91st (Argyllshire) Highlanders
1872–81	The 91st (Princess Louise's Argyllshire) Highlanders

PRINCIPAL CAMPAIGNS, BATTLES, etc.

1795–1802	Cape of Good Hope	1813	Nivelle
1808–14	Peninsula	1813	Nive
1808	Roleia	1814	Orthes
1808	Vimiera	1841–3	South Africa
1809	Corunna	1846–7	South Africa
1809	Talavera	1879	South Africa
1813	Pyrenees		

MOTTO

'Ne obliviscaris' (Forget not)

1881	Linked to the 93rd (Sutherland Highlanders) Regiment of Foot to form: THE PRINCESS LOUISE'S (ARGYLL AND SUTHERLAND HIGHLANDERS)
1921	The title was changed to: THE ARGYLL AND SUTHERLAND HIGHLANDERS (PRINCESS LOUISE'S)

see page 195 93rd (Sutherland Highlanders) Regiment of Foot
see page 250 The Argyll and Sutherland Highlanders (Princess Louise's)

The 92nd (Gordon Highlanders) Regiment of Foot

see page 175 75th (Stirlingshire) Regiment of Foot
see page 246 The Gordon Highlanders

TITLES

1794–8	The 100th (Gordon Highlanders) Regiment of Foot
1798–1861	The 92nd (Highland) Regiment of Foot; there had previously been three other regiments bearing this number, but none incorporated for more than four years.
1861–81	The 92nd (Gordon Highlanders) Regiment of Foot

PRINCIPAL CAMPAIGNS, BATTLES, etc.

1799	Egmont-op-Zee	1813	Nive
1801	Mandora	1814	Orthes
1801	Egypt	1815	Quatre Bras
1808–14	Peninsula	1814	Waterloo
1809	Corunna	1878–80	2nd Afghan War
1811	Fuentes d'Onor	1879	Charasiah
1812	Almaraj	1879	Kabul
1813	Vittoria	1880	Kandahar
1813	Pyrenees		

NICKNAME

The Gay Gordons

1881	Linked to the 75th (Stirlingshire) Regiment of Foot to form: THE GORDON HIGHLANDERS

The 93rd (Sutherland Highlanders) Regiment of Foot

Previous Units with which the Regiment claims no connection

1760–96 The 93rd Regiment of Foot; during this period three 93rds were raised and disbanded—1760–3; 1779–83 (American War); and 1793–6 (served in Demerara, Essequibo, and Berbice, and then was drafted into the 39th).

TITLES

1799–1861 The 93rd Highlanders (raised by General Wemyss)
1861–81   The 93rd (Sutherland Highlanders) Regiment of Foot

PRINCIPAL CAMPAIGNS, BATTLES, etc.

1806	Cape of Good Hope	1854	Balaclava
1814–15	New Orleans	1855	Sevastopol
1854–5	Crimea	1857	Indian Mutiny
1854	Alma	1857	Lucknow

MOTTO

'Sans peur' (Without fear)

1881 Linked to the 91st (Princess Louise's Argyllshire) Highlanders to form:
THE PRINCESS LOUISE'S (ARGYLL AND SUTHERLAND) HIGHLANDERS
1921 The title was changed to:
THE ARGYLL AND SUTHERLAND HIGHLANDERS (PRINCESS LOUISE'S)

see page 193 91st (Princess Louise's Argyllshire) Highlanders
see page 250 The Argyll and Sutherland Highlanders (Princess Louise's)

The 94th Regiment of Foot

The 94th of the period 1803–18 was a Scots Brigade which had been in the service of Holland almost continually from 1586–1793. In 1803 it was taken in the English service.

TITLES

1760–3	The 94th (Royal Welsh Volunteers) Regiment of Foot; disbanded.
1779–83	The 94th Regiment of Foot; disbanded.
1794–5	The 94th (Irish) Regiment of Foot; disbanded.
1803–18	The 94th (Scots Brigade) Regiment of Foot; disbanded.
1823–81	The 94th Regiment of Foot

PRINCIPAL CAMPAIGNS, BATTLES, etc.

1799	Seringapatam	1813	Nivelle
1809–14	Peninsula	1814	Orthes
1812	Badajos	1814	Toulouse
1812	Salamanca	1877–9	South Africa
1813	Vittoria		

NICKNAME

The Gawies

1881	Linked to the 88th (Connaught Rangers) Regiment of Foot to form:
	THE CONNAUGHT RANGERS

see page 190 88th (Connaught Rangers) Regiment of Foot
see page 249 The Connaught Rangers

The 95th or Derbyshire Regiment of Foot

Previous Units with which the Regiment claims no connection

1760–3	The 95th Regiment of Foot; disbanded.
1780–3	The 95th Regiment of Foot; disbanded.
1794–6	The 95th Regiment of Foot; disbanded.

TITLES

1823–5	The 95th Regiment of Foot
1825–81	The 95th or Derbyshire Regiment of Foot

PRINCIPAL CAMPAIGNS, BATTLES, etc.

1824	Malta	1857	Central Indian
1830–50	Greece, Ceylon, Hong		Campaign
	Kong		(Rowa, Kotah,
1854–5	Crimea		Kotah-ki-Serai,
1854	Alma		Gwalior, Powrie,
	Inkerman		Beejapore,
	Sevastopol		Koondrye)

NICKNAME

The Nails

May 1881	Linked to the 45th (Nottinghamshire Regiment) Sherwood Foresters to form: The Derbyshire Regiment (Sherwood Foresters)
July 1881	Title varied to: THE SHERWOOD FORESTERS (DERBYSHIRE REGIMENT)
1902	Title changed to: THE SHERWOOD FORESTERS (NOTTINGHAMSHIRE AND DERBYSHIRE REGIMENT)

see page 143 45th (Nottinghamshire Regiment) Sherwood Foresters
see page 230 The Sherwood Foresters (Nottinghamshire and Derbyshire Regiment)
see page 274 The Worcestershire and Sherwood Foresters Regiment (29th/54th Foot)

The 96th Regiment of Foot

TITLES

1760–3	The 96th Regiment of Foot (raised for service in the Carnatic); disbanded.
1780–3	The 96th (British Musketeers) Regiment; disbanded.
1793–8	The 96th (The Queen's Royal Irish) Regiment; dispersed.
1803–16	The 96th Regiment of Foot (raised as 2nd Bn 52nd Foot; renumbered the 95th, and as such disbanded in 1818)
1815–18	The 96th (Queen's Own) Regiment of Foot (raised in 1798 as The Queen's Germans; numbered the 97th in 1802; renumbered, in 1815, the 96th; disbanded in 1818—the Egyptian and Peninsular honours of this corps were assumed by the late 96th)
1824–81	The 96th Regiment of Foot

PRINCIPAL CAMPAIGNS, BATTLES, etc.

1801	Egypt
1808–11	Peninsula
1845–7	New Zealand

NICKNAME
The Bend-overs

1881	Linked to the 63rd (West Suffolk) Regiment of Foot to form:

THE MANCHESTER REGIMENT

see page 163 63rd (West Suffolk) Regiment of Foot
see page 240 The Manchester Regiment
see page 266 The King's Regiment

The 97th (The Earl of Ulster's) Regiment of Foot

TITLE

1824–81   The 97th (The Earl of Ulster's) Regiment of Foot

PRINCIPAL CAMPAIGNS, BATTLES, etc.

1854–5	Crimea	1857–8	Indian Mutiny
1855	Sevastopol	1858	Lucknow

NICKNAME

The Celestials

MOTTO

'Quo fas et gloria ducunt' (Whither right and glory lead)

1881   Linked to the 50th (Queen's Own) Regiment of Foot to form:
THE QUEEN'S OWN ROYAL WEST KENT REGIMENT

see page 149   50th (Queen's Own) Regiment of Foot
see page 234   The Queen's Own Royal West Kent Regiment
see page 271   The Queen's Regiment

The 98th (The Prince of Wales's) Regiment of Foot

TITLES

1760–3	The 98th Regiment of Foot; disbanded.
1779–84	The 98th Regiment of Foot; disbanded.
1793–1802	The 98th (Highland) Regiment of Foot; renumbered the 91st.
1805–15	The 98th Regiment of Foot; renumbered as The 97th and disbanded in 1818.
1805–18	The 99th (Prince of Wales's Tipperary) Regiment of Foot; renumbered the 98th in 1815, and afterwards disbanded.
1824–76	The 98th Regiment of Foot
1876–81	The 98th (The Prince of Wales's) Regiment of Foot

PRINCIPAL CAMPAIGNS, BATTLES, etc.

1842	China	1848–9	2nd Sikh War

1881	Linked to the 64th (2nd Staffordshire) Regiment of Foot to form: THE NORTH STAFFORDSHIRE REGIMENT (THE PRINCE OF WALES'S)

see page 164 64th (2nd Staffordshire) Regiment of Foot
see page 241 The North Staffordshire Regiment (The Prince of Wales's)
see page 267 **The Staffordshire Regiment (The Prince of Wales's)**

The 99th (The Duke of Edinburgh's) Regiment of Foot

TITLES

1760–3	The 99th Regiment of Foot; disbanded.
1780–3	The 99th (Jamaica) Regiment of Foot; disbanded.
1794–8	The 99th Regiment of Foot; disbanded.
1804–11	The 99th Regiment of Foot; renumbered the 98th (or Prince of Wales's Tipperary) Regiment of Foot; disbanded in 1818.
1805–15	The 100th Regiment of Foot; renumbered.
1815–18	The 99th (H.R.H. The Prince Regent's County of Dublin) Regiment of Foot; disbanded.
1824–74	The 99th (Lanarkshire) Regiment of Foot
1874–81	The 99th (The Duke of Edinburgh's) Regiment of Foot

PRINCIPAL CAMPAIGNS, BATTLES etc.

1845–7	New Zealand	1879–80	South Africa (Zulu War)
1860	China		
1860	Peking		

1881   Linked to the 62nd (Wiltshire) Regiment of Foot to form: THE WILTSHIRE REGIMENT (DUKE OF EDINBURGH'S)

see page 162 62nd (Wiltshire) Regiment of Foot
see page 239 The Wiltshire Regiment (Duke of Edinburgh's)
see page 267 The Duke of Edinburgh's Royal Regiment (Berkshire and Wiltshire)

The 100th (Prince of Wales's Royal Canadian) Regiment

TITLES

1761–3	The 100th (Highland) Regiment of Foot; disbanded.
1780–4	The 100th Regiment of Foot; disbanded.
1794–18??	The 100th (Gordon Highlanders) Regiment of Foot; the late 92nd, now 2nd Gordon Highlanders.
1805–19	The 100th (Prince Regent's County of Dublin) Regiment of Foot; disbanded as the 99th.
1816–18	The 100th (Duke of York's Irish) Regiment of Foot; raised as the 101st.
1858–81	The 100th (Prince of Wales's Royal Canadian) Regiment of Foot

PRINCIPAL CAMPAIGNS, BATTLES, etc.

1761–2	Martinique	1812–14	Canada
1761	Belle Isle	1813	Niagara
1783	Carnatic		

1881	Linked to the 109th (Bombay Infantry) Regiment to form: THE PRINCE OF WALES'S LEINSTER REGIMENT (ROYAL CANADIANS)

see page 211 109th (Bombay Infantry) Regiment
see page 251 The Prince of Wales's Leinster Regiment (Royal Canadians)

The 101st (Royal Bengal Fusiliers) Regiment

PRINCIPAL CAMPAIGNS, BATTLES, etc.

1757	Chandernagore	1826	Bhurtpore
1757	Plassey	1839–40	1st Afghan War
1758	Condore	1839	Ghuznee
1759	Masulipatam	1845–6	1st Sikh War
1757	Bandara	1845	Ferozeshah
1760	Windewash	1846	Sobraon
1763–5	Goojerat	1851–3	2nd Burma War
1764	Buxar	1857–8	Indian Mutiny
1774–94	Rohilcund	1857	Delhi
1783	Carnatic	1858	Lucknow
1805	Bhurtpore		

NICKNAMES

The Dirty Shirts

1881	Linked to the 104th (Bengal Fusiliers) Regiment to form: THE ROYAL MUNSTER FUSILIERS

The 102nd (Royal Madras) Fusiliers

TITLES

1760–3	The 102nd (Queen's Own Royal Volunteers) Regiment of Foot; disbanded.
1780–3	The 102nd Regiment of Foot; disbanded.
1793–4	The 102nd (Irish) Regiment of Foot; drafted.
1809–16	The 102nd Regiment of Foot; raised in 1798 as the New South Wales Corps; disbanded in 1818 as the 100th Foot.
1746–1830	The Hon. East India Company's European Regiment
1830–9	The Hon. East India Company's Madras (European) Regiment
1839–43	The Hon. East India Company's 1st Madras (European) Regiment
1843–58	The Hon. East India Company's 1st Madras (European) Fusiliers
1858–61	The 1st Madras Fusiliers
1861–81	The 102nd (Royal Madras) Fusiliers

PRINCIPAL CAMPAIGNS, BATTLES, etc.

1751	Arcot	1810	Amboyna
1757	Plassey	1810	Ternate
1758	Condore	1810	Banda
1760	Windewash	1817	Maheidpore
1760	Pondicherry	1824	1st Burma War
1780	Gujerat	1826	Ava
1781	Sholingar	1857–8	Indian Mutiny
1793	Pondicherry	1851	Lucknow

NICKNAME

The Lambs

MOTTO

'Spectamur agendo' (We are judged by our deeds)

1881	Linked to the 103rd (Royal Bombay Fusiliers) to form: THE ROYAL DUBLIN FUSILIERS

see page 205 103rd (Royal Bombay Fusiliers)
see page 253 The Royal Dublin Fusiliers

The 103rd Royal Bombay Fusiliers

PRINCIPAL CAMPAIGNS, BATTLES, etc.

1747–83	Carnatic	1821	Beni-Boo-Ally
1747–83	Mysore	1839	Aden
1757	Plassey	1848–9	2nd Sikh War
1764	Buxar	1849	Multan
1791	Nundy-Droog	1849	Gujerat
1792	Seringapatam	1852–3	2nd Burma War
1817	Kirkee	1857–8	Indian Mutiny

NICKNAME

The Old Toughs

1881	Linked to the 102nd (Royal Madras) Fusiliers to form: THE ROYAL DUBLIN FUSILIERS

see page 204 102nd (Royal Madras) Fusiliers
see page 253 The Royal Dublin Fusiliers

The 104th Bengal Fusiliers

TITLES

1761–3	The 104th (King's Volunteers) Regiment of Foot; disbanded.
1780–3	The 104th Regiment of Foot; disbanded.
1794–5	The 104th (Royal Manchester Volunteers) Regiment of Foot; drafted.
1806–16	The 104th Regiment of Foot; disbanded.
1839–50	The Hon. East India Company's 2nd Bengal (European) Regiment
1850–8	The Hon. East India Company's 2nd (Bengal European) Fusiliers
1858–61	The 2nd Bengal Fusiliers
1861–81	The 104th Bengal Fusiliers

PRINCIPAL CAMPAIGNS, BATTLES, etc.

1848–9	2nd Sikh War	1852–3	2nd Burma War
1849	Chillianwallah	1857	Indian Mutiny
1849	Gujerat	1857	Delhi

1881	Linked to the 101st (Royal Bengal Fusiliers) Regiment to form:
	THE ROYAL MUNSTER FUSILIERS

see page 203 101st (Royal Bengal Fusiliers) Regiment
see page 252 The Royal Munster Fusiliers

105th (Madras Light Infantry) Regiment

Previous Units with which the Regiment claims no connection

1761–3   The 105th (Queen's Own Royal Highlanders) Regiment; raised as a wedding escort to Queen Charlotte; disbanded.
1781–3   The 105th (Volunteers of Ireland) Regiment
1794–6   The 105th Regiment of Foot

TITLES

1839–58   The Hon. East India Company's 2nd Madras (European Light Infantry) Regiment
1858–61   The 2nd Madras (Light Infantry) Regiment
1861–81   The 105th (Madras Light Infantry) Regiment
(The Regiment was in the pay of the East India Company until 1861 when it became a Queen's Regiment. It came to England for the first time in 1874.)

PRINCIPAL CAMPAIGNS, BATTLES, etc.

1897   Tirah   1900–2   South Africa

MOTTO

'Cede Nullis' (Yield to none)

1881   Linked to the 51st (2nd Yorkshire West Riding) Regiment to form:
THE KING'S OWN YORKSHIRE LIGHT INFANTRY

see page 154 51st (2nd Yorkshire West Riding) Regiment
see page 235 The King's Own Yorkshire Light Infantry
see page 272 The Light Infantry

The 106th Bombay Light Infantry Regiment

The Regiment came to England for the first time in 1871.

TITLES

1826–40	The Hon. East India Co.'s 2nd Bombay European Regiment
1840–58	2nd Bombay European Light Infantry
1858–61	The 2nd Bombay Light Infantry Regiment
1862–81	The 106th Bombay Light Infantry Regiment

PRINCIPAL CAMPAIGNS, BATTLES, etc.

1856	Persia	1856	Bushire
1856	Reshire	1857	Kooshab

1881   Linked to the 68th (Durham Light Infantry) Regiment of Foot to form:
THE DURHAM LIGHT INFANTRY

see page 168 68th (Durham Light Infantry) Regiment of Foot
see page 243 The Durham Light Infantry
see page 272 The Light Infantry

The 107th Bengal Infantry Regiment

The 108th (Madras Infantry) Regiment

TITLES

1760–3	The 108th Regiment of Foot; disbanded.
1794–6	The 108th Regiment of Foot; disbanded, and troops dispersed between 64th and 85th Foot.
1854–8	The Honourable East India Company's 3rd (Madras Infantry) Regiment
1858–61	The 3rd (Madras) Regiment
1861–81	The 108th (Madras Infantry) Regiment

PRINCIPAL CAMPAIGNS, BATTLES, etc.

1857–8	Indian Mutiny	1878–80	2nd Afghan War

1881	Linked to the 27th (Inniskilling) Regiment of Foot to form:
	THE ROYAL INNISKILLING FUSILIERS

see page 124   27th (Inniskilling) Regiment of Foot
see page 213   The Royal Inniskilling Fusiliers
see page 273   The Royal Irish Rangers (27th (Inniskilling) 83rd and 87th)

The 109th (Bombay Infantry) Regiment

PRINCIPAL CAMPAIGNS, BATTLES, etc.

1858	Central India	1858	Jhansi
1858	Ratgur	1858	Kouch
1858	Barodia	1858	Calpe
1858	Sangor	1858	Morar
1858	Garrakota	1858	Gwalior
1858	Muddenpore	1900	South Africa
1858	Betura		

NICKNAMES

The German Mob   The Brass Heads

The Cameronians (Scottish Rifles)

1881	Formed by the linking of the 26th Cameronian Regiment and the 90th Perthshire Light Infantry, which became respectively the 1st and 2nd Battalions of the Regiment, the County Regiment of Lanarkshire and Scotland's only Rifle Regiment.

PRINCIPAL CAMPAIGNS, BATTLES, etc.

1899–1902	South Africa	1939–45	2ND WORLD WAR
1900	Spion Kop		Battle honours
	Relief of Ladysmith		selected to appear on the Colours:
1914–18	1ST WORLD WAR		Odon
	Battle honours		Scheldt
	selected to appear on		Rhineland
	the Colours:		Rhine
	Mons		North-West Europe,
	Marne, 1914, '18		1940, '44–5
	Neuve Chapelle		Sicily, 1943
	Loos		Anzio
	Somme, 1916, '18		Italy, 1943–4
	Ypres, 1917, '18		Chindits, 1944
	Hindenburg Line		Burma, 1942, '44
	Macedonia, 1916–18		
	Gallipoli, 1915–16	1950–3	Emergency in Malaya
	Palestine, 1917–18	1957	Operations in Muscat and Oman
1923	Punitive expedition in Kurdistan	1966–7	Aden
1936	Mufti's Revolt in Palestine		

14 May 1968	Being offered the alternatives of amalgamation or disbandment the Regiment chose disbandment. (*Note:* At a Council of the Colonels of all Scottish Regiments, held before publication of the White Paper of July 1967, it was unanimously agreed that there would be no further amalgamations and that it would be left to the Ministry of Defence to name the Regiment or Regiments which were to go.)

see page 123 26th Cameronian Regiment
see page 192 90th Perthshire Light Infantry

The Royal Inniskilling Fusiliers

1881   Formed by the linking of the 27th (Inniskilling) Regiment of Foot and the 108th (Madras Infantry) Regiment which became respectively the 1st and 2nd battalions of the Regiment.

PRINCIPAL CAMPAIGNS, BATTLES, etc.

1899–1902   South Africa
1900   Relief of Ladysmith

1914–18   1ST WORLD WAR
Battle honours selected to appear on the Colours:
Le Cateau
Somme, 1916, '18
Ypres, 1917, '18
St. Quentin
Hindenburg Line
France & Flanders
Macedonia, 1915–17
Landing at Helles
Gallipoli, 1915–16
Palestine, 1917–18

1939–45   2ND WORLD WAR
Battle honours selected to appear on the Colours:
North-West Europe, 1940
Djevel Tanngoucha
North Africa, 1942–3
Centuripe
Sicily, 1943
Garigliano Crossing
Cassino II
Italy, 1943–5
Yenangyaung, 1942
Burma, 1942–3

MOTTO

'Nec aspera terrent' (Nor do difficulties deter)

1 July 1968   Amalgamated with The Royal Ulster Rifles and The Royal Irish Fusiliers to form:
THE ROYAL IRISH RANGERS

see page 247   The Royal Ulster Rifles
see page 248   The Royal Irish Fusiliers
see page 273   The Royal Irish Rangers

The Gloucestershire Regiment

1881	Formed by the linking of the 28th (North Gloucestershire) Regiment of Foot and the 161st (South Gloucestershire) Regiment of Foot which became respectively the 1st and 2nd battalions of the Regiment.

PRINCIPAL CAMPAIGNS, BATTLES, etc.

1889–1902	South Africa	1939–45	2ND WORLD WAR
1899	Defence of Ladysmith		Battle honours
1900	Relief of Kimberley, Paardeburg		selected to appear on the Colours:
			Defence of Escaut
1914–18	1ST WORLD WAR		Cassel
	Battle honours		Mont Pincon
	selected to appear on		Falaise
	the Colours:		North-West Europe, 1940, '44–5
	Mons		Taukyan
	Ypres, 1914, '15, '17		Paungde
	Loos		Pinwe
	Somme, 1916, '18		Myitson
	Lys		Burma, 1942, '44–5
	Selle		
	Vittorio Veneto		
	Doiran, 1917	1950–1	KOREAN WAR
	Sari Bair		'Imjin', Korea, 1950–1
	Baghdad		

NICKNAMES

The Back Numbers   The Glorious Gloucestershires

The Worcestershire Regiment

1881	Formed by the linking of the 29th (Worcestershire) Regiment of Foot and the 36th (Herefordshire) Regiment of Foot which became respectively the 1st and 2nd battalions of the Regiment.

PRINCIPAL CAMPAIGNS, BATTLES, etc.

1900–2	South Africa	1939–45 2ND WORLD WAR
1914–18	1ST WORLD WAR	Battle honours

1900–2   South Africa

1914–18   1ST WORLD WAR
Battle honours
selected to appear on
the Colours:
Mons
Ypres, 1914, '15, '17,
  '18
Gheluvelt
Neuve Chapelle
Somme, 1916, '18
Cambrai, 1917, '18
Lys
Italy, 1917, '18
Gallipoli, 1915–16
Baghdad

1939–45   2ND WORLD WAR
Battle honours
selected to appear on
the Colours:
Mont Pincon
Seine, 1944
Geilenkirchen
Goch
North-West Europe,
  1940, '44–5
Keren
Gazala
Kohima
Mandalay
Burma, 1944–5

NICKNAMES

The Old and Bold   The Saucy Greens

MOTTO

Firm

28 February 1970	Amalgamated with The Sherwood Foresters to form: **THE WORCESTERSHIRE AND SHERWOOD FORESTERS REGIMENT** (29th/45th FOOT)

see page 230   The Sherwood Foresters
see page 274   The Worcestershire and Sherwood Foresters Regiment (29th/45th Foot)

The East Lancashire Regiment

| 1881 | Formed by the linking of the 30th (Cambridgeshire) Regiment of Foot, and the 59th (2nd Nottinghamshire) Regiment of Foot, which became respectively the 1st and 2nd battalions of the Regiment. |

PRINCIPAL CAMPAIGNS, BATTLES, etc.

1895	Chitral	1914–18	Kut al Amara, 1917
1900–2	South Africa		
		1939–45	2ND WORLD WAR
1914–18	1ST WORLD WAR		Battle honours
	Battle honours		selected to appear on
	selected to appear on		the Colours:
	the Colours:		Dunkirk, 1940
	Retreat from Mons		Falaise
	Marne, 1914		Lower Maas
	Aisne, 1914, '18		Ourthe
	Neuve Chapelle		Reichswald
	Ypres, 1915, '17, '18		Weeze
	Somme, 1916, '18		Aller
	Arras, 1917, '18		Madagascar
	Doiran, 1917, '18		Pinwe
	Helles		Burma, 1944–5

MOTTO

'Spectamur agendo' (By our deeds we are known)

| 1 July 1958 | Amalgamated with The South Lancashire Regiment to form: THE LANCASHIRE REGIMENT (PRINCE OF WALES'S VOLUNTEERS) |

see page 225 The South Lancashire Regiment
see page 265 The Lancashire Regiment (Prince of Wales's Volunteers)
see page 276 The Queen's Lancashire Regiment

The East Surrey Regiment

1881	Formed by the linking of the 31st (Huntingdonshire) Regiment of Foot, and the 70th (Surrey) Regiment of Foot, which became respectively the 1st and 2nd battalions of the Regiment.

PRINCIPAL CAMPAIGNS, BATTLES, etc.

1885	Suakin	1939–45	2ND WORLD WAR
1899–1902	South Africa		Battle honours
1900	Relief of Ladysmith		selected to appear on the Colours:
1914–18	1ST WORLD WAR		Dunkirk, 1940
	Battle honours		North-West Europe, 1940
	selected to appear on the Colours:		Oued Zarga
	Mons		Longstop Hill, 1943
	Marne, 1914		North Africa, 1942–3
	La Bassée, 1914		Sicily, 1943
	Ypres, 1915, '17, '18		Sangro
	Loos		Cassino
	Somme, 1916, '18		Italy, 1943–5
	Albert, 1916, '18		Malaya, 1941–2
	Cambrai, 1917, '18		
	Selle		
	Doiran, 1918		

14 October 1959	Amalgamated with The Queen's Royal Regiment (West Surrey) to form: THE QUEEN'S ROYAL SURREY REGIMENT
31 December 1966	Redesignated: The 1st Battalion THE QUEEN'S REGIMENT (QUEEN'S SURREYS)
1969	Redesignated: The 1st Battalion THE QUEEN'S REGIMENT and County affiliation ceased

see page 75   The Queen's Royal Regiment (West Surrey)
see page 271   The Queen's Regiment

The Duke of Cornwall's Light Infantry

1881	Formed by the linking of the 32nd (Cornwall) Light Infantry Regiment and the 46th (South Devonshire) Regiment which became respectively the 1st and 2nd battalions of the Regiment.

PRINCIPAL CAMPAIGNS, BATTLES, etc.

1882	Egypt	1914–18	Gaza
1882	Tel-el-Kebir		
1884–5	Nile	1939–45	2ND WORLD WAR
1889–1902	South Africa		Honours selected to appear on the Colours:
1914–18	1ST WORLD WAR		Hill 112
	Battle honours		Mont Pincon
	selected to appear on		Nederrijn
	the Colours:		Geilenkirchen
	Mons		Rhineland
	Marne, 1914		North-West Europe,
	Ypres, 1915, '17		1940, '44–5
	Somme, 1916, '18		Gazala
	Arras, 1917		Medjez Plain
	Passchendaele		Cassino II
	Cambrai, 1917, '18		Incontro
	Sambre		
	Doiran, 1917, '18		

NICKNAME

The Docs

MOTTO

One and All

6 October 1959	Amalgamated with The Somerset Light Infantry to form: **THE SOMERSET AND CORNWALL LIGHT INFANTRY**

see page 97 The Somerset Light Infantry
see page 268 The Somerset and Cornwall Light Infantry
see page 272 The Light Infantry

The Duke of Wellington's Regiment (West Riding)

1881   Formed by the linking of the 33rd (Duke of Wellington's) Regiment of Foot and the 76th Regiment of Foot, which became respectively the 1st and 2nd battalions of the Regiment. Until 1920, the Regiment was known as The Duke of Wellington's (West Riding Regiment).

PRINCIPAL CAMPAIGNS, BATTLES, etc.

1899–1902	South Africa	1939–45	1ST WORLD WAR
1900	Relief of Kimberley		Battle honours selected to appear on the Colours:
1914–18	1ST WORLD WAR		Dunkirk, 1940
	Battle honours selected to appear on the Colours:		St. Valery-en-Caux
	Mons		Fontenoy La Pesnil
	Marne, 1914, '18		North-West Europe, 1940, '44–5
	Ypres, 1914, '15, '17		Djebel Bou Aoukaz, 1943
	Hill 60		Anzio
	Somme, 1916, '18		Monte Ceco
	Arras, 1917, '18		Sittang, 1942
	Lys		Chindits, 1944
	Cambrai, 1917, '18		Burma, 1942–4
	Piave		
	Landing of Suvla		
1919	Afghanistan (3rd Afghan War)		

MOTTO

Virtutis fortuna comes (Fortune accompanies honour)

see page 130   33rd (Duke of Wellington's) Regiment of Foot
see page 176   76th Regiment of Foot

The Border Regiment

1881   Formed by the linking of The 34th (Cumberland) Regiment of Foot and The 55th (Westmoreland) Regiment of Foot, which became respectively the 1st and 2nd battalions of the Regiment.

PRINCIPAL CAMPAIGNS, BATTLES, etc.

1889–1902	South Africa	1919	Afghanistan (3rd
1900	Relief of Ladysmith		Afghan War)

1914–18

1ST WORLD WAR
Battle honours
selected to appear on
the Colours:
Ypres, 1914, '15, '17
Langemarck, 1914,
  '17
Somme, 1916, '18
Arras, 1917, '18
Cambrai, 1917, '18
Lys
France & Flanders,
  1914–18
Vittorio Veneto
Macedonia, 1915–18
Gallipoli, 1915–16

1939–45

2ND WORLD WAR
Battle honours
selected to appear on
the Colours:
Dunkirk, 1940
Arnhem, 1944
North-West Europe,
  1940, '44
Tobruk, 1941
Landing in Sicily
Imphal
Myinmu Bridgehead
Meiktila
Chindits, 1944
Burma, 1943–5

1 October 1959   Amalgamated with The King's Own Royal Regiment (Lancaster) to form:
THE KING'S OWN ROYAL BORDER REGIMENT

see page 79 The King's Own Royal Regiment (Lancaster)
see page 268 The King's Own Royal Border Regiment

The Royal Sussex Regiment

1881   Formed by the linking of the 35th Royal Sussex Regiment of Foot and the 107th (Bengal Infantry) Regiment, which became respectively the 1st and 2nd battalions of the Regiment.

PRINCIPAL CAMPAIGNS, BATTLES, etc.

1882	Egypt	1914–18	North-West Frontier,
1884–5	Nile		India, 1915,
1885	Abu Klea		1916–17
1900–2	South Africa		
		1939–45	2ND WORLD WAR
1914–18	1ST WORLD WAR		Battle honours
	Battle honours		selected to appear on
	selected to appear on		the Colours:
	the Colours:		North-West Europe,
	Retreat from Mons		1940
	Marne, 1914, '18		Abyssinia, 1941
	Ypres, 1914, '17, '18		Omars
	Somme, 1916, '18		Alam el Halfa
	Pilckem		El Alamein
	Hindenburg Line		Akarit
	Italy, 1917–18		North Africa, 1940–3
	Gallipoli, 1915		Cassino II
	Palestine, 1917–18		Italy, 1944–5
			Burma, 1943–5

NICKNAME

The Orange Lilies

31 December 1966   Redesignated:
The 3rd Battalion THE QUEEN'S REGIMENT (ROYAL SUSSEX)

1969   Redesignated:
The 3rd Battalion THE QUEEN'S REGIMENT and County affiliation ceased.

see page 271   The Queen's Regiment

The Royal Hampshire Regiment

1881   Formed by the linking of the 37th (North Hampshire) Regiment of Foot, and the 67th (South Hampshire) Regiment of Foot, which became respectively the 1st and 2nd battalions of the Regiment.

TITLES

1881–1946   The Hampshire Regiment
1946–70   The Royal Hampshire Regiment

PRINCIPAL CAMPAIGNS, BATTLES, etc.

1855–7	Burma	1939–45	2ND WORLD WAR
1900–2	South Africa		Battle honours selected to appear on the Colours:
1914–18	1ST WORLD WAR Battle honours selected to appear on the Colours:		Dunkirk, 1940
	Retreat from Mons		Normandy Landing
	Ypres, 1915, '17, '18		Caen
	Somme, 1916, '18		Rhine
	Arras, 1917, '18		Tebourba Gap
	Cambrai, 1917, '18		Hunt's Gap
	Doiran, 1917, '18		Salerno
	Landing at Helles		Casino II
	Suvla		Gothic Line
	Gaza		Malta, 1941–2
	Kut al Amara, 1915, '17		

NICKNAME

The Hampshire Tigers

In 1970 the Regiment was reduced to one company, the Minden Company. In October 1971 the decision was taken to reconstitute the 1st Battalion at full strength.

The South Staffordshire Regiment

| 1881 | Formed by the linking of the 38th (1st Staffordshire) Regiment of Foot and the 80th (Staffordshire Volunteers) Regiment of Foot, which became respectively the 1st and 2nd battalions of the Regiment. |

PRINCIPAL CAMPAIGNS, BATTLES, etc.

1882	Egypt	1914–18	Suvla
1884–5	Nile		
	Kirbekan	1939–45	2ND WORLD WAR
1900–2	South Africa		Battle honours selected to appear on
1914–18	1ST WORLD WAR		the Colours:
	Battle honours		Caen
	selected to appear on		Noyers
	the Colours:		Falaise
	Mons		Arnhem, 1944
	Marne, 1914		North-West Europe,
	Aisne, 1914, '18		1940, '44
	Ypres, 1914, '17		North Africa, 1940
	Loos		Landing in Sicily
	Somme, 1916, '18		Sicily, 1943
	Cambrai, 1917, '18		Chindits, 1944
	St. Quentin Canal		Burma, 1944
	Vittorio Veneto		

| 31 January 1959 | Amalgamated with The North Staffordshire Regiment to form:
 THE STAFFORDSHIRE REGIMENT (PRINCE OF WALES'S) |

see page 241 The North Staffordshire Regiment
see page 267 The Staffordshire Regiment (Prince of Wales's)

The Dorset Regiment

<table>
<tr><td>1881</td><td>Formed by the linking of the 39th (Dorsetshire) Regiment of Foot and the 54th (West Norfolk) Regiment of Foot, which became respectively the 1st and 2nd battalions of the Regiment.
(Until 1951 the Regiment was called The Dorsetshire Regiment, after which the title was varied as above.)</td></tr>
</table>

PRINCIPAL CAMPAIGNS, BATTLES, etc.

1877–8	Tirah	1914–18	Shaiba
1899–1902	South Africa		Ctesiphon
1900	Relief of Ladysmith		
1900	Alleman's Nek	1939–45	2ND WORLD WAR Battle honours
1914–18	1ST WORLD WAR Battle honours selected to appear on the Colours:		selected to appear on the Colours: St. Omer-La-Bassee
	Marne, 1914		Normandy Landing
	Mons		Caen
	Ypres, 1915, '17		Arnhem, 1944
	Somme, 1916, '18		Aam
	Khan Bagdadi		Geilenkirchen
	Hindenburg Line		Landing in Sicily
	Suvla		Malta, 1940–2
	Sambre		Kohima
	Gaza		Mandalay

MOTTO

'Primus in Indis' (First in India)

17 May 1958	Amalgamated with The Devonshire Regiment of Foot to form: THE DEVONSHIRE AND DORSET REGIMENT

see page 93 The Devonshire Regiment
see page 265 The Devonshire and Dorset Regiment

The South Lancashire Regiment (The Prince of Wales's Volunteers)

1881   Formed by the linking of the 40th (2nd Somersetshire) Regiment of Foot and the 82nd (The Prince of Wales's Volunteers) Regiment of Foot, which became respectively the 1st and 2nd battalions of the Regiment.

PRINCIPAL CAMPAIGNS, BATTLES, etc.

1899–1902	South Africa	1914–18	Baluchistan, 1918
1900	Relief of Ladysmith		
		1939–45	2ND WORLD WAR
1914–18	1ST WORLD WAR		Battle honours
	Battle honours		selected to appear on
	selected to appear on		the Colours:
	the Colours:		Dunkirk, 1940
	Mons		Normandy Landing
	Aisne, 1914, '18		Bourguebus Ridge
	Messines, 1914, '17, '18		Falaise
	Ypres, 1914, '15, '17, '18		Rhineland
	Somme, 1916, '18		North-West Europe, 1940, '44–5
	Lys		Madagascar
	Doiran, 1917, '18		North Arakan
	Sari Bair		Kohima
	Baghdad		Nyaungu Bridgehead

1 July 1958   Amalgamated with The East Lancashire Regiment to form:

THE LANCASHIRE REGIMENT (PRINCE OF WALES'S VOLUNTEERS)

see page 216 The East Lancashire Regiment
see page 265 The Lancashire Regiment (Prince of Wales's Volunteers)
see page 276 The Queen's Lancashire Regiment

The Welch Regiment

1881	Formed by the linking of the 41st (The Welsh) Regiment of Foot and the 69th (South Lincolnshire) Regiment of Foot, which became respectively the 1st and 2nd battalions of the Regiment.

TITLES

1881–1920	The Welsh Regiment
1920–69	The Welch Regiment

PRINCIPAL CAMPAIGNS, BATTLES, etc.

1899–1902	South Africa	1939–45	2ND WORLD WAR
1900	Relief of Kimberley		Battle honours selected to appear on the Colours:
1914–18	1ST WORLD WAR		Falaise
	Battle honours		Lower Maas
	selected to appear on		Reichswald
	the Colours:		Croce
	Aisne, 1914, '18		Italy, 1943–5
	Ypres, 1914, '15, '17		Canea
	Gheluvelt		Kyauknyaung
	Loos		Bridgehead
	Somme, 1916, '18		Sittang, 1945
	Pilckem		Burma, 1944–5
	Cambrai, 1917, '18		
	Macedonia, 1915–18		
	Gallipoli, 1915	1951–2	KOREAN WAR
	Gaza		Korea, 1951–2

MOTTO

'Gwell angau na Chywilydd' (Death rather than dishonour)

June 1969	Amalgamated with The South Wales Borderers to form: THE ROYAL REGIMENT OF WALES (24th/41st FOOT)

see page 117 The South Wales Borderers
see page 274 The Royal Regiment of Wales (24th/41st Foot)

The Black Watch
(Royal Highland Regiment)

1881   Formed by the linking of the 42nd (Royal Highland–The Black Watch) and the 73rd (Perthshire) Regiment of Foot, which became respectively the 1st and 2nd battalions of the Regiment.

PRINCIPAL CAMPAIGNS, BATTLES, etc.

1882–4	Egypt	1914–18	Kut al Amara, 1917
1882	Tel-el-Kebir		
1884–5	Nile	1939–45	2ND WORLD WAR
1885	Kirbekan		Battle honours
1899–1902	South Africa		selected to appear on
			the Colours:
1914–18	1ST WORLD WAR		Falaise Road
	Battle honours		Rhine
	selected to appear on		Tobruk, 1941
	the Colours:		El Alamein
	Marne, 1914, '18		Akarit
	Ypres, 1914, '17, '18		Tunis
	Loos		Sicily, 1943
	Somme, 1916, '18		Cassino II
	Arras, 1917, '18		Crete
	Lys		Burma, 1944
	Hindenburg Line		
	Doiran, 1917	1952–3	KOREAN WAR
	Megiddo		Korea, 1952–3
			The Hook, 1952

see page 140   42nd (Royal Highland–The Black Watch)
see page 173   73rd (Perthshire) Regiment of Foot

The Oxfordshire and Buckinghamshire Light Infantry

1881	Formed by the linking of the 43rd (Monmouthshire Light Infantry) Regiment and the 52nd (Oxfordshire Light Infantry) Regiment, which became the 1st and 2nd battalions of the Regiment.

TITLES

1881–1908	The Oxfordshire Light Infantry
1908–58	The Oxfordshire and Buckinghamshire Light Infantry

PRINCIPAL CAMPAIGNS, BATTLES, etc.

1900–2	South Africa	1914–18	Defence of Kut al
1900	Relief of Kimberley		Amara

1914–18	1ST WORLD WAR	1939–45	2ND WORLD WAR
	Battle honours selected to appear on the Colours:		Battle honours selected to appear on the Colours:
	Mons		Cassel
	Ypres, 1914, '17		Ypres-Comines Canal
	Langemarck, 1914, '17		Normandy Landing
			Pegasus Bridge
	Nonne Bosschen		Reichswald
	Somme, 1916, '18		Rhine
	Cambrai, 1917, '18		Enfidaville
	Piave		Salerno
	Doiran, 1917, '18		Anzio
	Ctesiphon		Gemmano Ridge

7 November 1958	Redesignated 1st Green Jackets, 43rd and 52nd, and formed part of the: Green Jackets Brigade
1 January 1966	The Green Jackets Brigade was designated: THE ROYAL GREEN JACKETS

see page 275 The Royal Green Jackets
see page 141 43rd (Monmouthshire Light Infantry) Regiment
see page 151 52nd (Oxfordshire Light Infantry) Regiment

The Essex Regiment

1881	Formed by the linking of the 44th (East Essex) Regiment of Foot and the 56th (West Essex) Regiment of Foot, which became respectively the 1st and 2nd battalions of the Regiment.

PRINCIPAL CAMPAIGNS, BATTLES, etc.

1884–5	Nile	1939–45	2ND WORLD WAR
1899–1902	South Africa		Battle honours selected to appear on the Colours:
1914–18	1ST WORLD WAR Battle honours selected to appear on the Colours: La Cateau Marne, 1914 Ypres, 1916, '17 Loos Somme, 1916, '18 Arras, 1917, '18 Cambrai, 1917, '18 Selle Gallipoli, 1915–16 Gaza		Zetten North-West Europe, 1940, '44–5 Palmyra Tobruk, 1941 Defence of Alamein Line Enfidaville Sangro Villa Grande Cassino I Chindits, 1944

MOTTO

'Montis Insignia Calpe' (Arms of the rock of Gibraltar)

2 June 1958	Amalgamated with the Bedfordshire and Hertfordshire Regiment to form: THE 3rd EAST ANGLIAN REGIMENT (16th/44th FOOT) (Soubriquet—'Pompadours')
1 September 1964	The Regiment was redesignated: The 3rd (16th/44th Foot) Battalion THE ROYAL ANGLIAN REGIMENT
1 July 1968	'(16th/44th)' dropped from the title. County affiliation ceased.

see page 103 The Bedfordshire and Hertfordshire Regiment
see page 270 The Royal Anglian Regiment

The Sherwood Foresters (Nottinghamshire and Derbyshire Regiment)

1881   Formed by the linking of the 45th (Nottinghamshire Regiment) Sherwood Foresters and the 95th Derbyshire Regiment of Foot, which became the 1st and 2nd battalions respectively of the Regiment.

PRINCIPAL CAMPAIGNS, BATTLES, etc.

1882	Egypt	1914–18	Gallipoli, 1915
1882–8	Sikkim Expedition		
1897–8	Tirah	1922	Chanak (Turkish/ Greek War)
1899–1902	South Africa		

1914–18   **1ST WORLD WAR**
Battle honours selected to appear on the Colours:
Aisne, 1914, '18
Neuve Chapelle
Loos
Somme, 1916, '18
Ypres, 1917, '18
Cambrai, 1917, '18
St. Quentin Canal
France & Flanders, 1914–18
Italy, 1917–18

1939–40   **2ND WORLD WAR**
Battle honours selected to appear on the Colours:
Norway, 1940
Gazala
El Alamein
Tunis
Salerno
Anzio
Campoleone
Gothic Line
Coriana
Singapore Island

28 February 1970   Amalgamated with The Worcestershire Regiment to form: THE WORCESTERSHIRE AND SHERWOOD FORESTERS REGIMENT (29th/45th FOOT)

see page 215   The Worcestershire Regiment
see page 274   The Worcestershire and Sherwood Foresters Regiment (29th/45th Foot)

The Loyal Regiment (North Lancashire)

1881	Formed by the linking of the 47th (Lancashire) Regiment of Foot and the 81st (Loyal Lincoln Volunteers) Regiment of Foot, which became respectively the 1st and 2nd battalions of the Regiment.

PRINCIPAL CAMPAIGNS, BATTLES, etc.

1899–1902 South Africa

1914–18 1ST WORLD WAR
Battle honours selected to appear on the Colours:
Mons
Aisne, 1914, '18
Ypres, 1914, '17, '18
Somme, 1916, '18
Lys
Hindenburg Line
Suvla
Gaza
Baghdad
Kilimanjaro

1939–45 **2ND WORLD WAR**
Battle honours selected to appear on the Colours:
Djebel Kesskiss
Gueriat el Atach Ridge
North Africa, 1943
Anzio
Fiesole
Monte Grande
Italy, 1944–5
Johore
Singapore Island

MOTTO

'Loyaute m'oblige' (My loyalty compels me)
(This Motto was originally the family motto of Colonel Albermarle Berti, later 9th Earl of Lindsey, who raised The Loyal Lincoln Volunteers which later became the 81st Foot.)

March 1970	Amalgamated with The Lancashire Regiment (Prince of Wales's Volunteers) to form: THE QUEEN'S LANCASHIRE REGIMENT

see page 265 The Lancashire Regiment (Prince of Wales's Volunteers)
see page 276 The Queen's Lancashire Regiment

The Northamptonshire Regiment

1881 — Formed by the linking of the 48th (Northamptonshire) Regiment of Foot and the 58th (Rutlandshire) Regiment of Foot, which became respectively the 1st and 2nd battalions of the Regiment.

PRINCIPAL CAMPAIGNS, BATTLES, etc.

1897	Tirah	1939–45	2ND WORLD WAR
1899	Modder River		Battle honours
1899–1902	South Africa		selected to appear on the Colours:
1914–18	1ST WORLD WAR		North-West Europe, 1940, '45
	Battle honours		North Africa, 1942–3
	selected to appear on the Colours:		Garigliano Crossing
	Mons		Anzio
	Marne, 1914		Cassino II
	Aisne, 1914, '18		Italy, 1943–5
	Ypres, 1914, '17		Yu
	Neuve Chapelle		Imphal
	Loos		Myinamnu Bridgehead
	Somme, 1916, '18		Burma, 1943–5
	Arras, 1917, '18		
	Epehy		
	Gaza		

MOTTO
'Montis Insignia Calpe' (The arms of Gibraltar)

1 June 1960 — Amalgamated with The Royal Lincolnshire Regiment to form:
THE 2nd EAST ANGLIAN REGIMENT (DUCHESS OF GLOUCESTER'S OWN LINCOLNSHIRE AND NORTHAMPTONSHIRE)

1 September 1964 — The above unit was redesignated:
The 2nd (Duchess of Gloucester's Own Lincolnshire and Northamptonshire) Battalion
THE ROYAL ANGLIAN REGIMENT

1 July 1968 — Redesignated:
2nd Battalion THE ROYAL ANGLIAN REGIMENT
and the County affiliation ceased.

see page 91 — The Royal Lincolnshire Regiment
see page 270 — The Royal Anglian Regiment

The Royal Berkshire Regiment (Princess Charlotte of Wales's)

1881	Formed by the linking of the 49th Princess Charlotte of Wales's Hertfordshire Regiment of Foot and the 66th (Berkshire) Regiment of Foot, which became respectively the 1st and 2nd battalions Princess Charlotte of Wales's Berkshire Regiment. In 1885 the title 'Royal' was conferred. In 1921 the title was varied to The Royal Berkshire Regiment (Princess Charlotte of Wales's).

PRINCIPAL CAMPAIGNS, BATTLES, etc.

1882	Egypt	1914–18	Vittorio Veneto
1885	Suakim		Doiran, 1917, '18
1885	Nile		
1885	Tofrek	1939–45	2ND WORLD WAR
1899–1902	South Africa		Battle honours
			selected to appear on
1914–18	1ST WORLD WAR		the Colours:
	Battle honours		Dyle
	selected to appear on		Dunkirk, 1940
	the Colours:		Normandy Landing
	Mons		Rhine
	Ypres, 1914, '17		Sicily, 1943
	Neuve Chapelle		Damiano
	Loos		Anzio
	Somme, 1916, '18		Kohima
	Arras, 1917, '18		Mandalay
	Cambrai, 1917, '18		Burma, 1943–5
	Selle		

9 June 1959	Amalgamated with The Wiltshire Regiment (Duke of Edinburgh's) to form: THE DUKE OF EDINBURGH'S ROYAL REGIMENT (BERKSHIRE AND WILTSHIRE)

see page 239 The Wiltshire Regiment (Duke of Edinburgh's)
see page 267 The Duke of Edinburgh's Royal Regiment (Berkshire and Wiltshire)

The Queen's Own Royal West Kent Regiment

1881	Formed by the linking of the 50th (The Queen's Own) Regiment of Foot and the 97th (The Earl of Ulster's) Regiment of Foot, which became respectively the 1st and 2nd battalions of the Regiment. Till 1921 the title was the Royal West Kent Regiment (Queen's Own).

PRINCIPAL CAMPAIGNS, BATTLES, etc.

1882	Egypt	1914–18	Sharqat
1884–5	Nile		
1900–2	South Africa	1938	Palestine
1914–18	1ST WORLD WAR Battle honours selected to appear on the Colours: Mons Ypres, 1914, '15, '17, '18 Hill 60 Somme, 1916, '18 Vimy, 1917 Italy, 1917–18 Gallipoli, 1915 Gaza Defence of Kut al Amara	1939–45	2ND WORLD WAR Battle honours selected to appear on the Colours: North-West Europe, 1940 El Alamein Medjez Plain Centuripe Sangro Cassino Trasimene Line Argenta Gap Malta, 1940–2 Defence of Kohima
		1951	Malaya

MOTTO
'Quo fas et gloria ducunt' (Whither right and glory lead)

1 March 1961	Amalgamated with The Buffs (Royal East Kent) Regiment to form: THE QUEEN'S OWN BUFFS, ROYAL KENT REGIMENT
31 December 1966	Redesignated: 2nd Battalion THE QUEEN'S REGIMENT
see page 77	The Buffs (Royal East Kent) Regiment
see page 271	The Queen's Regiment

The King's Own Yorkshire Light Infantry

1881	Formed by the linking of the 51st (2nd Yorkshire West Riding) Regiment and the 105th (Madras Light Infantry) Regiment, which became respectively the 1st and 2nd battalions of the Regiment.

PRINCIPAL CAMPAIGNS, BATTLES, etc.

1885–7	3rd Burma War	1939–45	2ND WORLD WAR
1889–1902	South Africa		Battle honours selected to appear on the Colours:
1914–18	1ST WORLD WAR		Norway, 1940
	Battle honours selected to appear on the Colours:		Fontenay le Pesnil
	Le Cateau		North-West Europe, 1944–5
	Marne, 1914, '18		Argoub Sellah
	Messines, 1914, '17, '18		Sicily, 1943
	Ypres, 1914, '15, '17, '18		Salerno
	Somme, 1916, '18		Minturno
	Cambrai, 1917, '18		Anzio
	Havrincourt		Germano Ridge
	Sambre		Burma, 1942
	Italy, 1917–18		
	Macedonia, 1915–17		

MOTTO

'Cede nullis' (Yield to none)

10 July 1968	Amalgamated with The Somerset and Cornwall Light Infantry, and The King's Shropshire Light Infantry, and The Durham Light Infantry to form: THE LIGHT INFANTRY

see page 268 The Somerset and Cornwall Light Infantry
see page 236 The King's Shropshire Light Infantry
see page 243 The Durham Light Infantry
see page 272 The Light Infantry

The King's Shropshire Light Infantry

1881   Formed by the linking of the 53rd (Shropshire) Regiment of Foot and the 85th (Bucks Volunteers) (The King's Light Infantry) Regiment, which became respectively the 1st and 2nd battalions of the Regiment.

Originally the Regiment was named The Shropshire Regiment (King's Light Infantry), then The King's Light Infantry (Shropshire Regiment), then The King's (Shropshire Light Infantry). The present title was adopted in 1920.

PRINCIPAL CAMPAIGNS, BATTLES, etc.

1882	Égypt	1930–1	North-West Frontier
1885	Suakin		
1889–1902	South Africa	1939–45	2ND WORLD WAR
	Modder River, Relief		Battle honours
	of Kimberley,		selected to appear on
	Paardeberg, Orange		the Colours:
	Free State,		Dunkirk, 1940
	Transvaal		Normandy Landing
			Antwerp
1914–18	1ST WORLD WAR		Venraij
	Battle honours		Hochwald
	selected to appear on		Bremen
	the Colours:		North-West Europe,
	Armentieres, 1914		1940, '44–5
	Ypres, 1915, '17		Tunis
	Frezenberg		Anzio
	Somme, 1916, '18		Italy, 1943–5
	Arras, 1917, '18		
	Cambrai, 1917, '18	1945–6	Palestine
	Bligny	1951–2	KOREAN WAR
	Epehy		Korea, 1951–2
	Doiran, 1917, '18		Kowang-San
	Jerusalem	1955–6	Kenya

MOTTO

'Aucto splendore resurgo' (I rise again with increased splendour)

| 10 July 1958 | Amalgamated with The Somerset and Cornwall Light Infantry, and The King's Own Yorkshire Light Infantry, and the Durham Light Infantry to form: THE LIGHT INFANTRY |

see page 268 The Somerset and Cornwall Light Infantry
see page 235 The King's Own Yorkshire Light Infantry
see page 243 The Durham Light Infantry
see page 272 The Light Infantry

The Middlesex Regiment (Duke of Cambridge's Own)

1881	Formed by the linking of the 57th (West Middlesex) Regiment of Foot and the 77th (East Middlesex) Regiment of Foot, which became respectively the 1st and 2nd battalions of the Regiment.

PRINCIPAL CAMPAIGNS, BATTLES, etc.

1900–2	South Africa	1939–45	2ND WORLD WAR
1900	Relief of Ladysmith		Battle honours selected to appear on the Colours:
1914–18	1ST WORLD WAR		Dunkirk, 1940
	Battle honours selected to appear on the Colours:		Normandy Landing
			Caen
	Mons		Mont Pincon
	Marne, 1914		Rhine
	Ypres, 1915, '17, '18		El Alamein
	Albert, 1916, '18		Akarit
	Bazentin		Sicily, 1943
	Cambrai, 1917, '18		Anzio
	Hindenburg Line		Hong Kong
	Suvla		
	Jerusalem	1950–1	KOREAN WAR
	Mesopotamia, 1917–18		Naktong Bridgehead
			Korea, 1950–1

31 December 1966	Redesignated: The 4th Battalion THE QUEEN'S REGIMENT (MIDDLESEX)
1 July 1968	Redesignated: 4th Battalion THE QUEEN'S REGIMENT and the County affiliation ceased.

see page 271 The Queen's Regiment
see page 156 57th (West Middlesex) Regiment of Foot
see page 177 77th (East Middlesex) Regiment of Foot

The Wiltshire Regiment
(Duke of Edinburgh's)

1881   Formed by the linking of the 62nd (Wiltshire) Regiment of Foot and the 99th (The Duke of Edinburgh's) Regiment of Foot, which became respectively the 1st and 2nd battalions of the Regiment.

PRINCIPAL CAMPAIGNS, BATTLES, etc.

1900–2   South Africa   1914–18   Baghdad

1914–18	1ST WORLD WAR	1939–45	2ND WORLD WAR
	Battle honours selected to appear on the Colours:		Battle honours selected to appear on the Colours:
	Mons		Defence of Arras
	Messines, 1914, '17, '18		Hill 112
			Maltot
	Ypres, 1914, '17		Mont Pincon
	Somme, 1916, '18		Seine, 1944
	Arras, 1917		Garigliano Crossing
	Bapaume, 1918		Anzio
	Macedonia, 1915–18		Rome
	Gallipoli, 1915–18		North Arakan
	Palestine, 1917–18		

9 June 1959   Amalgamated with The Royal Berkshire Regiment to form:
THE DUKE OF EDINBURGH'S ROYAL REGIMENT (BERKSHIRE AND WILTSHIRE)

see page 233   The Royal Berkshire Regiment
see page 267   The Duke of Edinburgh's Royal Regiment (Berkshire and Wiltshire)

The Manchester Regiment

<table>
<tr><td>1881</td><td colspan="3">Formed by the linking of the 63rd (West Suffolk) Regiment of Foot and the 96th Regiment of Foot, which became respectively 1st and 2nd battalions of the Regiment.</td></tr>
</table>

PRINCIPAL CAMPAIGNS, BATTLES, etc.

1882	Egypt	1914–18	Baghdad
1899–1902	South Africa		
1900	Defence of Ladysmith	1939–45	2ND WORLD WAR
			Battle honours
1914–18	1ST WORLD WAR		selected to appear on
	Battle honours		the Colours:
	selected to appear on		Dyle
	the Colours:		Defence of Arras
	Mons		Caen
	Givenchy, 1914		Scheldt
	Ypres, 1915, '17, '18		Lower Maas
	Somme, 1916, '18		Roer
	Hindenburg Line		Reischswald
	Piave		Gothic Line
	Macedonia		Malta, 1940
	Gallipoli, 1915		Kohima
	Megiddo		

1 September 1958 — Amalgamated with The King's Regiment (Liverpool) to form:
THE KING'S REGIMENT (MANCHESTER AND LIVERPOOL)

1969 — The title became:
THE KING'S REGIMENT
and the County affiliation ceased.

see page 87 The King's Regiment (Liverpool)
see page 266 The King's Regiment

The North Staffordshire Regiment (The Prince of Wales's)

1881	Formed by the linking of the 64th (2nd Staffordshire) Regiment of Foot and the 98th (The Prince of Wales's) Regiment of Foot, which became respectively the 1st and 2nd battalions of the Regiment.

PRINCIPAL CAMPAIGNS, BATTLES, etc.

1896	Hafir (Dongola Expedition)	1919	Afghanistan (3rd Afghan War)
1900–2	South Africa	1939–45	2ND WORLD WAR
1914–18	1ST WORLD WAR		Battle honours selected to appear on the Colours:
	Battle honours selected to appear on the Colours:		Dyle
	Armentieres, 1914		Ypres-Comines Canal
	Somme, 1916, '18		Caen
	Arras, 1917		Brieux Bridgehead
	Messines, 1917, '18		Medjez Plain
	Ypres, 1917, '18		North Africa, 1943
	St. Quentin Canal		Anzio
	Selle		Rome
	Sari Bair		Marradi
	Kut al Amara		Burma, 1943
	North-West Frontier, India, 1915		

31 January 1959	Amalgamated with The South Staffordshire Regiment to form: THE STAFFORDSHIRE REGIMENT (PRINCE OF WALES'S)

see page 223 The South Staffordshire Regiment
see page 267 The Staffordshire Regiment (Prince of Wales's)

The York and Lancaster Regiment

1881   Formed by the linking of the 65th (2nd Yorkshire, North Riding) Regiment of Foot and the 84th (York and Lancaster) Regiment of Foot, which became respectively the 1st and 2nd battalions of the Regiment.

PRINCIPAL CAMPAIGNS, BATTLES, etc.

1882–4	Egypt	1914–18	Selle
1882	Kassassin		Piave
1882	Tel-el-Kebir		Macedonia, 1915–18
1884	El Teb		Gallipoli, 1915
1884	Tamai		
1891–7	South Africa	1939–45	2ND WORLD WAR
1896	Matabele War		Battle honours
1899–1902	South Africa		selected to appear on
1900	Relief of Ladysmith		the Colours:
			Fontenay le Pesnil
1914–18	1ST WORLD WAR		Antwerp Turnhout
	Battle honours		Canal
	selected to appear on		Tobruk, 1941
	the Colours:		Mine de Sed jenane
	Ypres, 1915, '17, '18		Sicily, 1943
	Somme, 1916, '18		Solerno
	Messines, 1917, '18		Minturno
	Passchendaele		Crete
	Cambrai, 1917, '18		North Arakan
	Lys		Chindits, 1944

NICKNAMES

The Young and Lovelies   The Tigers
Cat and Cabbage

14 December 1968   The Regiment was disbanded.

see page 165 65th (2nd Yorkshire, North Riding) Regiment of Foot
see page 185 84th (York and Lancaster) Regiment of Foot

The Durham Light Infantry

1881   Formed by the linking of the 68th (Durham Light Infantry) Regiment of Foot and the 106th Bombay Light Infantry Regiment, which became respectively the 1st and 2nd battalions of the Regiment.

PRINCIPAL CAMPAIGNS, BATTLES, etc.

1899–1902	South Africa	1939–45	2ND WORLD WAR
1900	Relief of Ladysmith		Battle honours selected to appear on the Colours:
1914–18	1ST WORLD WAR		Dunkirk, 1940
	Battle honours selected to appear on the Colours:		Tilly-sur-Seulles
	Aisne, 1914, '18		Defence of Rauray
	Ypres, 1915, '17, '18		Gheel
	Hooge, 1915		Tobruk, 1941
	Loos		El Alamein
	Somme, 1916, '18		Mareth
	Arras, 1917, '18		Primosole Bridge
	Messines, 1917		Salerno
	Lys		Kohima
	Hindenburg Line	1952–3	KOREAN WAR
	Sambre		Korea, 1952–3
1919	Afghanistan (3rd Afghan War)		

10 July   Amalgamated with The King's Own Yorkshire Light
1968   Infantry, the Somerset and Cornwall Light Infantry, and The King's Shropshire Light Infantry to form:
THE LIGHT INFANTRY

see page 168 68th (Durham Light Infantry) Regiment of Foot
see page 208 106th Bombay Light Infantry Regiment
see page 235 The King's Own Yorkshire Light Infantry
see page 236 The King's Shropshire Light Infantry
see page 97 The Somerset and Cornwall Light Infantry
see page 272 The Light Infantry

The Highland Light Infantry (City of Glasgow Regiment)

1881 — Formed by the linking of the 71st (Highland Light Infantry) Regiment and the 74th (Highlanders) Regiment, which became respectively the 1st and 2nd battalions of the Regiment.

PRINCIPAL CAMPAIGNS, BATTLES, etc.

1882	Tel-el-Kebir	1919	Archangel, 1919
1899–1902	South Africa		
		1939–45	2ND WORLD WAR
1914–18	1ST WORLD WAR		Battle honours
	Battle honours		selected to appear on
	selected to appear on		the Colours:
	the Colours:		Odon
	Mons		Scheldt
	Ypres, 1914, '15, '17, '18		Walcheren Causeway
	Loos		Rhine
	Somme, 1916, '18		Reichswald
	Arras, 1917, '18		North-West Europe, 1940, '44–5
	Hindenburg Line		Keren Cauldron
	Gallipoli, 1915–16		Landing in Sicily
	Palestine, 1917–18		Greece, 1944–5
	Mesopotamia, 1916–18		

MOTTO

'Montis Insignia Calpe' (The arms of Gibraltar)

20 January 1959 — Amalgamated with The Royal Scots Fusiliers to form: THE ROYAL HIGHLAND FUSILIERS (PRINCESS MARY'S OWN GLASGOW AND AYRSHIRE REGIMENT)

see page 112 The Royal Scots Fusiliers
see page 266 The Royal Highland Fusiliers (Princess Mary's Own Glasgow and Ayrshire Regiment)

Seaforth Highlanders (Ross-shire Buffs, The Duke of Albany's)

1881	Formed by the amalgamation of the 72nd Duke of Albany's Own Highlanders with the 78th Highlanders (Ross-shire Buffs) which became respectively the 1st and 2nd battalion Seaforth Highlanders.

PRINCIPAL CAMPAIGNS, BATTLES, etc.

1882	Egypt	1914–18	Cambrai, 1917, '18
1882	Shaluf		Valenciennes
1882	Kassassin		Palestine, 1918
1882	Tel-el-Kebir		Baghdad
1888	Hazara		
1891	Hazara	1930	North-West Frontier of India
1898	The Atbara		
1898	Omdurman	1939–45	2ND WORLD WAR
1899–1902	South Africa		Battle honours
1899	Magersfontein		selected to appear on
1900	Paardeberg		the Colours:
1908	North-West Frontier of India		St. Valery-en-Caux
			Caen
1914–18	1ST WORLD WAR		Rhineland
	Battle honours		El Alamein
	selected to appear on		Akarit
	the Colours:		Sicily, 1943
	Marne, 1914, '18		Anzio
	Loos		Madagascar
	Ypres, 1915, '17, '18		Imphal
	Somme, 1916, '18		Burma, 1942–4
	Arras, 1917, '18	1945–6	Java
	Vimy, 1917	1948–51	Malaya

MOTTOES

'Cuidich 'n Righ' (Save the King)
'Caber Feidh' (The antlers of the deer)
'Tulloch Ard' (The High Hillock)

7 February 1961	Amalgamated with the Queen's Own Cameron Highlanders to form: QUEEN'S OWN HIGHLANDERS (SEAFORTH AND CAMERONS)

see page 179 The Queen's Own Cameron Highlanders
see page 269 Queen's Own Highlanders (Seaforth and Camerons)

The Gordon Highlanders

1881   Formed by the linking of the 75th (Stirlingshire) Regiment of Foot and the 92nd (Gordon Highlanders) Regiment of Foot, which became respectively the 1st and 2nd battalions of the Regiment.

PRINCIPAL CAMPAIGNS, BATTLES, etc.

1882–4	Egypt	1914–18	Arras, 1917, '18
1882	Tel-el-Kebir		Cambrai, 1917, '18
1884–5	Nile		Vittoria Veneto
1884	El Teb		
1895	Chitral	1939–45	2ND WORLD WAR
1897–8	Tirah		Battle honours
1899–1902	South Africa		selected to appear on the Colours:
			Odon
1914–18	1ST WORLD WAR		Reichswald
	Battle honours		Goch
	selected to appear on		Rhine
	the Colours:		North-West Europe,
	Mons		1940, '44–5
	Le Cateau		El Alamein
	Marne, 1914, '18		Mareth
	Ypres, 1914, '15, '17		North Africa, 1942–3
	Loos		Sferro
	Somme, 1916, '18		Anzio
	Ancre, 1916		

MOTTO

'Bydand' (Watchful)

see page 175   75th (Stirlingshire) Regiment of Foot
see page 194   92nd (Gordon Highlanders) Regiment of Foot

The Royal Ulster Rifles

1881   Formed by the linking of the 83rd (County of Dublin) Regiment of Foot and the 86th (Royal County Down) Regiment of Foot, which became respectively the 1st and 2nd battalions of the Regiment.
Until 1921 the Regiment was known as The Royal Irish Rifles.

PRINCIPAL CAMPAIGNS, BATTLES, etc.

1899–1902	South Africa	1914–18	Courtrai
			Struma
1914–18	1ST WORLD WAR		Suvla
	Following its conversion to a rifle regiment the honours on the Colours were placed on the Officer's Shoulder Belt Plate. Principal battle honours awarded were:		Jerusalem
		1939–45	2ND WORLD WAR Principal battle honours awarded were:
	Mons		Dunkirk
	Marne, 1914		Normandy Landing
	Ypres, 1914, '15, '17, '18		Caen
			Rhine
	Neuve Chapelle		Bremen
	Somme, 1916, '18	1950–1	KOREAN WAR Korea, 1950–1 Seoul, Imjin
	Albert, 1916		

NICKNAME

The Stickies

MOTTO

'Quis Separabit' (Who shall separate us?)

1 July 1968   Amalgamated with other regiments of the North Irish Brigade, The Royal Inniskilling Fusiliers and The Royal Irish Fusiliers to form:
THE ROYAL IRISH RANGERS

see page 213   The Royal Inniskilling Fusiliers
see page 248   The Royal Irish Fusiliers
see page 273   The Royal Irish Rangers

The Royal Irish Fusiliers
(Princess Victoria's)

1881   Formed by the linking of the 87th (The Royal Irish Fusiliers) Regiment of Foot and the 89th (Princess Victoria's) Regiment of Foot, which became respectively the 1st and 2nd battalions of the Regiment.

PRINCIPAL CAMPAIGNS, BATTLES, etc.

1882	Egypt	1914–18	Lys
1882	Tel-el-Kebir		Macedonia, 1915—17
1884	Egypt		Suvla
1884	El Teb & Tamaii		Palestine, 1917–18
1889–1902	South Africa		
1900	Relief of Ladysmith, Talana, Tugela Heights	1939–45	2ND WORLD WAR Battle honours selected to appear on the Colours:
1914–18	1ST WORLD WAR Battle honours selected to appear on the Colours:		St. Omer-La Bassée
	Le Cateau		Bou Arada
	Marne, 1914		Oued Arada
	Ypres, 1915, '17, '18		Djebel Tanngoucha
	Somme, 1916, '18		Argenta Gap
	Arras, 1917		Centruipe
	Messines, 1917, '18		Termoli
			Sangro
			Cassino II
			Malta, 1940

MOTTO

'Faugh-a-Ballagh' (Clear the way)

1 July 1968   Amalgamated with the Regiments of the North Irish Brigade, The Royal Inniskilling Fusiliers, and the Royal Ulster Rifles to form:
THE ROYAL IRISH RANGERS

see page 213 The Royal Inniskilling Fusiliers
see page 247 The Royal Ulster Rifles
see page 273 The Royal Irish Rangers

The Connaught Rangers

1881	Formed by the linking of the 88th (Connaught Rangers) Regiment of Foot and the 94th Regiment of Foot, which became respectively the 1st and 2nd battalions of the Regiment.

PRINCIPAL CAMPAIGNS, BATTLES, etc.

1899–1902	South Africa	1914–18	Ypres, 1914, '15, '17
1914–18	1ST WORLD WAR Battle honours selected to appear on the Colours: Mons Aisne, 1914 Messines, 1914, '17		Guillemont Cambrai, 1918 Kosturino Scimitar Hill Megiddo Kut al Amara

MOTTO

'Quis separabit' (Who shall separate us?)

31 July 1922	Disbanded.

see page 190 88th Connaught Rangers (Regiment of Foot)
see page 196 94th Regiment of Foot

The Argyll and Sutherland Highlanders (Princess Louise's)

1881   Formed by the linking of the 91st (Princess Louise's Argyllshire) Highlanders and the 93rd (Sutherland Highlanders) Regiment of Foot, which became respectively the 1st and 2nd battalions of the Regiment.

PRINCIPAL CAMPAIGNS, BATTLES, etc.

1897–8	Tochi Valley	1939–45	Odon
1899–1902	South Africa		Rhine
1899	Modder River		Sidi Barrani
1900	Paardeberg		El Alamein
			Akarit
1914–18	1ST WORLD WAR		Longstop Hill, 1943
	Battle honours		Italy, 1943–4
	selected to appear on		Crete
	the Colours:		Grik Road
	Mons		Malaya, 1941–2
	Le Cateau		
	Marne, 1914, '18	1945–8	Palestine
	Ypres, 1915, '17, '18	1950–1	KOREAN WAR
	Loos		Korea, 1950–1
	Somme, 1916, '18		Pakchon
	Arras, 1917, '18		
	Cambrai, 1917, '18	1953–4	British Guiana
	Doiran, 1917, '18	1956	Suez Operation
	Gaza	1957–9	Cyprus
		1964–6	Borneo
1935	Mohmand Operations	1967	Aden
1937	Waziristan Operations		
1939–45	2ND WORLD WAR		
	Battle honours		
	selected to appear on		
	the Colours:		

MOTTOES

'Ne obliviscaris' (Forget not)
'Sans peur' (Without fear)

October 1971   The 1st Battalion, which had been reduced to the strength of a company (Balaclava Company) in 1970, was reconstituted.

see page 193   91st (Princess Louise's Argyllshire) Highlanders
see page 195   93rd (Sutherland Highlanders)

The Prince of Wales's Leinster Regiment (Royal Canadians)

1881   Formed by the linking of the 100th (Prince of Wales's Royal Canadian) Regiment and the 109th (Bombay Infantry) Regiment which became respectively the 1st and 2nd battalions of the Regiment.

PRINCIPAL CAMPAIGNS, BATTLES, etc.

1899–1902   South Africa

1914–18   1ST WORLD WAR
Battle honours
selected to appear on
the Colours:
Aisne, 1914
Ypres, 1915, '17, 18
Somme, 1916, '18

1914–18   Guillemont
Vimy, 1917
Messines, 1917
St. Quentin
Macedonia, 1915–17
Gallipoli, 1915
Jerusalem

31 July   The Regiment was disbanded.
1922

see page 202   100th (Prince of Wales's Royal Canadian) Regiment
see page 211   109th (Bombay Infantry) Regiment

The Royal Munster Fusiliers

1881   Formed by the linking of the 101st (Royal Bengal Fusiliers) Regiment and the 104th Bengal Fusiliers, which became respectively the 1st and 2nd battalions of the Regiment.

PRINCIPAL CAMPAIGNS, BATTLES, etc.

1885–7	3rd Burma War	1914–18	Aubers
1899–1902	South Africa		Guillemont
			St. Quentin
1914–18	1ST WORLD WAR		Drocourt-Queant
	Battle honours		Selle
	selected to appear on		Landing at Helles
	the Colours:		Landing at Suvla
	Retreat from Mons		Jerusalem
	Ypres, 1914, '17		

MOTTO

'Spectamur agendo' (We are judged by our deeds)

31 July 1922   The Regiment was disbanded.

see page 203   101st (Royal Bengal Fusiliers) Regiment
see page 206   104th Bengal Fusiliers

The Royal Dublin Fusiliers

1881   Formed by the linking of the 102nd (Royal Madras Fusiliers) and the 103rd (Royal Bombay Fusiliers), which became respectively the 1st and 2nd battalions of the Regiment.

PRINCIPAL CAMPAIGNS, BATTLES, etc.

1899–1902	South Africa	1914–18	Ypres, 1915, '17, '18
1900	Relief of Ladysmith		Somme, 1916, '18
			Cambrai, 1917, '18
1914–18	1ST WORLD WAR		Hindenburg Line
	Battle honours		Selle
	selected to appear on		Macedonia, 1915–17
	the Colours:		Gallipoli, 1915–16
	Retreat from Mons		Jerusalem
	Marne, 1914		

MOTTO

'Spectamur agendo' (We are judged by our deeds)

31 July 1922   The Regiment was disbanded.

see page 204   102nd (Royal Madras Fusiliers)
see page 205   103rd (Royal Bombay Fusiliers)

The West India Regiment

Formed circa 1779 from Malcolm's Black Rangers and St. Vincent's Black Rangers, which became respectively the 1st and 2nd battalions of the Regiment.

PRINCIPAL CAMPAIGNS, BATTLES, etc.

1779	Savannah	1853–5	Sabbajee
1780	Charlestown	1864	Ashantee
1781	Hobkirk's Hill	1865	Jamaica
1781	Entwa Springs	1872	Orange Walk
1794	Martinique	1873–4	Ashantee
1794	Guadaloupe	1887	West Africa
1795	St. Lucia	1892–4	West Africa
1795	St. Vincent	1898–9	Sierra Leone
1796	St. Lucia	1900	Ashantee
1805	Dominica		
1809	Martinique	1914–18	1ST WORLD WAR
1809	San Domingo		One battalion of the
1810	Guadaloupe		Regiment served.
1815	New Orleans		Battle honours
1815	Mobile		selected to appear on
1823	Mahaica		the Colours:
1848	Coomassie		Duala
1853–4	Christenbourg		Cameroons, 1914–16

1928   The Regiment was disbanded.

NOTE: This regiment, though disbanded, is included because of its long existence and place on the British Home Establishment.

The Marines

From 1664 onwards a number of the Line regiments served as marines for various periods, and a number of regiments were raised specially as marines in the late 17th century and the first half of the 18th century.

When the present corps of Royal Marines was raised by the Board of Admiralty in 1755, it was ranked next to the 49th Foot (from 1881 the 1st battalion The Royal Berkshire Regiment) thus providing a link with the army.

PRINCIPAL CAMPAIGNS, BATTLES, etc.

1705	Gibraltar	1709	West Indies
1706	Spain	1709	Dunkirk
1708	Minorca	1741	Carthagena
1708	Nice	1746	Culloden
1708	Ostend	1747–8	Aria-Coupang
1708	Sardinia	1747–8	Pondicherry
1709	Nova Scotia	1747–8	Coromandel Coast

NOTE: This corps though subordinate to the Admiralty, not the War Office, is included because of its members' status as 'sea-soldiers'.

The Glider Pilot Regiment

The Regiment was raised in 1942, its personnel consisting of trained pilots. During the 2nd World War the Regiment piloted the Gliders carrying the Airborne Soldiers for the invasions of Sicily, Normandy, South of France, for the battle of Arnhem, and on the crossing of the Rhine. Post war the Regiment flew liaison aircraft and helicopters in Korea, Malaya, Cyprus, and Kenya.

In 1957 the Regiment was disbanded on the re-formation of the Army Air Corps and its personnel were absorbed by the new Corps.

PRINCIPAL CAMPAIGNS, BATTLES, etc.

1939–45	2ND WORLD WAR Battle honours selected to appear on the Colours: Normandy Landing Pegasus Bridge Merville Battery	1939–45	Rhine South France North-West Europe, 1944–5 Landing in Sicily Sicily, 1943

MOTTO
Nothing is impossible

see page 295 The Army Air Corps

NOTE: This regiment is included as it is one of the ancestors of the Army Air Corps.

The Parachute Regiment

1 August 1942 Established as a Regiment of the Army Air Corps.

A completely Volunteer Regiment its personnel remaining on the strength of their own parent Corps or Regiments. This remained until 1953 when soldiers and NCO's were permitted to transfer to the Regiment as permanent cadre. Officers were later permitted to do so in 1958. All personnel are still volunteers but only 25% are now seconded from other Corps or Regiments.

PRINCIPAL CAMPAIGNS, BATTLES, etc.

1939-45

2ND WORLD WAR
Battle honours
selected to appear on
the Colours:
Bruneval
Normandy Landing
Breville
Arnhem, 1944
Rhine
Southern France
Oudna

1939-45

Tamera
Primosole Bridge
Athens

Since the 2nd World War the Regiment has taken part in the following campaigns: Palestine; Egypt (Suez); Malaya; Borneo; Cyprus; Radfan; Aden.

MOTTO
'Utrinque Paratus' (Ready for anything)

NICKNAME
Red Devils

see page 295 The Army Air Corps

2nd King Edward VII's Own Gurkha Rifles (The Sirmoor Rifles)

January 1948	Together with the other three regiments of the Brigade of Gurkhas, the Regiment became part of the British Army. The Regiment was raised in 1815 from Gurkha soldiers who enlisted in the British Army after the first phase of the Nepal campaign was over.

Originally known as The Sirmoor Battalion, the unit greatly distinguished itself during the Indian Mutiny, and was granted a Truncheon for its service at Delhi.

In 1858 when the Crown assumed responsibility for the government of India, it was taken on the establishment of the Bengal Army.

PRINCIPAL CAMPAIGNS, BATTLES, etc.

1826	Bhurtpore	1914–18	Tigris, 1916
1846	Aliwal		Kut-al-Amara, 1917
1846	Sobraon		Baghdad
1857	Delhi		Persia, 1918
1878–80	2nd Afghan War		
1879	Kabul	1939–45	2ND WORLD WAR
1880	Kandahar		Principal battle honours:
1897	Tirah		El Alamein
	Punjab Frontier		Akarit
1914–18	1ST WORLD WAR		Tunis
	Principal battle honours:		Cassino I
			Gothic Line
	La Bassée, 1914		Jitra
	Festubert, 1914–15		Slim River
	Givenchy, 1914		North Arakan
	Neuve Chapelle		Irrawaddy
	Aubers		Tamandu
	Loos		

6th Queen Elizabeth's Own Gurkha Rifles

January 1948

Together with the other three regiments of the Brigade of Gurkhas, the Regiment became part of the British Army. The Regiment was raised at Chaubiagang in Cuttack in 1917. From 1823 to 1901 it was a Light Infantry Regiment. In 1901 it was designated the 42nd Gurkha Rifles and in 1903, was designated the 6th Gurkha Rifles. From 1 January 1959, it was designated the 6th Queen Elizabeth's Own Gurkha Rifles in recognition of its magnificent war record, especially the eight years it operated in the Malayan jungles.

PRINCIPAL CAMPAIGNS, BATTLES, etc.

1885–7	Burma	1919	3rd Afghan War

1914–18	1ST WORLD WAR
	Principal battle
	honours:
	Helles
	Krithia
	Suvla
	Sari Bair
	Gallipoli, 1915
	Suez Canal
	Khan Baghdad
	Mesopotamia,
	    1916–18
	Persia, 1918
	North-West Frontier,
	    India, 1915
		1939–45	2ND WORLD WAR
			Principal battle
			honours:
			Monte Chicco
			Medicina
			Italy, 1944–5
			Kyaukmyaung
			    Bridgehead
			Mandalay
			Fort Dafferin
			Rangoon Road
			Sittang, 1945
			Chinditis, 1944
			Burma, 1944–5

7th Duke of Edinburgh's Own Gurkha Rifles

January
1948

Together with the other three regiments of the Brigade of Gurkhas, the Regiment became part of the British Army. The Regiment was raised in 1902 at Thayet-myo and the following year became the 2nd battalion, 10th Gurkha Rifles. In 1907, however, it assumed its identity as the 7th Gurkha Rifles and in the same year a second battalion was raised.

On 1 January 1959, it was designated the 7th Duke of Edinburgh's Own Gurkha Rifles, in recognition of its magnificent war record.

PRINCIPAL CAMPAIGNS, BATTLES, etc.

1914–18

1ST WORLD WAR
Principal battle
honours:
Egypt, 1915
Megiddo
Sharon
Palestine, 1918
Kut-al-Amara,
    1915–17
Ctesiphon
Defence of
    Kut-al-Amara
Baghdad
Sharqat

1914–18   Mesopotamia,
                1915–18
1919   3rd Afghan War

1939–45   2ND WORLD WAR
           Principal battle
           honours:
           Cassino I
           Poggio del Grillo
           Tavoleto
           Sittang, 1942, '45
           Kyaukse, 1942
           Imphal
           Bishenpur
           Meiktila
           Rangoon Road

10th Princess Mary's Own Gurkha Rifles

1 January 1948	Together with the other three regiments of the Brigade of Gurkhas, the Regiment became part of the British Army. The Regiment was raised in 1890 from Kubo Valley Police Battalion, as the 10th (Burma) Regiment of Madras Infantry.
	In 1901 it became the 10th Gurkha Rifles and in 1949 was granted the title of the 10th Princess Mary's Own Gurkha Rifles.

PRINCIPAL CAMPAIGNS, BATTLES, etc.

1914–18	1ST WORLD WAR Principal battle honours: Helles Krithia Suvla Sari Bair Gallipoli, 1915 Suez Canal Egypt, 1915 Sharqat Mesopotamia, 1916–18	1939–45	2ND WORLD WAR Principal battle honours: Coriano Santarcangelo Bologna Imphal Tuitam Tengnoupal Mandalay Myinmu Bridgehead Meiktila Rangoon Road
1919	Afghanistan (3rd Afghan War)		

The Rifle Brigade
(Prince Consort's Own)

Formed in 1800 by detachments from various regiments.

TITLES

1800–2	Experimental Corps of Riflemen; also the Rifle Corps.
1802–16	The 95th (Rifle) Regiment
1816–62	Rifle Brigade
1862–81	The Prince Consort's Own Rifle Brigade
1881–1920	Rifle Brigade (The Prince Consort's Own)
1920–58	The Rifle Brigade (Prince Consort's Own)

PRINCIPAL CAMPAIGNS, BATTLES, etc.

1801	Copenhagen	1855	Sevastopol
1806	Buenos Aires	1857–8	Indian Mutiny
1807	Monte Video	1858	Lucknow
1807	Copenhagen	1874	Ashantee
1808–14	Peninsula	1878–9	Afghanistan
1808	Roliea	1878	Ali Masjid
1808	Vimiera	1885–7	Burma
1809	Corunna	1899	Khartoum
1809	Flushing	1899–1902	South Africa
1810	Busaco		
1811	Barossa	1914–18	1ST WORLD WAR
1811	Sabugal		Principal battle
1811	Fuentes d'Onor		honours were as
1811	Tarifa		follows:
1812	Cuidad Rodrigo		Le Cateau
1812	Badajoz		Neuve Chapelle
1812	Salamanca		Ypres, 1915, '17
1813	Vittoria		Somme, 1916–18
1813	St. Sebastian		Arras, 1917, '18
1813	Nivelle		Messines, 1917
1813	Nive		Cambrai, 1917, '18
1814	Orthes		Hindenburg Line
1814	Toulouse		France & Flanders,
1814	Antwerp		1914–18
1814–15	Netherlands		Macedonia, 1915–18
1815	New Orleans	1939–45	2ND WORLD WAR
1815	Waterloo		The principal battle
1846–53	South Africa		honours were as
1854–5	Crimea		follows:
1854	Alma		Calais, 1940
1854	Inkerman		

1939–45	North-West Europe, 1940, '44–5	1939–45	North Africa, 1940–3
	Beda Fomm		Cassino II
	Sidi Rezegh, 1941		Capture of Perugia
	Alam el Halfa		Italy, 1943–5
	El Alamein	1954–6	Kenya
		1956–7	Malaya

NICKNAMES

The Sweeps   Green Jackets

7 November 1958	Redesignated: THE 3rd GREEN JACKETS, THE RIFLE BRIGADE so becoming part of the Green Jacket Brigade.
1 January 1966	Further redesignated The 3rd Battalion, The Royal Green Jackets (The Rifle Brigade), thus amalgamating with the other units of the Green Jackets Brigade to form: THE ROYAL GREEN JACKETS
June 1968	Sub-title (The Rifle Brigade) was dropped.

see page 275 The Royal Green Jackets

The Special Air Service Regiment

The 22nd S.A.S. is the regular battalion of the Special Air Service Regiment. The earliest elements of the Regiment saw action in North Africa in 1940 and 1941. Later the Regiment saw action in Italy, Greece, and North-West Europe (before and after 'D' Day).

The Regiment was re-consituted in 1947 and became a separate Corps in 1950. The Regiment has since seen service in Malaya, Muscat, Radfan, and Borneo.

MOTTO
'Who Dares Wins'

The Prince of Wales's Own Regiment of Yorkshire

25 April 1958	Formed by the amalgamation of The West Yorkshire Regiment (The Prince of Wales's Own) and The East Yorkshire Regiment (The Duke of York's Own)

PRINCIPAL CAMPAIGNS, BATTLES, etc.

1958–9	Aden	1965–6	Aden (Operational)
1959–61	Gibraltar	1967	Aden (Emergency
1961–3	Germany		operations)
1963–5	Berlin		

MOTTO
'Nec Aspera Terrent' (Nor do difficulties deter)

see page 99 The West Yorkshire Regiment (The Prince of Wales's Own)

see page 101 The East Yorkshire Regiment (The Duke of York's Own)

The Devonshire and Dorset Regiment

17 May 1958   Formed from the amalgamation of The Devonshire Regiment and The Dorset Regiment

The Lancashire Regiment (Prince of Wales's Volunteers)

1 July 1958   Formed from an amalgamation of The East Lancashire Regiment and The South Lancashire Regiment.

PRINCIPAL CAMPAIGNS, BATTLES, etc.

1967   Aden

March 1970   Amalgamated with The Loyal Regiment (North Lancashire) to form:
THE QUEEN'S LANCASHIRE REGIMENT

The King's Regiment

1 September 1958   Formed by the amalgamation of The King's Regiment (Liverpool) and The Manchester Regiment
Until 1969 the title was The King's Regiment (Manchester and Liverpool).

see page 87   The King's Regiment (Liverpool)
see page 163   The 63rd (West Suffolk) Regiment of Foot
see page 240   The Manchester Regiment

The Royal Highland Fusiliers (Princess Margaret's Own Glasgow and Ayrshire Regiment)

20 January 1959   Formed by the amalgamation of The Royal Scots Fusiliers and The Highland Light Infantry (City of Glasgow Regiment).

see page 112   The Royal Scots Fusiliers
see page 171   The 71st (Highland Light Infantry) Regiment
see page 174   The 74th (Highlanders) Regiment
see page 198   The 96th Regiment of Foot
see page 244   The Highland Light Infantry

The Staffordshire Regiment
(The Prince of Wales's)

31 January 1959   Formed by the amalgamation of The South Staffordshire Regiment and The North Staffordshire Regiment (The Prince of Wales's).

The Duke of Edinburgh's
Royal Regiment (Berkshire
and Wiltshire)

9 June 1959   Formed from the amalgamation of The Royal Berkshire Regiment (Princess Charlotte of Wales's) and The Wiltshire Regiment (Duke of Edinburgh's).

The King's Own Royal Border Regiment

1 October 1959	Formed by the amalgamation of The King's Own Royal Regiment (Lancaster) and The Border Regiment.

see page 220 The Border Regiment
see page 79 The King's Own Royal Regiment (Lancaster)
see page 131 The 34th (Cumberland) Regiment of Foot
see page 154 The 55th (Westmorland) Regiment of Foot

The Somerset and Cornwall Light Infantry

6 October 1959	Formed by the amalgamation of The Duke of Cornwall's Light Infantry and The Somerset Light Infantry.
10 July 1968	Was amalgamated with other regiments of the Light Infantry Brigade to form: THE LIGHT INFANTRY

see page 272 The Light Infantry

Queen's Own Highlanders
(Seaforth and Camerons)

7 February 1961	Formed by the amalgamation of The Queen's Own Cameron Highlanders and the Seaforth Highlanders (Ross-shire Buffs, The Duke of Albany's).

PRINCIPAL CAMPAIGNS, BATTLES, etc.

1962	Brunei	1963	Borneo

see page 179   The Queen's Own Cameron Highlanders
see page 245   Seaforth Highlanders (Ross-shire Buffs, The Duke of Albany's)
see page 172   The 72nd Duke of Albany's Own Highlanders
see page 178   The 78th Highlanders (The Ross-shire Buffs)

The Royal Anglian Regiment

1 September-
ber 1964

Formed from the following regiments:
The 1st East Anglian Regiment (Royal Norfolk and Suffolk)
The 2nd East Anglian Regiment (Duchess of Gloucester's Own)
The 3rd East Anglian Regiment (16th/44th Foot)
The Royal Leicestershire Regiment
These regiments were redesignated as follows:
The 1st (Norfolk and Suffolk) Battalion The Royal Anglian Regiment
The 2nd (Duchess of Gloucester's Own Lincolnshire and Northamptonshire Battalion) The Royal Anglian Regiment
The 3rd (16th/44th Foot) Battalion The Royal Anglian Regiment
The 4th (Leicestershire Battalion) The Royal Anglian Regiment

1 July 1968

The battalions were redesignated as follows:
The 1st Battalion The Royal Anglian Regiment
The 2nd Battalion The Royal Anglian Regiment
The 3rd Battalion The Royal Anglian Regiment
The 4th Battalion The Royal Anglian Regiment
On this date therefore all County affiliation ceased.
The pre-1958 regiments of the line which went to form the Royal Anglian Regiment were as follows:

see page 89 The Royal Norfolk Regiment
see page 95 The Suffolk Regiment
see page 91 The Royal Lincolnshire Regiment
see page 232 The Northamptonshire Regiment
see page 229 The Essex Regiment
see page 103 The Bedfordshire and Hertfordshire Regiment
see page 105 The Royal Leicestershire Regiment
4th Battalion reduced to company strength (Tiger Company)

NICKNAME

The 2nd Battalion retains 'The Poachers'

see page 142 The 44th (East Essex) Regiment of Foot
see page 147 The 48th (Northamptonshire) Regiment of Foot
see page 155 The 56th (West Essex) Regiment of Foot
see page 157 The 58th (Rutlandshire) Regiment of Foot

The Queen's Regiment

31 December 1966	Formed from the following regiments:
	The Queen's Royal Surrey Regiment
	The Queen's Own Buffs, The Royal Kent Regiment
	The Royal Sussex Regiment
	The Middlesex Regiment (Duke of Cambridge's Own)
	These regiments were redesignated as follows:
	The 1st Battalion The Queen's Regiment (The Queen's Surreys)
	The 2nd Battalion The Queen's Regiment (The Queen's Own Buffs)
	The 3rd Battalion The Queen's Regiment
	The 4th Battalion The Queen's Regiment (Middlesex)
1969	Sub-titles were discontinued and County affiliations therefore ceased.
	The pre-1958 regiments which went to form the Queen's Regiment were:

see page 75	The Queen's Royal Regiment (West Surrey)
see page 217	The East Surrey Regiment
see page 77	The Buffs (Royal East Kent Regiment)
see page 234	The Queen's Own Royal West Kent Regiment
see page 221	The Royal Sussex Regiment
see page 238	The Middlesex Regiment
	4th Battalion reduced to company strength

MOTTO

'Unconquered I Serve'

see page 128	The 31st (Huntingdonshire) Regiment
see page 132	The 35th (Royal Sussex) Regiment of Foot
see page 149	The 50th (The Queen's Own) Regiment of Foot
see page 156	The 57th (West Middlesex) Regiment of Foot
see page 170	The 70th (Surrey) Regiment of Foot
see page 177	The 77th (East Middlesex) Regiment of Foot
see page 199	The 97th (The Earl of Ulster's) Regiment of Foot
see page 209	The 107th Bengal Infantry Regiment

The Royal Regiment of Fusiliers

23 April 1968 Formed by the amalgamation of The Royal Northumberland Fusiliers, The Royal Warwickshire Fusiliers, The Royal Fusiliers (City of London Regiment) and The Lancashire Fusiliers.
4th Battalion disbanded

The Light Infantry

10 July 1968 Formed from the regiments of the Light Infantry Brigade:
The Somerset and Cornwall Light Infantry
The King's Own Yorkshire Light Infantry
The King's Shropshire Light Infantry
The Durham Light Infantry
The above regiments were organized to form the 1st, 2nd, 3rd, and 4th Battalions The Light Infantry.
On the 31 March 1969 the 4th Battalion The Light Infantry was disbanded.

The Royal Irish Rangers (27th [Inniskilling] 83rd and 87th)

1 July 1968   Formed from an amalgamation of the regiments constituting the North Irish Brigade:
The Royal Inniskilling Fusiliers
The Royal Ulster Rifles
The Royal Irish Fusiliers

1970   The 3rd Battalion of the Royal Irish Rangers disbanded

The Royal Regiment of Wales
(24th/41st Foot)

June 1969   Formed by the amalgamation of The South Wales Borderers and The Welch Regiment.

MOTTO
'Gwell angan na Chywilydd' (Death before Dishonour)

see page 117 The South Wales Borderers
see page 226 The Welch Regiment
see page 138 The 41st (The Welsh) Regiment of Foot
see page 169 The 69th (South Lincolnshire) Regiment of Foot

The Worcestershire and Sherwood Foresters Regiment
(29th/54th Foot)

March 1970   Formed by the amalgamation of The Worcestershire Regiment and The Sherwood Foresters.

see page 215 The Worcestershire Regiment
see page 230 The Sherwood Foresters
see page 126 The 29th (Worcestershire) Regiment of Foot
see page 133 The 36th (Herefordshire) Regiment of Foot
see page 143 The 45th (Nottinghamshire Regiment) Sherwood Foresters
see page 197 The 95th or Derbyshire Regiment of Foot

The Royal Green Jackets

1 January 1966	Formed from the units which, from 7 November 1958 to 31 December 1965, had constituted The Green Jackets Brigade
	The 1st Green Jackets (43rd and 52nd), which was re-designated:
	The 1st Battalion, Royal Green Jackets (43rd and 52nd)
	The 2nd Green Jackets, The King's Royal Rifle Corps, which was redesignated:
	The 2nd Battalion, The Royal Green Jackets (The King's Royal Rifle Corps)
	The 3rd Green Jackets, The Rifle Brigade, which was re-designated:
	The 3rd Battalion, The Royal Green Jackets (The Rifle Brigade)
June 1968	The sub-titles were dropped.
	Before the formation of the Green Jackets Brigade on 7 November 1958 the titles of these regiments were as follows:
	The Oxfordshire and Buckinghamshire Light Infantry
	The King's Royal Rifle Corps
	The Rifle Brigade (Prince Consort's Own)
	In October 1971 the 3rd Battalion, which had been reduced three months earlier to company strength, was reconstituted.

see page 159 The King's Royal Rifle Corps
see page 262 The Rifle Brigade
see page 228 The Oxfordshire and Buckinghamshire Light Infantry
see page 141 The 43rd (Monmouthshire Light Infantry) Regiment
see page 151 The 52nd (Oxfordshire Light Infantry) Regiment

The Queen's Lancashire Regiment

The Royal Regiment of Artillery

When guns were needed to serve at home or abroad, a train of artillery had to be authorized by a royal warrant, and it was disbanded again on the cessation of hostilities. This system led to much confusion and delay, and in the Jacobite Rebellion of 1715 it took so long to mobilize a train that the rebellion was over before the guns were ready.

It was then decided to organize a permanent force of artillery, and so on the 26 May 1716 two companies of artillery were created by royal warrant of King George I and were formed at Woolwich. Six years later on 1 April 1722 these two companies were grouped together with the companies at Gibraltar and Minorca to form the Royal Regiment of Artillery, Colonel Albert Borgard being appointed as its first Colonel.

During the eighteenth century the Regiment continued to grow and by 1757 there were 24 companies apart from the Cadet Company formed in 1741. They were divided into two battalions of 12 companies each, with appropriate staffs. In 1771 there were four battalions consisting of eight companies and an additional two Invalid companies each, the latter being raised for garrison duties in order to free other companies for active service overseas.

Civilian wagons and horses were still being hired to move the guns and it was only in 1794 that the 'Corps of Captains Commisaries and Drivers' was formed to provide drivers and teams for the field guns. (The RHA formed in 1793 already had its own horses and teams for each troop.) In 1801 this Corps was replaced by a similar organization called the Corps of Gunner Drivers. This was also unsatisfactory, and in 1806 its title was changed to the Royal Artillery Drivers. Finally in 1822 this Corps—already greatly reduced in establishment since 1815—was disbanded and recruits were enlisted as 'Gunner and Driver'. This continued until after 1918 when enlistments were made as Gunner only.

In 1833 King William IV granted the Regiment the privilege of bearing the Royal Arms over a gun with the

continued overleaf

Motto UBIQUE (Everywhere), followed by QUO FAS ET GLORIA DUCUNT (Whither right and glory lead). In 1855 the Board of Ordnance was abolished, and the Royal Artillery, together with the Royal Engineers, came under the Commander-in-Chief and the War Office like the rest of the Army.

In 1859 the companies ceased to be organized into battalions, and were brigaded instead, at the same time being referred to as batteries instead of companies. In 1861 after the Indian Mutiny the Royal Artillery received the addition of 21 troops of Horse Artillery and 48 batteries Royal Artillery from the three Indian Presidencies, and so now comprised 29 RHA batteries, 73 field batteries, and 88 garrison batteries.

On 1 June 1899 the Royal Artillery was divided into two distinct branches—mounted and dismounted. A royal warrant established the Royal Garrison Artillery as a separate Corps from Royal Horse and Field Artillery, and decided that it was to man the Coast Defence Units, the Mountain Batteries, and the Heavy and Siege batteries. However, this decision was reversed in 1924 and both branches were united into a single corps—the Royal Artillery.

In 1938 the decision was taken to mechanize the Horse and Field Artillery, and to adopt a new organization for these units, and for the medium artillery. In place of 'brigade' the term 'regiment' was substituted.

On 1 April 1947 all batteries except Royal Horse Artillery were placed on a single roll. Batteries were numbered on this roll throughout the whole regiment, so that there was only one battery bearing any particular number.

Changes after the 2nd World War comprised the abolition of Anti-Tank Artillery, and in the middle of the 1950s the abolition of the Anti-Aircraft Command and the entire Coast Artillery organization.

NICKNAME

The Gunners

MOTTOES

Ubique (Everywhere)
Quo Fas et Gloria Ducunt (Whither right and glory lead)

The Royal Horse Artillery

Until the end of the 18th century gunners had to walk beside their guns which meant that movement was slow. On many occasions the officers (who were mounted) had to manhandle the guns into action before their men arrived.

The solution was obvious and in January 1793 two troops of Horse Artillery were raised, differing from field units in that all personnel were mounted. Two more troops were formed in November of that year, and each troop had six 6-pounder guns with 45 drivers and 186 horses on their establishment, a self-contained mobile fighting unit of artillery had at last come into existence. The superior organization of the RHA troops enabled them to develop from the first a very high standard of discipline and efficiency which has never been allowed to weaken.

After Waterloo seven troops RHA were disbanded between 1816 and 1819 (including 2nd Rocket Troop) and the others were reduced to a skeleton establishment, barely sufficient to man two guns apiece. The history of the Horse Artillery from Waterloo to the Crimea was a blank page, soldiering in England or Ireland being all that was offered. Nevertheless the corps survived, and after the Crimean War the Royal Horse Artillery was formed into a Horse Brigade. In 1861 the Horse Artillery batteries from the Indian establishment increased the strength by four brigades, making a total of five. In 1871, under the stimulus of the Franco-Prussian War, a further reorganization took place, whereby one RHA battery was added to the Regiment, making a total of 31 batteries RHA. Six years later, however, the RHA was again reorganised into three brigades (10 batteries and one Depot Battery to each brigade). In 1882 the brigades were reduced to two (each of 13 batteries) and a depot—a reduction of five batteries. Following the outbreak of the South African War in 1900 there was an increase of seven batteries, and during the 1st World War the Regiment expanded to 50 batteries RHA. But the end of the war brought the inevitable reductions, and by 1936 the strength was three brigades and five unbrigaded batteries, a total of 14 batteries. By

continued overleaf

1940 the batteries were mechanised, except for a ceremonial RHA troop in London.

In 1947 the Riding Troop which had been formed for ceremonial duties was inspected at St. John's Wood by King George VI. He created history by erasing the title of the troop and inserting the words 'The King's Troop'—a title which the present Queen was pleased to leave unchanged.

In 1959 there were five RHA regiments with a total of 15 batteries and the King's Troop making the sixteenth. But by 1969 further reductions had taken place and the strength now comprises:

The King's Troop RHA
1st Regiment RHA
3rd Regiment RHA
7th Parachute Regiment RHA

The Royal Tank Regiment

16 February 1916	Six companies of tanks were formed. The first name, Tank Detachment, was quickly dropped for security reasons in favour of Armoured Car Section of the Motor Machine Gun Service. In May it was re-named Heavy Section, Machine Gun Corps.
16 November 1916	Re-named Heavy Branch, Machine Gun Corps.
27 July 1917	Re-named the Tank Corps, by royal warrant. Initially the battalions were identified by letters, but in March 1918 they were numbered. Twenty-five battalions were formed, of which eighteen were in action in France by November 1918.
18 October 1923	Granted the prefix 'Royal', becoming The Royal Tank Corps.
4 April 1929	Re-named The Royal Tank Regiment, upon the formation of The Royal Armoured Corps, combining mechanized cavalry and yeomanry regiments with the tank battalions in a single corps. Units of The Royal Tank Regiment were known colloquially throughout the 2nd World War as battalions. Units equipped with 'Infantry' tanks in Army Tanks Brigades—later Tank Brigades—were officially described as battalions in tables of organization until 18 January 1945, when Tank Brigades became Armoured Brigades. Thereafter the major units of The Royal Tank Regiment were known as regiments, i.e. 2nd Royal Tank Regiment. After 1919 the following units remained on the permanent establishment: 1 (Depot) Bn, Tank Corps 2, 3, 4, 5 Bns, Tank Corps 1 to 12 Armoured Car Companies, Tank Corps.
April 1933	6th Bn RTC was re-formed.
April 1934	1st (Light) Bn RTC re-formed. (The term 'Light' was dropped in December 1938.)
May 1937	7th Bn RTC was re-formed.
May 1938	8th Bn RTC was re-formed.

continued overleaf

Between 1929 and 1938 the Armoured Car Companies were variously disbanded or reorganized as Light Tank Companies to suit their role and equipment. In 1938, 1, 2, 6, 7, 9, and 11 Light Tank Companies remained.

1940–1   From the eight regular battalions serving at the outbreak of war, four more were formed:
November 1940—9th and 10th Bns RTR
December 1940—12th Bn RTR
January 1941—11th Bn RTR
When the 4th and 7th Bns were captured at Tobruk in June 1941 they ceased to exist. Subsequently they were re-formed:
4th RTR—by re-naming 144th Regiment, Royal Armoured Corps (formerly 8th Bn, the East Lancashire Regiment) on 1 March 1945.
7th RTR—by renumbering 10th Bn RTR on 1 April 1943.

1945   Regular establishment reduced to eight regiments, numbered 1 to 8, e.g. 1st Royal Tank Regiment.

1951   In November of this year No. 1 Independent Squadron RTR was formed for service in Berlin. It was disbanded in October 1957.

1963   In March of this year The Independent Squadron RTR was formed for service in Berlin. In January 1965 it was disbanded.

1959–60   The following amalgamations took place to effect a reduction of three regiments:
3 April 1959—4th and 7th RTR to form the new 4th Royal Tank Regiment.
31st October 1959—3rd and 6th RTR to form the new 3rd Royal Tank Regiment.
1 July 1960—5th and 8th RTR to form the new 5th Royal Tank Regiment.
To effect a further reduction the 5th Royal Tank Regiment was disbanded on 7 December 1969.

PRINCIPAL CAMPAIGNS, BATTLES, etc.

Battle honours are held by the Royal Tank Regiment as a whole and not by any individual regiment. Principal battle honours are as follows:

1914–18   **1ST WORLD WAR**
Somme, 1916–18

1914–18
Arras, 1917–18
Messines, 1916
Ypres, 1917
Cambrai, 1917
Villers Bretonnaux
Amiens
Bapaume, 1918
Hindenburg Line
France & Flanders, 1916–18

1939–45	2ND WORLD WAR	1939–45	Sicily, 1943
	Rhine		Italy, 1943–5
	North-West Europe, 1940, '44–5		Greece, 1941
			Burma, 1942
	Abyssinia, 1940		
	Tobruk, 1941	1951–3	KOREAN WAR
	El Alamein		Korea, 1951–3
	North Africa, 1940–43		

MOTTO

'Fear Naught'

The Corps

The Royal Armoured Corps

April 1939　Formed as a parent Corps to the Royal Tank Corps (retitled Royal Tank Regiment on joining) and those cavalry regiments which had been mechanized. Other cavalry regiments were included as they mechanized and eventually all the Cavalry of the Line were drawn into the new Corps. During the Second World War a number of Territorial Infantry battalions, which had been mechanized for operational reasons, were given numbers as Regiments of the R.A.C. (107th–116th Regiments and 141st–163rd Regiments, R.A.C.). A small number of training and specialized regiments were also formed as Regiments of the R.A.C. during the Second World War.

In 1944 the R.A.C. absorbed the Reconnaissance Corps (formed 8 January 1941, disbanded August 1946). Since the end of the Second World War the Royal Armoured Corps has reverted to the status of an administrative corps.

It should be noted that the Household Cavalry regiments, though armoured, do not belong to it.

The Corps of Royal Engineers

from Norman and Plantagenet times	Military Engineers employed permanently by the Crown under Letters Patent.
circa 1414	King's Military Engineers employed by newly-formed Board of Ordnance responsible for the control of the King's Works and Arsenals.
1716	The Artillery and Engineers of the Board of Ordnance constituted on separate establishments as the Royal Regiment of Artillery and the officer Corps of Engineers.
1772	Formation of Soldier Artificer Company at Gibraltar for the construction of fortifications. They were the first permanent engineer soldiers of the British Army and were commanded by officers of the Corps of Engineers.
1787	Corps of Engineers given Royal title. In the same year a Corps of Royal Military Artificers was formed for the construction of seaward defences at home and overseas as a precaution against a French invasion. Officers for this Corps were supplied by the Corps of Royal Engineers.
1797	The Gibraltar Soldier Artificers were absorbed into the Corps of Royal Military Artificers.
1812	Title of Royal Military Artificers changed to Royal Sappers and Miners to denote the changing combat role of the military engineers during the Peninsular War.
1855	Board of Ordnance abolished and the Royal Artillery and the officer Corps of Royal Engineers together with the Corps of Royal Sappers and Miners came directly under the control of the Commander-in-Chief of the Army.
1856	Corps of Royal Sappers and Miners absorbed into the Corps of Royal Engineers, thus ending the long-existing anomaly of the officers and soldiers of the Engineer Arm of the British Army belonging to two separate Corps.
1862	British officers and NCOs of the Hon. East India Company, Bengal, Madras, and Bombay Engineer Corps absorbed into the Corps of Royal Engineers after the Indian Mutiny. The Royal Engineers however continued to

supply officers and NCO instructors to the Corps of Sappers and Miners retained in the Indian Army until India and Pakistan received their independence in 1947.

1912   Royal Flying Corps (Naval and Military Wings) formed from the Air Battalion RE. From 1862 to 1912 the Royal Engineers had been responsible for the development of military aviation.

1920   Royal Corps of Signals formed from the RE Signal Service.

1965   RE Transportation and Movement Control Services incorporated, with the Royal Army Service Corps, into the Royal Corps of Transport.

The Corps of Royal Engineers can trace its ancestry back to the Military Engineers brought over from Normandy by William the Conqueror. Their task was to build roads, bridges, and castles to subjugate Saxon England. These road-served castles became important military and administrative centres upon which the internal security and local government of the country depended. The Military Engineers of Edward I were employed on castle building on a vast scale during his wars against the Welsh and the Scots. They also were responsible for the conduct of all siege operations and the construction and firing of 'engines of war' designed to batter down hostile defences. From those early days the British Military Engineer has been both a professional engineer and a professional fighting soldier.

With the introduction of the cannon a Board of Ordnance was set up in the early fifteenth century to administer all matters connected with the King's fortifications and works, his arsenals and warlike equipment, and the military engineers, surveyors, and artillerymen required for these tasks were held on the Board's permanent establishment. Ordnance Trains, officered by the 'military gentlemen of the Board of Ordnance' and consisting of impressed skilled engineer tradesmen and gunners, were raised as required for specific campaigns and disbanded when no longer required. The engineers were traditionally responsible for all siege operations and the siting of batteries. The distinction between engineer and artillery officers of the Board was however an indistinct one and, as a result of the lessons learned during Marlborough's Campaigns during the War of the Spanish Succession, 1702 to 1713, the Artillery and

continued overleaf

Engineers were in 1716 constituted as separate establishments. The Board of Ordnance continued to administer the Royal Artillery and Royal Engineers until it was abolished in 1855 towards the end of the Crimean War when both Arms came directly under the control of the Commander-in-Chief.

NICKNAME

The Sappers

MOTTOES

'Ubique' (Everywhere)
'Quo Fas et Gloria Ducunt' (Whither right and glory lead)

The Gurkha Engineers

When the Gurkha Brigade came on to the British Army Establishment in 1948 the 67th Gurkha Field Squadron RE was raised. In October 1949 it became an independent unit.

In 1950 the 68th Gurkha Field Squadron RE was raised and in the following year served alongside the 67th in Hong Kong.

In June 1951 the 50th Field Engineer Regiment was formed as the Field Engineer Regiment of the Gurkha Brigade.

On 28 September 1955 the Gurkha Engineers became an independent unit.

In 1958 the unit was affiliated to the Corps of Royal Engineers.

70th Gurkha Field Park Squadron was raised in Malaya in 1960, and 69th Gurkha Field Squadron on 1 April 1961.

MOTTOES

'Ubique' (Everywhere)
'Quo fas et Gloria Ducunt' (Whither right and glory lead)

The Royal Corps of Signals

Early systems of transmitting intelligence were normally either visual, such as beacon fires or semaphore machines, or by hand, whether on foot or horseback. The invention of the morse code in 1835 and the electric telegraph in 1837 greatly widened the possibilities and in the Crimean War in 1854 the British Army first used the electric telegraph in war, and a new era had begun.

In 1870 the first Royal Engineer unit to specialize in signalling came into being, namely C (Telegraph) Troop RE later to become the Telegraph Battalion RE and this unit took part in campaigns in Ashanti 1873, Zululand 1879, Egypt 1882, Bechuanaland 1884, the Nile 1884, Ashanti 1896, the South African War 1899–1902, and Somaliland 1903–4.

The Bell telephone had been invented in 1876 and was seen in England the following year. Royal Engineer officers immediately set to and produced their own telephones. They were used near Peshawar on Frontier operations in 1877 and there were probably as many telephones in use at the siege of Sherpur in Afghanistan in 1879 as there were in London at the same time. There were seven connected to the London Telephone Exchange.

The first victory to be reported by telegraph direct from the battlefield was that of Tel-el-Kebir in 1882 when the Commander-in-Chief in the field received H.M. Queen Victoria's reply to his report within 45 minutes.

As a result of the experience of the South African War it was decided to co-ordinate all means of communication under one service, and in 1908 the RE Signal Service was formed. In the meantime wireless had been invented and the motor-cycle had become available and these means were added to the telephones, telegraphs, visual, and horse despatch riding activities of the signal companies.

In the 1st World War the RE Signal Service took part in every land battle fought by the British Army using every means of signalling, visual, line, wireless, despatch riders, message carrying rockets, pigeons, and dogs.

In 1920 the Corps of Signals separated from the Royal Engineers and became the Royal Corps of Signals. In the

2nd World War it expanded from a permanent establishment of 541 officers and 9,837 soldiers to a figure of 8,518 officers and 142,472 soldiers.

From 1925 to 1947 Royal Signals were amalgamated with the Indian Signal Corps.

Since 1945 the Royal Corps has been on active service in Palestine, Korea, Kenya, Malaya, Cyprus, Suez, Jordan, Kuwait, Aden, and Borneo, and there are Royal Signals Troops aboard some of Her Majesty's Ships and the Corps also serves the Royal Air Force.

In 1970 staffs at corps, division, and brigade headquarters are provided with automatic trunk dialling facilities, high speed teleprinters, a facsimile system, and, where practicable, closed circuit television. In addition they have access to a modern range of radio sets and a manual telephone exchange for personal service.

MOTTO

'Certa cito' (Swift and sure)

Gurkha Signals

Soon after the Gurkha Brigade came on to the British Army Establishment there was formed in 1949 a Signals Training and Holding Wing in Kuala Lumpur, Malaya, and called Royal Signals Gurkha.

In 1952 the 3rd Squadron of the 17th Gurkha Division Signal Regiment had four Signal Troops in operation. In 1955 the 1st and 3rd Squadrons were incorporated to form the 17th Gurkha Division Signal Regiment.

In September 1955 the Gurkha Signals became an independent unit.

In 1958 the unit was affiliated to the Royal Corps of Signals.

MOTTO

'Certa Cito' (Swift and Sure)

The Army Air Corps

1878	Military experiments with balloons begun at Woolwich Arsenal. Five balloons in service by following year.
1880 & 1882	Balloon Section at Aldershot Manœuvres.
1884	Balloon Detachment accompanied Sir Charles Warren's force to Bechuanaland.
1885	Balloons employed in Sudan at El Teb and Tamai.
1890	Balloon Section introduced into British Army as a unit of the Royal Engineers. Depot formed at Farnborough. (Later R.A.E.)
1899	Four Balloon Sections took active part in South African War.
1907	First British Army airship 'Nulli Secundus' passed its trials.
Spring 1911	The Air Battalion formed.
November 1911	Prime Minister asked Committee of Imperial Defence under Lord Haldane to consider future of military aviation. Recommended creation of a Royal Flying Corps to consist of a Naval Wing, a Military Wing and a Central Flying School.
13 April 1912	The Royal Flying Corps created by Royal Warrant. It absorbed the Air Battalion and its Reserves. Admiralty and War Office went their separate ways.
1914	R.F.C. took the field in France with a Headquarters, Nos. 2, 3, 4, and 5 Aeroplane Squadrons and an Aircraft Park. H.Q. left Farnborough 11th August and arrived Amiens 13th August. Squadrons flew to France. This was the first organized national force to fly to a war overseas.
19 August 1914	First air reconnaissance by R.F.C.
August 1914	Lord Kitchener ordered plans to be made for the formation of a large number of new squadrons.
November 1914	Wings formed to support Corps mainly on reconnaissance and artillery spotting duties.
1915	When order of battle for New Army was produced it was decided that 100 service squadrons would be required.

continued overleaf

1916	Work so great (air fighting was by then a commonplace) that squadrons were increased from 12 to 18 aircraft with 20 pilots.
April 1916	32 R.F.C. squadrons on Western Front.
June 1916	C.-in-C. (Haig) asked for 56 squadrons.
July 1916	Some RNAS squadrons posted to France to help fill gap.
Spring 1917	38 R.F.C. squadrons on Western Front.
August 1917	General Smuts Committee reports on need for unity of control by an Air Department.
November 1917	C.-in-C. (Haig) asks for 179 squadrons (66 for long distance bombing). Approved establishment at time 86 squadrons.
November 1917	Air Force (Constitution) Bill presented to Parliament.
December 1917	Order in Council creating the Air Council.
1 April 1918	Easter Monday. Royal Air Force created. At that time R.F.C. on Western Front numbered about 1,600 aircraft. Numbers had grown from 150 aircraft and 250 officers in 1914 to 22,000 aircraft and 30,000 officers at the time of the Armistice.
1918–39	On the absorption of the Royal Flying Corps into the Royal Air Force the link between ground and air was maintained by R.A.F. army co-operation units, with which some officers seconded from the army served. In 1939 the B.E.F. was accompanied to France by an Air Component of 13 R.A.F. squadrons.
1940	The Central Landing School began training parachutists in July at Ringway. In September a glider training section and a technical research section were added and the school was renamed Central Landing Establishment. These later split off becoming No. 1 Glider Training School and Airborne Forces Experimental Establishment. No. 1 Parachute Training School remained at Ringway.
August 1941	Approval given for formation of an Air Observation Post Squadron, Royal Artillery.
November 1941	G.O.C. Airborne Forces appointed and also Commanders of 1st Parachute Brigade and 1st Air Landing Brigade.
1942	The Glider Pilot Regiment was formed in January. R.A.F. No. 38 Wing (later Group) formed to provide transport for airborne forces in February and The Army Air Corps was founded to act as an administrative centre for the Glider Pilot Regiment and the Parachute Regiment, also formed that year.

1950	The Army Air Corps was disbanded.
1957	The Army Air Corps was reformed. The Glider Pilot Regiment was officially dissolved and it and the Air Observation Post Squadrons Royal Artillery were merged in the new corps which was henceforth a true corps with a combatant role and its own complement of men and machines. The Army Air Corps now performs observation and transport missions for the army.

The Corps has seen service in Cyprus, Radfan, Malaya, Arabian Peninsula (Muscat), Brunei, Borneo, South Arabia and Aden.

MOTTO

'Per Ardua ad Astra'

The Royal Army Chaplains' Department

It is often claimed that the 'Royal Army Chaplains' Department has an unbroken record of existence since 1796'. In fact, though the official formation of the Department dates from that year, clergymen have been closely associated with the soldiers of his country from the earliest days of history of these islands. It is probably true to say that up to the time of Edward I no army was raised which did not have amongst its leaders many of the foremost clergy of the land. In about 1300 there appeared on the army's pay roll the Army Chaplain, Capellanus Magnificus, who received 1s. per day and Capellanus Vulgaris, a lower-class who received only 6d. per day for his work.

At Crecy (1345) and again at Agincourt (1414) Chaplains are listed. In 1621 in the reign of Elizabeth I regimental chaplains are mentioned for the first time. In both the Royalist and Parliamentary Armies of the Civil War, chaplains had their official status, one for every regiment. By 1648 chaplains were appointed by the Headquarters Council of Cromwell's Army, replacing the older system whereby the gift of a chaplaincy was in the Commanding Officers' hands. The earliest known commission as a Chaplain dates from 1653, whilst the Articles of War published in 1662 specifies the duties of Garrison Chaplains and laid down that 'any soldier missing prayers should forfeit one day's pay'.

As the 18th century ended, chaplains took their duties far from seriously, often employing deputies to do their duties or virtually absenting themselves from barracks. Such a situation could not be permitted to continue and finally by the Royal Warrant of 23 September 1796, regimental chaplaincies were abolished and the Army Chaplains' Department came into being. After Waterloo and up to the Crimean War, the Department was reduced drastically in strength with consequences similar to those found by all arms on the outbreak of the Crimean War.

Prior to 1827 only Church of England Chaplains were authorized for the Army as chaplains. In 1827 Presbyterians were recognized, whilst in 1836 Roman Catholic chaplains were accepted on an equal footing with their colleagues in the Church of England and Presbyterian

Churches but whereas the latter came directly under the Chaplain General, Roman Catholic chaplains reported direct to the Principal Chaplain (RC) at the War Office.

In 1816 chaplains were given seniority equivalent to military rank, according to their class, i.e. the Chaplain General ranked as a Major-General; a 3rd Class Chaplain as a Major and a 4th Class as a Captain. In 1860 Chaplains first wore military uniform, their earlier dress virtually being normal civilian pattern.

In 1881 Wesleyans were officially recognized, whilst the first Jewish Chaplain to the Forces was appointed in 1892. In 1914 there were 117 Chaplains in the Department (including 17 RC and 11 Presbyterians). By 1918 there were 3,475 Chaplains. The title 'Royal' was conferred on 22 February 1919.

In the 2nd World War Chaplains served in all theatres of War.

NICKNAME
The Padres

MOTTO
'In This Sign Conquer'

The Royal Corps of Transport

The officers did not belong to the Corps but were supplied by the War Office. During this period three other Corps existed for short periods:

When the Royal Army Service Corps became the Royal Corps of Transport there was a change in function. The responsibility for supply was transferred to the Royal Army Ordnance Corps but the Corps took over from the Royal Engineers (Transportation) and the Movement Control Service many of their duties.

NICKNAMES

Farmer records the following but without stating his source:

The London Thieving Corps (from the initials of the London Transport Corps)

The Moke (or Muck) Train (because at one period Spanish mules were employed instead of horses)

The Murdering Thieves (from the initials of the Military Train)

More common are:

Aly Sloper's Cavalry

The Galloping Grocers

The Gurkha Transport Regiment

28 and 30 Companies were first formed on 1 July 1958 as the Gurkha Army Service Corps, and in 1959, 31 and 34 Companies were raised. Headquarters Gurkha ASC was formed on 1 July 1960.

With the formation of the Royal Corps of Transport on 15 July 1965 the Gurkha Army Service Corps became the Gurkha Transport Regiment.

The Royal Army Medical Corps

From 1661 to the Crimean War almost two centuries later medical officers were employed on a regimental basis. The Duke of Marlborough instituted what were called 'Marching Hospitals' and 'Flying Hospitals' which might be called the forerunners of the Field Ambulance Companies. It was not until 1812 in the Peninsula that the first organized medical service was instituted by Wellington. On 10 January that year he appointed Dr. James McGrigor his Principal Medical Officer and consulted him almost daily. McGrigor introduced a system for evacuating casualties and set up pre-fabricated hospital huts sent out from England. He also caused casualties to be registered, so making statistical recording possible.

After Waterloo, the experience in the Peninsula was largely forgotten, and when the Army went to the Crimea in 1854 it was with medical officers on a regimental basis only. When the administrative services broke down, the War Office reluctantly sent 300 decrepit pensioners to form a Hospital Conveyance Corps. This proved quite useless. The following year the Medical Staff Corps was formed, composed of 'Men able to read and write, of regular steady habits and good temper and of a kindly disposition'. In 1857 The Medical Staff Corps was reorganized into the Army Hospital Corps, a title which it retained until 1884 when it reverted to its previous title. On 1 July 1898 the Royal Army Medical Corps was formed by amalgamating the Medical Staff (officers) and the Medical Staff Corps (men).

NICKNAMES

The Poultice Wallopers   The Linseed Lancers
The Pills

MOTTO

'In Arduis Fidelis' (Steadfast in adversity)

The Royal Army Ordnance Corps

Originated in the old Ordnance Department, the first official record dating back to 1418 when John Louth was appointed Clerk to the Ordnance.

In 1855 the Board of Ordnance ceased to exist and its duties were taken over from the Secretary of State for War. The present Corps dates from 1875. The title 'Royal' was conferred in 1918.

TITLES

The Military Store Staff Corps
The Ordnance Store Corps
Army Ordnance Corps
Royal Army Ordnance Corps

NICKNAME

The Sugar Stick Brigade

MOTTO

'Sua Tela Tonanti' (Of Jupiter—'Thundering forth his weapons')

The Corps of Royal Electrical and Mechanical Engineers

The Corps was formed from the Royal Army Ordnance Corps on 19 May 1942. It has borne the title 'Royal' from its formation. It is responsible for all electrical and mechanical repairs which cannot be carried out within units. It also provides Light Aid Detachments to repair and maintain equipment in mechanized fighting units. Its own main sub-units are called Workshops and its private soldiers bear the rank of Craftsman.

The Corps of Royal Military Police

In 1855, 12 N.C.O.s from Cavalry Regiments were selected to act as Mounted Police. During the years which followed their numbers increased and the Military Mounted Police was formed.

In 1885 the Military Foot Police was formed.

In 1926 the two detachments were amalgamated to form the Corps of Military Police.

In 1946 the title 'Royal' was granted.

The Royal Army Pay Corps

In the Peninsular War paymasters served on a regimental basis.

In 1878 the Army Pay Department was formed.

In 1899 the Army Pay Corps was formed.

The Corps was formed in 1920 by the amalgamation of the above. The title 'Royal' was conferred shortly afterwards.

NICKNAMES

The Quill Drivers   The Ink Slingers

MOTTO

'Fide et Fiducia' (In faith and trust)

The Royal Army Veterinary Corps

In the 17th and 18th centuries the care of horses was entrusted to farriers.

The first Veterinary Surgeon to serve with the British Army appears to have been Mr. John Ship who was appointed to the 11th Light Dragoons in 1796.

In 1858 the Veterinary Medical Department was formed.

In 1881 this was recognized as the Army Veterinary Department. All regimental appointments, except those to the Household Cavalry, were abolished.

In 1891 officers were given substantive military rank.

In 1903 the Army Veterinary Corps (composed of other ranks only) was formed.

In 1906 this amalgamated with the Army Veterinary Department, to form the present Corps.

In 1918 the title 'Royal' was conferred.

NICKNAMES

The Vets   The Horse Doctors

The Small Arms School Corps

The Small Arms School Corps is the descendant of the Corps of Instructors of Musketry established at the School of Musketry at Hythe in 1854. In 1929 the instructors of that school (renamed the Small Arms School in 1919) joined those of the Machine Gun School, Netheravon, to form a new Corps, the Small Arms School Corps. None of its members hold lower rank than that of Sergeant.

The Military Provost Staff Corps

The Military Provost Staff Corps, originally the Military Prison Staff Corps, was established in 1901 and re-designated in 1906. It provides the staff for military prisons and its members are all of non-commissioned rank or senior.

The Royal Army Educational Corps

On 2 July 1846 a Corps of Army Schoolmasters was created by royal warrant. In 1857 a Council of Military Education was set up which soon afterwards took over all army schools and libraries and became responsible for the administration and policy of the Corps of Schoolmasters. A survey carried out in 1858 showed that one-fifth of the troops could neither read nor write, another fifth could read but not write, and only five per cent enjoyed any 'superior degree of education'. Ten years later the Council could show that the illiteracy rate had been halved. In 1870 the Royal Commission on Military Education was set up which resulted in the appointment of a Director-General of Military Education. At this time, however, the Caldwell reforms came into operation, and the ranks became full of short-service men. Time for education became restricted and by 1885 the Commission's recommendations were largely undermined. In 1887, when a Special Committee was convened, the opponents of education were only defeated by the efforts of Sir Garnet Wolseley, who argued that the better a man was educated the better soldier he became. However, it was not until 1913 that recruits were compelled to attend school until they gained 3rd-Class certificates. In 1920 by royal warrant the Corps of Army Schoolmasters was disbanded and the Army Educational Corps formed. Its duty in war was 'to assist by all means in the maintenance of a high spirit of devotion and wellbeing'. In 1923 the strength of the Corps was halved by the Geddes axe; and the outbreak of war in 1939 saw the scattering of personnel and the virtual end of education among the troops. In 1940, however, the Haining Scheme linked education and welfare in a major effort to keep the troops informed on the progress of the war. By 1945 the operations of the Corps had increased enormously, and the view of education as an integral part of training was recognized throughout the service.

The title 'Royal' was granted on 28 November 1946.

The Royal Army Dental Corps

In the 1st World War of 1914–18 dental officers had served on the establishment of all medical units.

In 1921 the Army Dental Corps was formed.
In 1946 the title 'Royal' was conferred.

MOTTO

'Ex Dentibus Ensis' (From the teeth a sword)

The Royal Pioneer Corps

A Corps of Royal Pioneers was formed in 1762 but was disbanded the following year.

A Labour Corps was formed on 21 February 1917 to relieve the fighting services of duties which they had formerly carried out on returning from the front line for 'rest' periods and to assist the Services in carrying out their work. This Corps was disbanded in 1919.

On 17 October 1939 the Auxiliary Military Pioneer Corps was formed and on 22 November 1940 the title was changed to Pioneer Corps. The Corps was fully combatant and at its peak in May 1945 included 12,000 officers, 166,000 United Kingdom personnel and about 400,000 pioneers from other parts of the Empire. In addition, Pioneers were responsible for a civilian labour force of 1,074,000 and a prisoner of war force of 173,000.

The Corps served in all theatres of operations in the 2nd World War.

On 26 November 1946 the title 'Royal' was granted.

The Royal Pioneer Corps became part of the Regular Army in 1950.

Since 1945 the Corps served in Egypt, Korea, Malaya, Suez, Cyprus, Jordan/Lebanon, Kuwait, Southern Cameroons, Borneo, Radfan, and Aden.

The Royal Pioneer Corps is the Army's specialist in the handling of stores using both manual and mechanical means. It provides military labour for the Army in U.K. and overseas in peace and war; also, in certain circumstances, assists the Royal Navy and Royal Air Force.

The Corps provides the personnel for the Defence and Employment Platoons for the Brigade Headquarters of the Strategic Reserve.

In addition to Military labour the Corps is responsible in certain overseas theatres in peace, and all overseas theatres in war, for recruiting and administering civilian labour employed by the Services.

MOTTO

'Labor Omnia Vincit' (Labour conquers all things)

The Intelligence Corps

The Intelligence Corps operated throughout the 1st and 2nd World Wars and in subsequent Theatres of Operations. In addition, historical research has established that it may have existed in the South African War of 1899–1902 when units of Guides, mainly men with knowledge of the country and speaking the Dutch and Kaffir dialects, were organized for intelligence work in the Field. A pamphlet on 'Field Intelligence', published in 1904, certainly referred to the Intelligence Corps as such.

It is, therefore, difficult to separate the Intelligence Corps from the whole field of military intelligence as the development of both has gone hand in hand.

Some of the leading personalities connected with the historical background of military intelligence are:

Lieutenant-Colonel Colquhoun Grant, Head of Intelligence to Wellington at Waterloo.

General Sir George Murray, Quartermaster-General to Wellington who formed a Corps of Guides for the collection of intelligence.

General Sir Harry Lumsden, who as a subaltern, formed the Indian Corps of Guides for intelligence collection on the North-West Frontier.

General Rimington who raised a unit of Guides in the Boer War to collect intelligence, known as 'Rimington's Tigers'.

Lieutenant-Colonel Baden Powell who collected intelligence at the outbreak of the Boer War.

Lieutenant-Colonel David Henderson who was Director of Military Intelligence South Africa under Lord Roberts from 1901 to 1902. He wrote a pamphlet on the principles of intelligence, based on his experience in the Boer War, proposing the formation of a permanent Intelligence Corps. This was finally accepted by the War Office in 1913, when an Establishment for an Intelligence Corps was drawn up to comprise personnel of any arm, wearing their own unit cap badges but carrying out intelligence duties. Thus throughout the 1st World War all personnel connected with intelligence were known as Intelligence Corps.

At the outbreak of the 2nd World War there was no Intelligence Corps as all officers and soldiers employed on intelligence duties either remained in their regiments or were commissioned or enlisted on the General List.

Intelligence with all its ramifications and duties became so vast and grew so rapidly that it was impossible to control personnel properly or obtain that esprit de corps that was so essential. The War Office subsequently accepted the fact that an Intelligence Corps was necessary and therefore gave approval for its formation which came into effect on 19 July 1940.

MOTTO

'Manui Dat Cognitio Vires' (Knowledge Gives Strength to the Arm)

The Army Catering Corps

An Army School of Cookery was established at Aldershot after the 1st World War. With the great need for cooks after the rapid expansion of the army following the outbreak of the 2nd World War in 1939 it was decided that more comprehensive arrangements would have to be made for recruitment and training. All unit cooks were therefore transferred to one Corps which controlled their training, administration and deployment.

The Corps was formed in March 1941.

The Army Physical Training Corps

Its forerunner was the Army Physical Training Staff.

In 1940, to provide the central administration necessary to meet the great need for instructors, the Army School of Physical Training formed the basis of the present Corps.

Queen Alexandra's Royal Army Nursing Corps

An Army Nursing Service was formed in 1881. To ensure that an adequate supply of trained nurses would be available in time of war an Army Nursing Reserve was established in 1897. In 1902 this was reorganized and named 'Queen Alexandra's Imperial Military Nursing Service'.

In 1949 Queen Alexandra's Royal Army Nursing Corps was formed and took on the duties of the above.

MOTTO

'Sub Cruce Candida' (Under the White Cross)

The Women's Royal Army Corps

The Corps was formed on 1 February 1941. Its forerunners were the Women's Auxiliary Corps, formed in 1917, and renamed Queen Mary's Auxiliary Army Corps in 1918, just before disbandment; and the Auxiliary Territorial Service, formed in 1938, which served throughout the 2nd World War.

MOTTO

'Suavita in modo fortita in re' (Gentle in manner strong in deed)

The Mutiny Act, 1689

Anno Regni

GULIELMI

et

MARIÆ

REGIS & REGINA

Angliæ, Scotiæ, Franciæ & Hiberniæ

PRIMO

On the Twenty-third Day of December,
Anno Dom. 1689. In the First Year of
Their Majesties Reign, This ACT
Passed the Royal Assent

LONDON

*Printed by Charles Bill and Thomas Newcomb, Printers
to the King and Queens most Excellent Majesties*

MDCLXXXIX

Whereas the raising or keeping a Standing Army Within this Kingdom in time of Peace, unless it be with Consent of Parliament, is against Law; And Whereas it is judged necessary by Their Majesties and this present Parliament, That during this time of War, several of the forces which are now on foot, should be continued, and others raised for the Safety of the Kingdom, for the Commen Defence of the Protestant Religion, and for the Reducing of Ireland. And Whereas no man may be forejudged of Life or Limb, or subjected to any kind of Punishment by Martial Law, or in any other manner then by the Judgment of his Peers, and according to the known and established Laws of this Realm; Yet nevertheless, it being requisite for retaining such Forces as are or shall be Raised during this Exigence of Affairs, in their Duty, That an exact Discipline be observed, and that Soldiers who shall Mutiny or Stir up Sedition, or shall Desert Their Majesties Service, be brought

continued overleaf

to a more Exemplary and speedy Punishment than the usual Forms of Law will allow.

Be it therefore Enacted by the King and Queens most Excellent Majesties, by and with the Advice and Consent of the Lords Spiritual and Temporal, and Commons in this present Parliament Assembled, and by Authority of the same, That from and after the Twentieth day of December, in the Year of our Lord One Thousand six hundred eighty nine, every Person being in Their Majesties Service in the Army, and being Mustered and in pay as an Officer or Soldier, who shall at any time before the Twentieth day of December, in the Year of our Lord One Thousand six hundred and ninety, Excite, Cause, or Joyn in any Mutiny or Sedition in the Army, or shall Desert Their Majesties Service in the Army, or being a Soldier actually Listed in any Regiment, Troop or Company, shall List himself into any other Regiment, Troop or Company, without a Discharge produced in Writing from the Captain of the Troop or Company wherein he is first Listed, shall suffer Death, or such other Punishment as by a Court-Martial shall be Inflicted.

And it is hereby further Enacted and Declared, That Their Majesties, or the General of Their Army for the time being, may by Virtue of this Act, have full Power and Authority to grant Commissions to any lieutenant General, or other Officers, not under the Degree of a Field-Officer, or Commander in Chief of a Garison, from time to time to Call and Assemble Court-Martials for punishing such Offences as aforesaid.

And it is hereby further Enacted and Declared, That no Court Martial which shall have Power to Inflict any Punishment by Virtue of This Act, for the Offences aforesaid, shall consist of fewer then Thirteen,

whereof none to be under the Degree of a Commission Officer, and the President of Such Court Martial not to be under the Degree of a Field-Officer, or the then Commander in Chief of the Garison where the Offender shall be Tryed.

Provided always, That no Field Officer be Tried by other then Field Officers, and that such Court-Martial shall have Power and Authority to Administer an Oath to any Witness, in order to the Examination or Trial of the Offences aforesaid.

Provided always, That nothing in this Act contained, shall extend, or be construed to extend to concern any of the Militia Forces of this Kingdom.

Provided also, That this Act shall continue and be in Force until the said Twentieth day of December in the said Year of our Lord One Thousand six hundred and ninety, and no longer.

Provided always, and be it Enacted, That in all Trials of Offenders by Courts Martial to be held by virtue of this Act, where the Offence may be punished by Death, every Officer present at such Trial, before any Proceeding be had thereupon, shall take an Oath upon the Evangelists before the Court, and the next Justice of the Peace, Judge Advocate or his Deputy, or one of them, are hereby respectively Authorized to Administer the same in these Words; That is to say,

You shall Well and Truly Try and Determine, according to your Evidence, the Matter now before you, between our Sovereign Lord and Lady the King and Queens Majesties, and the Prisoner to be Tried.

So help you God.

And no Sentence of Death shall be given against any Offender in such Case by any Court-Martial, unless

Nine of Thirteen Officers present shall concur therein, and if there be a greater number of Officers present, then the Judgment shall pass by the Concurrence of the greater part of them so Sworn, which major part shall not be less than Nine, and not otherwise; and no Proceedings, Tryal or Sentence of Death shall be had or given against any Offender, but between the hours of Eight in the Morning, and One in the Afternoon.

And for the preventing of Fraud and Deceit in Mustering of Soldiers, Be it further Enacted by the Authority aforesaid, That if any Person shall make or give, or procure to be made or given, any false or untrue Certificate, Whereby to Excuse any Soldiers for their Absence from any Muster or other Service which they ought to attend or perform, upon a pretence of Sickness, or other Cause, That then every such person so making, giving or procuring such Certificate, shall forfeit for every such Offence the Sum of Fifty Pounds, and shall be forthwith Cashiered and Displaced from such his Office, and shall be thereby utterly disabled to have or hold any Military Office or Imployment within this Kingdom, or in Their Majesties Service.

And be it further Enacted by the Authority aforesaid, That every Officer that shall make any false or untrue Muster of Man or Horse, and every Commissary, Muster-master, and other Officer, that shall wittingly or knowingly Allow or Sign the Muster-Roll wherein such false Muster is contained, or any Duplicate thereof, upon Proof thereof upon Oath made by two Witnesses before a Court-Martial to be thereupon called, (which is hereby Authorized and Required to Administer such Oath) shall for such their Offence be forthwith Cashiered and Displaced

from such their Office, and shall be thereby utterly disabled to have or hold any Military Office or Employment within this Kingdom, or in Their Majesties Service, and shall likewise forfeit the Sum of Fifty pounds.

And be it further Enacted by the Authority aforesaid, That every Commissary or Muster-Master, upon any Muster to be made, had or taken by him or them, shall by a convenient time before such Muster made, give notice to the Mayor or other Chief Magistrate or Officer of the Place where the Soldiers so to be Mustered shall be Quartered, who are hereby Required to be present at every such Muster, and give his utmost Assistance for the discovering any false or untrue Muster there made, or offered to be made; And that every such Commissary or Muster-Master making or taking such Muster, that shall neglect to give such notice, as aforesaid, or shall refuse to take the Aid and Assistance of such Mayor, Chief Magistrate or Officer where the Soldiers so to be Mustered shall be Quartered, shall forfeit the Sum of Fifty pounds, and be Discharged from his Office.

And also be it further Enacted by the Authority aforesaid, That if any Person shall be falsly Mustered, or offer himself falsly and deceitfully to be Mustered, every such person, if no Soldier, upon Proof thereof made upon Oath by two Witnesses before the next Justice of Peace of the County where such Muster shall be made, and every such person so falsly Mustered, or offering to be falsly Mustered, upon Certificate thereof in Writing under the Hand of the Officer Commanding in Chief at the Muster, or of the Commissary of the Musters, or any other Person, made to such Justice of the Peace, the said Justice is thereupon, and is

continued overleaf

hereby Authorized and Required to Commit such Offender to the House of Correction, there to remain for the space of Three Months, and to be kept at hard Labour, with convenient Correction.

And if any Person shall wittingly or willingly lend or furnish a Horse to be Mustered, which shall not truly belong to the Trooper or Troop so Mustered, the said Horse so falsly Mustered, shall be forfeited to the Informer, if the same doth belong to the Person lending or furnishing the said Horse, or otherwise the Person lending or furnishing the said Horse, shall forfeit the Sum of Twenty pounds, upon Oath made by Two Witnesses before the next Justice of the Peace, or be Committed to the House of Correction for Six months, unless he shall pay the same, there to be kept at hard Labour.

And be it also further Enacted by the Authority aforesaid, That the said Forfeitures shall be to such Person or Persons that shall Inform, immediately to be paid out of the Arrears of such Officers Pay as shall so offend, upon Conviction before the Court-Martial, by Order of the said Court to the Paymaster, if such Officer so offending shall have an Arrear, and if there shall be no Arrear, the Court-Martial shall immediately give Order to seize the Goods of such Officer so offending, and sell them for payment of such Forfeiture to the Informer, rending the overplus to the Owner; And the said Court-Martial is hereby obliged to Discharge such Informer, if a Soldier, from any further Service, if he shall demand the same.

And be it further Enacted, That if any Pay-Master, Agent, or Clerk of any Regiment, Troop, or Company, shall Detain or Withhold, by the space of One Month, the Pay of any Officer or Soldier (Cloathes and all other just Allowances being De-

ducted) after such Pay shall be by him or them Received, or if any Officer having received their Soldiers Pay, shall refuse to pay each respective Common Soldier their respective Pay, when it shall become due, that upon proof thereof before a Court-Martial, as aforesaid, every such Pay-Master, Agent, Clerk, and Officer so offending, shall be discharged from his Employment, and shall forfeit to the Informer, upon Conviction before the said Court-Martial, One hundred pounds, to be raised, as aforesaid, and the Informer, if a Soldier, if he Demands it, shall be, and is hereby Discharged of any further Service; Anything in this Act contained to the contrary notwithstanding.

And it is hereby Enacted and Declared, That the Commanding Officer of every Troop or Company at the time of Muster, shall bring in a Certificate Signed of the names of such Persons as are Sick, or have leave to be absent upon Furlows, and of such Persons as are Dead and Deserted since the last Muster, with the Days of their Deaths or Desertions, and if such Certificate shall prove false, upon Conviction thereof before a Court-Martial, the Officer Signing such Certificate, shall suffer such Penalties, and in such manner as is Declared and Inflicted by this Act upon those that make False Musters.

And it is hereby further Enacted, That if any Officer shall Muster any Person that is a Servant, or receives Wages from any Officer, or that shall atend any Officer, as a Servant, in the absence of the said Officer from his Quarters, or shall Muster any Person by a Wrong Name knowingly, upon Conviction thereof before a Court-Martial, the said Officer or Commissary shall suffer such penalties, and in such manner as is Inflicted and Declared by this Act upon those that shall make false Musters.

And Whereas by the Petition of Right in the Third Year of King Charles the First, It is Enacted and Declared, That the People of this Land are not by the Laws to be Burthened with the Sojourning of Soldiers against their Wills; And by a Clause in one Act of Parliament made in the One and Thirtieth Year of the Reign of King Charles the Second, for Granting a Supply to his Majesty of Two hundred and Six thousand four hundred and sixty two pounds seventeen shillings and three pence, for Paying and Disbanding the Forces, It is Declared and Enacted, That no Officer Military or Civil, nor any other Person whatsoever, shall from henceforth presume to Place, Quarter or Billett any Soldier or Soldiers upon any Subject or Inhabitants of this Realm, of any Degree, Quality or Profession whatsoever, without his Consent; And that it shall and may be Lawful for any such Subject and Inhabitants to refuse to Sojourn or Quarter and Soldier or Soldiers, notwithstanding any Command, Order, Warrant or Billetting whatsoever; But forasmuch as at this present time there is a Rebellion in Ireland, and a War against France, whereby there is occasion for the Marching of many Regiments, Troops and Companies in several parts of this Kingdom towards the Sea Coats, and otherwise:

Be it further Enacted by the Authority aforesaid, That for and during the Continuance of this Act, and no longer, It shall and may be Lawful for the Constables, Tythingmen, Headboroughs, and other Chief Officers and Magistrates of Cities, Towns and Villages, and other Places in the Kingdom of England, Dominion of Wales, and Town of Berwick upon Tweed, and for no others, to Quarter and Billett the Officers and Soldiers in Their Majesties Service, in Inns, Livery Stables, Ale-houses, Victualling-houses, and all Houses selling Brandy, Strong-Waters, Sider, or Metheglin by Retail, to be drank in their Houses, and no other, and in no Private Houses whatsoever.

And if any Constable, Tythingman, or such like Officer or Magistrate, as aforesaid, shall presume to Quarter or Billett any such Officer or Soldier in any Private House, Withour the Consent of the Owner or Occupier, in such case such Owner or Occupier shall have his or their Remedy at Law against such Magistrate or Officer, for the Damage that such Owner or Occupier shall sustain thereby.

Provided nevertheless, And it is hereby Enacted, That the Officers and Soldiers so Quartered and Billetted, as aforesaid, shall pay such reasonable prices as shall be appointed from time to time by the Justices of the Peace in their Quarter Sessions of each County, City or Division, or Place Within their respective Jurisdictions; And the Justices of the Peace aforesaid are hereby Impowered and Required to Set and Appoint in their Quarter Sessions aforesaid, such reasonable Rates for all necessary Provisions for such Officers and Soldiers, for One or more Nights, in their Marching through their Cities, Towns, Villages, and other Places, and for the First Night only in such Places as shall be appointed for their Residence or Quarters.

Provided, That the said Price so Set by the said Justices, be within the compass of the Subsistence Money paid to the Soldiers; which Subsistence Money is hereby declared to be for each Trooper Two

continued overleaf

shillings per diem; For each Dragoon One shilling and two pence per diem; And for each Foot Soldier, Sixpence; And after the said First Night in their Quarters, the Owners and Occupiers of the Inns, Alehouses, and other Publick Houses, as aforesaid, are hereby required to furnish such Officers and Soldiers so Quartered and Billetted, as aforesaid, with dry Lodgings, Stable-room for Horses, and with Fire and Water, and necessary Utensils to Dress their Meat, and not otherwise, without the said Officers or Soldiers shall make a Contract or Agreement for their Provisions with the said Owners or Occupiers.

Provided always, and be it Enacted, That if any Officer or Soldier shall take any Money of any Person for Excusing the Quartering of Officers or Soldiers, or any of them, in any house allowed by this Act, every such Officer or Soldier shall be Cashiered, and made incapable of Serving in any Military Employment whatsoever.

And be it further Enacted by the Authority aforesaid, That from and after the One and thirtieth day of December next ensuing, no Pay-Master of the Army, Secretary of War, Commissary, or Muster-Master, or their under Officers, shall receive any Fees, or make any Deductions whatsoever out of the Pay of any Officer or Soldier in Their Majesties Army, or from theor Agents, which shall grow due from and after the said One and thirtieth Day of December, other then the usual Deductions for Cloathing, and the Twelve Pence in the Pound, to be disposed of as Their Majesties shall think fit, and the One Days Pay in the Year for the Use of the Royal Hospital at Chelsey.

And be it further Enacted, That this Act shall be Read at the Head of every respective Regiment, Troop, or Company, at every respective Muster, by the Commissary or Muster-Master, before such Muster shall be made, that no Soldier may pretend Ignorance.

FINIS

Index

Index

M

Composition by Gloucester Typesetting Co. Ltd.,
Market Parade, Gloucester
and printed by
The Camelot Press Ltd., London and Southampton